GOING WILD
Adventures of a Zoo Vet

"Adventures of zoo vet Taylor, walk-about extraordinaire:

"DANGER—walking in an open tiger reserve (all tigers in the compound, of course) in a fog so dense you cannot see your feet, when suddenly the dying torch picks out 'two shimmering orange discs'; being treed by an onager with a brain tumor:

"HUMOR—the search for replacements for a flea circus; deBrazza monkeys that hole up in the warm air ducts of their monkey house:

"PATHOS—an alcoholic Capuchin monkey owned by an equally alcoholic spinster; a mother hippo standing ferocious over her dead baby.

"Taylor ties it all together with his love affair with Cuddles the killer whale; his camelopardthantophobia, and Andrew Greenwood who is 'always popping up' and becomes Taylor's partner when Molly and the giraffe (with Andrew's help) survives anesthesia. I'll bet there's another book there!"

—Voice of Youth Advocates

"The author writes humorously of his experiences yet his authentic concern and affection for all animals are visible throughout."

—ALA Booklist

"Entertaining book for animal lovers. The stories reflect his love for his charges and his bewilderment at the cruelty, conscious or unconscious, of too many people."
—*United Press International*

"Really wild stuff. Most people interested in nature will like it."
—*Southbridge (Ma.) News*

"More fun than 10 barrels of monkeys, drunk or sober."
—*St. Louis Post-Dispatch*

"Taylor writes with a light touch, so his story is most often amusing. But, there are moments of tragedy and worry to balance out the emotions. Good, light reading."
—*Charlston (S.C.) Evening Post*

"Lively good humor."
—*Minneapolis Tribune*

Also by David Taylor:

NEXT PANDA, PLEASE!

ZOOVET: THE WORLD OF A WILDLIFE VET

DOCTOR IN THE ZOO

Going Wild

Adventures of a Zoo Vet

DAVID TAYLOR

STEIN AND DAY/Publishers/New York

STEIN AND DAY PAPERBACK EDITION 1984
Going Wild was first published in hardcover in the
United States of America in 1981,
by Stein and Day/*Publishers*
Copyright © 1980 by David Taylor
All rights reserved, Stein and Day, Incorporated
Printed in the United States of America
STEIN AND DAY/*Publishers*
Scarborough House
Briarcliff Manor, N.Y. 10510
Library of Congress Catalog Card No. 80-18432
ISBN 0-8128-8024-2

To Lorchen

Photographs

GOING WILD

Adventures of a Zoo Vet

One

Have you ever seen a black polar bear? The first one will be worth a fortune, and it looked as though Belle Vue might have struck lucky. The coats of their polar bears were becoming darker and darker, giving a fair impression of bottle-blonde barmaids who had been slack and let their hair-roots grow through the bleach.

Belle Vue was the city zoo in Manchester, set in an old Victorian pleasure garden, where I had taken my first steps in wild animal medicine and to which I was still veterinarian. My family often found themselves involved in my work there, especially my wife, Shelagh, who had helped me pull back from the brink of death two new-born polar bear cubs after their mother had deserted them.* One summer Sunday a few months later, she and I watched delightedly with our two daughters as the cubs, vigorous and lively now, played by the edge of their pool.

It was Shelagh who first noticed the bears' colour. 'The babies are lovely,' she said, 'but the others are just plain—well—filthy!'

My daughters agreed and wagged admonitory fingers at me. 'The polar bears are turning brown like Mum says,' chirped five-year-old Lindsey. 'Why don't you give them a good bath in Omo?'

'In my view,' opined Stephanie, with the solemnity of a nine-year-old newly embarked upon biology studies at school, 'they're mutating into brown bears.'

*See *Doctor in the Zoo*

1

I had to admit that there was something in what they said. Only in picture books are polar bears portrayed as being white as snow; in their native Arctic they are actually a creamy colour. But compared with the shining pearly coats of the bears I had seen at other zoos, and even allowing for the Manchester atmosphere, our bears were not the right colour. I raised the matter with the zoo's director, Ray Legge.

'Funny you should mention it,' he said. 'I've watched this darkening of the fur for a couple of weeks now. I wondered if my eyes were playing tricks.'

'My girls said the colour reminded them of caramel cream.'

'That's it,' Ray replied. 'Caramel describes the shade exactly. What's more, it gets deeper every day. At this rate, within two months you won't be able to tell them apart from the real brown and black bears.'

What could be the reason? The animals had a deep pool of sweet water in which they swam during daylight hours and they were hosed down regularly. Surely this was more than just grime.

'Let's dope one of the most café-au-lait individuals,' I suggested, 'and have a look at the skin.'

On close inspection, the skin of the slumbering beast appeared to the naked eye to be healthy, the coat was thick and shining and the animal was generally in tip-top shape, yet without doubt the hairs were more like those of a seal-point Siamese cat. I took a small bunch of hair clippings for microscopical examination, and in due course these revealed, loosely speaking, that the polar bears were growing seaweed! Under the microscope thousands of minute brown plants could be seen clinging to each hair. These algae, the sort of primitive vegetation that forms the green scum on pond water, are the smaller relatives of the various types of seaweed. In the case of the polar bears, they were not invading the hair and causing disease as, say, ringworm fungi do; they were just camping out and multiplying in the warm, moist forest of the bears' coats.

It was the same little plant which made the stone steps at home as slippery as oiled ice in damp weather. Shelagh tried to keep it at bay with scrubbing brush, chlorine solution and copper sulphate crystals, but her methods were never successful for very long and anyway could not be applied to living animals. After a long hunt I found a chemical manufactured in the USA which was lethal for algae but completely non-toxic for every other living animal or plant except, oddly, rice sprouts. As there are no paddy fields in Belle Vue I felt safe in using the stuff, which we sprayed over the bears and added to their pool water. Within three weeks our Manchester polars looked as if they had just come back from the laundromat. It is not true that bears are pure white only in picture books; maybe in the Arctic they are not white as snow, but they were for a time in the icy wastes of north-west England.

A small, whitewood coffin lay on the back doorstep. The sunlight glinted off the brass knobs, brass handles and oblong brass plates with which it was fitted. I stood looking down at the doleful box, my hand frozen in mid-air on its way to pull my keys from my jacket pocket. The family had appeared hale and hearty at breakfast a few hours before, as far as I could remember I had never brushed with the Rochdale branch of the Cosa Nostra if it existed, and my wine-merchant would have had difficulty in fitting my monthly order into the rather shallow sarcophagus even if he had for some reason started to deliver his wares in so funereal a fashion. The brass plate on the coffin lid was unengraved but the corner of a piece of white paper had been slipped under it. Stooping down, I read the words scribbled in pencil on the protruding part: 'Having a drink at White Lion. L. Fazakerly, Undertaker.' I was intrigued. Shelagh was out shopping, the girls were both at school. I decided to go down

3

to the pub for a beer and find out why Mr Fazakerly had taken to leaving samples of his craft on my back doorstep.

It was 1968 and I had only recently taken the plunge and left general veterinary practice to set up on my own as the world's sole independent, full-time veterinarian for zoo animals and other wild, exotic creatures. Working from my home on the outskirts of Rochdale, the most unlikely and unexotic cotton-mill town in drizzly north-west England, I had not found the first few days of my new venture very encouraging. As part of a bustling practice in Rochdale for the previous dozen years, I had been gradually expanding my wild animal work: from seeing the odd parrot or lizard once in a blue moon, I had taken over the care of the animals at Belle Vue Zoo on behalf of the partnership, travelled increasingly to patients all over the world, and gained my Fellowship of the Royal College of Veterinary Surgeons in the specialised area of zoo primate diseases. But during all those years I had been backed up by my partner and assistants in the practice, there had been a full range of surgical and diagnostic equipment in our clinic, I had been able to fall back on pigs, cattle, dogs and cats when ailing armadillos and infirm elephants were hard to come by, and there had been a secure, regular income from the practice of medicine round the cobbled streets and rainswept Pennine farms of this grey and gritty industrial town.

Now all my connections with my old practice had been severed. A legal document dissolving my partnership had been drawn up and I was forbidden to treat anything other than exotic species within a ten-mile radius of Rochdale Town Hall. There were three named and specific exceptions to this. One was the stock owned by Farmer Schofield, my next-door neighbour, and then there were two dogs which I had personally attended to from puppyhood to old age. They were old, old friends and everyone had been agreed that the animals might not take kindly to a switch of physician so late in life. So the lawyers, in dissolving the partnership, had taken solemn and formal note of my two remaining pet patients: 'Bouncer', a beagle owned by the Brown family, and 'Fly', a spaniel belonging to Mr and Mrs Phillips.

I had also brought with me from my previous practice veterinary responsibility for the large collection of zoo animals at Belle Vue, but otherwise it was a matter of waiting for the telephone to ring. It did ring, and often, but invariably the caller was someone with a horse, a cat, a cow, or something else that was not in any way outlandish or untamed or might fall into my new province of 'exotica'. Already I had begun to wonder what had happened to the population of unusual pet animals out there. I knew that there were parrots and bush-babies and snakes and monkeys around for I had treated many of them in my old practice, but where were they now? Had they all been blessed simultaneously by uncommonly good health or had they been decimated, unknown to me, by some undiscriminating pandemic? Had folk with a penchant for cobras in the greenhouse or otters in the bathroom recanted and taken up pigeon-flying or suddenly seen the virtues of Siamese cats? Had they forgotten about me, now ready, willing and anxious to devote myself to their bizarre beasts or had they, more likely, never heard of me? Professionally prevented from advertising my presence as a zoo vet, I sat in the white-tiled dairy of my farmhouse that Shelagh had converted into an office, and began to consider whether my planned exotic animal practice was not only invisible but illusory.

To resist such gloomy fancies I filled my abundant spare time with reading, losing myself in piles of books and manuscripts about the care and treatment of wild creatures, which I found in the University library at Manchester. And now, coming home for lunch after a morning poring over such esoteric works as *Captain Bob's Experiences with Walruses, 1888–95*, I had found the undertaker's macabre visiting card.

The snug of my local pub, the White Lion, was almost

empty when I entered. Mr Fazakerly, whom I had heard of but never met, was instantly recognisable as he leaned against the copper-topped bar with a pint of bitter before him. Black jacket, faintly striped dark grey trousers, white shirt and black tie, the whole outfit clothed a slight and stooping figure surmounted by the pale face of a Low Church ecclesiastic and the Brylcreemed hair of a British Rail buffet car attendant. Coal-black eyes flanked a waxy, pointed nose.

'In nomine Patris, Filii . . .' the unmistakable undertaker was intoning as I walked over. I saw that he had a saucer of mussels in front of him, and that with one hand he was shaking drops of tabasco sauce from a small bottle over the plump bodies of the molluscs.

'Mr Fazakerly?' I asked.

The undertaker nodded but continued his invocation: '. . . et Spiritus Sancti.' When he was satisfied that each mussel had been splashed with the red sauce, he picked one up between black-gloved fingers and popped it into his mouth. Then he beckoned to the landlord before turning to me with a thin smile as delicate as hoar-frost on a thread of gossamer.

'Dr Taylor? Will you have a drink? How about a mussel?'

'Thank you,' I replied. 'I got your note on the, er, the box. What's it about?'

Mr Fazakerly wagged one glistening leather finger at me and drops of tabasco and mussel juice ran down onto his curling shirt cuff. 'Casket, Dr Taylor, casket, I beg you.'

'The casket, then, the one on my doorstep,' I went on correctly. 'Is it meant for me?'

The undertaker's whole face miraculously reformed itself into the spitting image of a saint or martyr as conceived by an Italian Baroque artist: the diagonally uptilted face, the lowered eyelids, the half-open, inverted crescent of pale lips, it was all there. He pressed his gloved palms gently together and breathed his next words towards me. 'The bereaved gave me your name, Dr Taylor. Normally we would not need assistance, but as this is a, well, rather unusual loved one. . .'

6

'Something's died?' I whispered awkwardly over the rim of my tankard.

'Some*one*, yes indeed. Sorely to be missed, I'm sure. A good, a loyal, an abiding friend.'

'Who?'

Mr Fazakerly cleared his throat and looked at me solemnly. I expected any moment that he would reach out, grasp my shoulder resolutely and support me as he delivered the sad tidings. 'Phillips—Lumbutts Lane. . .' He hesitated for a moment as if to give me a chance to take it all in, then he went on, 'The dear spaniel, Fly by name, I believe.'

Fly Phillips; so that was it. The epileptic spaniel with an incompetent mitral valve, who had uncomplainingly gobbled down each day a shower of multicoloured capsules, digitalis, tocopherol, primidone and phenytoin, was dead. Half of my remaining canine practice had passed on.

'How did it happen and how do you fit in?' I asked.

Mr Fazakerly looked about to break into tears. 'The loved one. . .'

'The dog,' I interrupted tetchily.

'. . . died suddenly in its sleep this morning. Mr and Mrs Phillips called you but you were not at home, so they contacted us.'

'To bury him, I presume?'

'No, Dr Taylor, to prepare him.'

Now I was stumped. As far as I knew, the Phillipses were not any sort of religious eccentrics. They were devoted to their pet, but I had never heard them mention anything special that should happen to Fly after he died. They were well-off, and I could imagine them forking out the cash to have the dog properly buried, but what was this about preparation?

I wondered if Mr Fazakerly, despite all this solemnity, was playing some sort of joke, fuelled by the White Lion's best bitter. Grinning, I thumped my companion in the ribs. 'Come on,' I said, 'you can't be serious. What do you mean by preparing him?'

Mr Fazakerly did not allow his pious expression to slip so much as a millimetre; there was no hint of a smile, no relaxation of his frown. 'Dr Taylor, the loved. . ., that is the dog, Fly Phillips, is to be buried in a plot at Mumbles on the Welsh coast, where he used to run on the cliffs as a puppy. Mumbles is over two hundred miles from here. My firm has been asked to embalm him.'

'Embalm the dog!' I exclaimed. 'You must be pulling my leg.'

The undertaker sighed and looked round conspiratorially to make sure that he was not being overheard. 'Not at all, Doctor. He is to be embalmed in a running position, albeit lying on his side, with his ears tastefully disposed as if blowing in the wind as he gaily bowls along.'

Astounded, I could still detect no chink in the under-taker's grave countenance. To give myself time to collect my thoughts, I invited him to have another pint.

'No, thank you. We can't possibly discuss matters further here. Let's go to your home. I'll meet you there.'

We left the pub and I climbed into my car. As I pulled out onto the main road moments later, I glanced into the driving mirror. A few yards behind me was cruising a highly polished Daimler hearse with Mr Fazakerly at the wheel.

Back at the house, the coffin was still lying on the door-step. Soundly asleep on top of it was Lupin, my cat. There was nobody about although Henry, our pet goat, with his head as usual poking inquisitively through the market-garden gate, did seem to be straining his ears in our direc-tion. The undertaker eyed Henry and motioned me away out of the goat's earshot.

'The dog must be embalmed, as I explained. I have all my equipment and materials with me, but as you will appreci-ate, my, er, subjects are normally humans. Of dogs I have no anatomical knowledge. That is why I need you to help me achieve a perfect closed circuit.'

'Closed circuit?'

8

'Yes, indeed, the touchstone of one in my profession, Dr Taylor: absence of bubbles.'

Mr Fazakerly had lost me again. What had all this flatulent talk to do with circuits and dead dogs? I decided to push on and tackle the bubbles when they appeared.

'So you want me to help you at the embalming?' I said.

'Yes.'

'Where is the body?'

'In the casket.'

I looked across at Lupin, blissfully unconscious with his head resting on the twinkling brass plate.

'Couldn't we have done this at your premises?' I asked. Fazakerly's Chapel of Rest was a sizeable building near the Town Hall.

The undertaker looked alarmed and tut-tutted. 'Oh, I'm afraid not, dear sir. We have our other loved ones and their bereaveds and their bereaveds' feelings to think of. I mean, if it got around the Freemasons and the Catenians and all the rest of our clientèle that Fazakerly's wasn't exclusively for, er, homo sapiens. . . Oh no! Quite out of the question. Hence the need for some degree of secrecy.'

A few minutes later Henry the goat watched soberly as Mr Fazakerly and I carried the coffin into the shed that I was planning to use for autopsying the cadavers of exotic birds, reptiles and small mammals which would, I hoped, soon begin to arrive by post from all over the world. Mr Fazakerly went back to the hearse and returned with a large black box which he placed on the floor near the examination table. Then he unscrewed the brass knobs of the little coffin, took off the lid and brought out the body of the cocker spaniel. I was intrigued, and waited expectantly for the undertaker to begin his arcane rites.

Fazakerly opened his black box, which was split into two equal halves. One side contained two large glass flasks, one empty and the other full of clear, pink liquid; there were also coils of rubber tubing and a shiny, dagger-like instrument.

The other side of the box was crammed with cosmetics: creams, powders, make-up sticks, eye-liners, rouges.

'Leichner,' said Fazakerly proudly, when he saw me staring at his collection. 'We always use Leichner—nothing but the best for Fazakerly's.' He fished in the box and pulled out a lipstick. 'The latest spring fashion—crusty pearl. May I offer this as a present for your wife, Doctor? Or would she prefer some gunmetal mascara?'

Hastily, I made up some story about Shelagh being allergic to the stuff.

Fazakerly returned the cosmetics to their compartment, then put the two flasks, the tubing and the dagger instrument on the table near the body. 'In order to preserve the loved one's appearance and presentability for the inspection of the bereaved between now and the interment in Wales,' he began, 'I shall now replace all the loved . . . the dog's blood with this pink solution of formalin in water coloured with cochineal. In humans I would set up an airtight closed-circuit pumping system by attaching one rubber tube via a glass cannula to an ankle vein. This tube leads into the empty flask, and a second tube links the empty flask to the one containing pink fluid. A third runs from there to this trocar'—Mr Fazakerly picked up the dagger-like instrument—'which is inserted by a deft thrust through the upper abdomen and diaphragm into the left ventricle of the heart. By squeezing this rubber enema pump clipped into the system, I can cause blood to enter the empty flask and be replaced via the heart and arterial system by the suitably coloured preserving fluid in the other container.'

Mr Fazakerly's enthusiastic exposition of his art had left him slightly breathless. He turned to me. 'So now you see why you are required, Doctor. Since my anatomical knowledge extends only to the human, you must find me an ankle vein on the dog and, more importantly, the left ventricle. I needn't say how vital it is that the loved one isn't mutilated unnecessarily.'

10

I thought about it. The 'ankle' vein would be no problem, and it took only a second to attach the first tube to a blood vessel below the right hock joint. The precise point at which to insert the dagger-like trocar was far trickier. Fazakerly was right. For his pumping system to work efficiently without air entering the system, the trocar had to be placed absolutely correctly; anywhere else and the strange postmortem circulation of liquids just would not take place. The problem was that a dog's heart is quite small, and the left ventricle forms only one quarter of the heart. Its position in the living animal is fairly precise, but it is much less easily located from outside after death and least of all with a big instrument designed for the larger human species.

After much careful consideration I selected a spot and inserted the undertaker's grim weapon. He connected all the tubes, checked for obvious leaks and began to pump vigorously. I watched the two flasks with fascination, feeling a bit like Igor, Dr Frankenstein's idiot assistant.

Some dark blood fell into the empty flask, while the level of pink fluid in the other fell slightly. Then, with a friendly chuffing sound, the empty flask began to fill with great big pink bubbles. All the tubes began to gurgle and vibrate.

'Holy Harry!' exclaimed Fazakerly irritably and pumping ever more furiously. 'Look at those bubbles. The circuit's faulty. You've got it wrong!'

It was not much use explaining that cardiac punctures on stiff and lifeless cadavers were hardly everyday work for veterinarians, so I began to fiddle with the tubes, made sure the connections were tight and adjusted the position of the trocar. My anatomical expertise and reputation were at stake.

The undertaker pumped some more and the froth multiplied. Bubbles danced prettily and inexplicably through the pink embalming fluid which was now certainly not going down. Mr Fazakerly positively growled at me. He couldn't have looked more deadly serious. He pumped on with wild abandon. Suddenly, the flask containing the fluid hiccupped and blew its lid off. Smelly formalin ran over Mr Fazakerly's black boots.

'There—you see! Look at that! That's never happened in all Fazakerlys' seventy-eight years!' He lowered his voice to a passionate whisper. 'Imagine what our bereaveds would say if that happened in the home!'

My future as a mortician's apprentice had never looked bleaker, but try as I might, I could not re-adjust the trocar in a way that started the exchange of liquids. Air was entering the system somehow. We both waggled the tubes, pushed and pulled, but it was no use. Eventually the undertaker reluctantly suggested that I operate on the dead animal, correctly place and sew in the trocar and then stitch everything up neatly beneath the long hair. For the first time since I was a student I practised surgery on a dead animal, but an hour later I had managed to link up Fazakerly's confounded plumbing system and the fluids began to flow. Fly was embalmed.

Mr Fazakerly was by now a trifle less indignant. He bent down to his black box again and rummaged among the cosmetics.

'You're not . . .' I began incredulously.

'I am indeed,' he replied, straightening up with a fistful of tubes and waxy sticks. 'Fazakerlys' are rightly appreciated for their thoughtful and realistic attention to every detail.'

Still keeping his gloves on, he began to reflect the lips of the dead spaniel and to reinforce the pale pink tinge produced by the embalming fluid with a liberal application of coloured cream. A glazed, partly-open eye was given a liquid glint by dropping in some glycerine, and the dried-up nose was freshened into the counterfeit dampness of health through the vigorous application of Nivea cream.

When my companion was satisfied with his artistry he stood back to admire the overall effect. 'Hmm. That seems fine,' he said. 'D'you see how I've got the shading of the tongue just right?' It was indeed a glorious salmon pink.

'I've done the make-up for Littleshaw Amateur Players for years, you know.'

Not with the same black boxful of cosmetics, I hoped.

It was time to box Fly's remains, now eternally glorious. The little coffin was neatly lined with white satin. We placed Fly inside. 'Now for the final effect,' said the undertaker. He flapped the two ears up over the head and, straining with all his might against the hold of rigor mortis, gradually persuaded the fore limbs to creak forwards and the hind limbs to groan backwards. Fly was silently galloping over the heath.

'There,' said Mr Fazakerly. With a sigh of satisfaction, he put the lid on the coffin and tightened the screws. 'The bereaveds will be satisfied and reassured, I think,' he said solemnly. 'Now, Doctor, would you be so good as to help me carry the casket out in proper fashion? In case there's anybody about, I don't want Fazakerly's to be thought capable of levity or lack of propriety.'

I guessed correctly what he meant. With Mr Fazakerly at the front and me at the back, the coffin was hoisted onto our left shoulders. When the undertaker gave the word the cortège trooped out of the shed and, at a pace that Fazakerlys' over seventy-eight years had no doubt found appropriately sedate and impressive, bore its burden towards the waiting hearse. Only Henry looked on as we slid the coffin in and Mr Fazakerly gravely shut the doors.

'Well, good afternoon then, Doctor,' said the undertaker, shaking my hand and leaving my fingers smelling of pickled mussels, formalin and greasepaint. 'I'll leave you my card. Perhaps Fazakerlys' can be at your service some time.'

After he had driven off at a sedate speed, I gave the business card to Henry, who quickly gobbled it down. 'Do you think that might have been some sort of ill omen for the future?' I asked the old goat.

Henry said nothing but his wise eyes, with their pupils like ever-open letter boxes, twinkled. No, it was going to be all right.

Two

Autumn was upon us shortly after Fly, the embalmed spaniel, had been lowered to his rest overlooking the Welsh coastline. Autumn in Manchester meant chill, clammy air and sulphureous mists that stung the eyes and clutched at the throat. It was the time for smog, the yellow blend of water vapour and industrial smoke, and smog time was always busy for the veterinarian of a city zoo. Each year as October came round, cases of disease and death among the animals at Belle Vue began to soar. Peacocks hacked away like chain-smokers, tigers heaved their chests with the desperate concentration of asthmatics, and chimpanzees wiped running eyes and nostrils with the backs of hairy hands. And animals died. Some, experiencing all this for the first time, died quickly from pneumonia. Others, the time-servers, finally gave up the struggle against fibrous lungs and chronically enlarged hearts and wheezed their last. Most animals do not live long enough to develop the chronic degenerative changes seen in humans, but at Manchester, in the bodies of big cats, rhinoceroses, apes and the like, I saw all the post-mortem signs associated with old human city-dwellers.

That year, not only was the smog particularly bad, but Winter must have been snapping at Autumn's heels. The leaves browned, fell and were whisked away by the moist wind, and within a few days precocious atoms of ice silvered the bare trees in Belle Vue's Victorian gardens. What was more, as if Matt Kelly, the zoo's Irish head keeper, was not busy enough breaking the ice on moated paddocks to prevent inmates walking their way to freedom, the small boys

14

who daily invade the zoo grounds free by scaling unscalable walls, outrunning corpulent gate keepers and various other means, became unusually active: perhaps it was the early frost that kept them on the move.

Worse still, there was a positive epidemic of animals going 'over the wall' in the other direction. The keepers had neglected to re-clip the flight feathers of the flamingoes at six-monthly intervals, and on a suitably windy day a gang of the gorgeous birds took off and cleared the zoo walls, never to be seen again. With even less chance of survival unless they could reach some centrally heated building, complete with a supply of mice for food, a posse of young rattlesnakes set forth from the reptile house one day after sneaking through a broken pane of glass. When he found seven of the venomous reptiles absent without leave, the keeper in charge decided to keep quiet about it in the hope that either they would turn up or the low temperatures outside would finish the little wanderers and so remove any threat to the local population. If it were known that such creatures were on the loose, he could foresee a drastic reduction in the numbers of visitors coming to the zoo to walk round the exhibits with their children on a Sunday morning. This in turn would undoubtedly lead to the zoo director giving him the boot.

The keeper tried to conceal his loss by stuffing rocks, logs and vegetation of all sorts into the rattlesnake vivarium, so that what had been a fair simulation of the dry, sun-baked environment of a Californian rattler, with coiled serpents easily seen against a sandstone background, was transformed into a dripping, dense and inappropriate jungle, in which the rattlesnakes could rarely be glimpsed, let alone counted. This trick worked until two little girls, coming through the main gates on their way to the fairground, came across a pretty, if rather sluggish, little snake wearily making in the general direction of the bus stop. They picked it up, were quick to spot that it was not a worm, were relieved to see that it had not got a V-mark behind its head—the little

15

girls had been learning about Britain's only poisonous snake, the adder at natural history lessons—and popped it into one of their purses. Their brother would just love to have a grass snake as a pet.

Later that day, back at home, Dad wound the little snake round his fingers, remarking how the warmth was making the little fellow much more agile and alert. Then he noticed the curious rings of loosely jointed dried skin at the tail. For some reason, although he was a builder's mate and this was the middle of Manchester, something worried him about those rings and he reached for a copy of *Pears Cyclopaedia*. Two minutes later he broke into a sweat and dashed to phone the police.

Matt Kelly, the head keeper, was the one who had to clear the mess up, calm down the builder's mate and his family, defuse the concern of the constabulary and divert the Press with blarney. He then fired the reptile keeper.

To add still more to our troubles that autumn, the numbers of animals being bodily purloined rose dramatically. All zoos have stock stolen from time to time: a guinea-pig or two from the Pets' Corner, tortoises from the reptile house, birds particularly parrots and cockatoos, and a variety of small mammals. Although it appeared that 'fences' did not want to touch gorillas, tigers or ostriches, that autumn saw some sizeable creatures disappear. One almost had to admire the thieves who got clean away with a five-foot alligator of irascible temperament in broad daylight, while the two little urchins who were collared half a mile from the zoo, breathlessly lugging home a trio of outraged coatimundi bundled inside a sack, must otherwise have led sainted lives not to have been severely injured by the hard-biting beasts.

Matt Kelly had hardly finished giving the crestfallen young culprits a lecture which, despite his soft Irish brogue, set their ears burning, when he was summoned to the scene of more animals gone a-missing. Two valuable De Brazza monkeys had vanished from the monkey house and the monkey keeper was certain that they had been stolen. A party had been round just before they had gone, a boisterous bunch of noisy schoolchildren. Matt quickly inspected the De Brazza cage; just possibly someone could have forced apart the vertical wires that formed the front. But how could they have grabbed hold of a big, tough species that could bite harder than a dog? Still, Matt had known it happen in the past—a jacket thrown over the animal, or even bare hands and bravado and never mind the bites and the blood when showing off in front of your pals. Before now the head keeper had stopped a coach laden with children before it left the park and had retrieved from under a seat a penguin with its powerful beak safely immobilised by rubber bands, and a wallaby hog-tied by a blushing schoolgirl's black lisle stockings. Anything could happen.

Matt rushed off to the car park with the monkey keeper. They were too late; the school party's coach had gone. The school was traced and its headmaster contacted, but the pair of monkeys, to my mind the most attractive of all primate species with their olive coat, brown and white face and goatee beard, were not forthcoming. Matt cursed and worried. Both of us could imagine the two monkeys stuffed into a dark, cramped rabbit hutch somewhere in Greater Manchester and pressed to take a diet of sweetmeats and peanuts.

The next crisis of that eventful autumn for Belle Vue was not long in coming. Someone was pinching food. Fruit, vegetables and other things were being stolen, particularly from the great ape house, the modern, self-contained unit which housed the chimpanzees, orang-utans and gorillas. Len, the senior great ape keeper, was up in arms about it. Food pilfering by keepers is an unpleasant but not uncommon problem facing all zoos, but a particularly severe outbreak at Belle Vue a few years earlier had led to the most rigid controls being imposed there. Ration sheets were printed for each species, and a cook dispensed all the food to the keepers.

The system recommended by Jimmy Chipperfield at his safari parks of chopping all fruit before sending it from the stores was adopted—nobody wants to take home a pocketful of sliced apple or pear—and I personally presented the zoo with a fruit and vegetable chopper of the sort used by farmers for mashing turnips.

I discussed this latest problem with Len and Matt Kelly. 'Whoever's doing it, they're damned sharp at it,' said Len, as he told us how some 'hands' of bananas had vanished during the tea break. 'Funny thing is, I didn't pass any keepers on my way back from the cafeteria.'

The great ape house stood apart from the other units, so anyone entering or leaving the house would have had to cross an area of open ground. The nearest unit was the Pets' Corner.

'Mebbe it's that new feller in there, the one that's lookin' after the goats and the donkeys,' growled Matt. 'Oi'll wander over and root around.'

But Matt found nothing to incriminate anybody in the Pets' Corner in any way—no banana skins in the dustbin, nothing secreted in the staff rest room. Two weeks passed. Each day one section or another reported losses of food. Apples here, tomatoes there, but always Len's great ape house was hardest hit.

Then came the nastiness. First it was a fountain pen that went, then a cigarette lighter. Finally, when a packet of cheroots disappeared while Len nipped over to the men's room, the great ape keeper had had enough. He stormed into the director's office, white-faced behind his spectacles.

'Get the police in,' he demanded. 'This light-fingered sneak-thief's gone too far.'

A report was made to the police and a detective-constable made a perfunctory visit, but there was nothing to show him and even less to be done, except to keep a sharp eye open.

'Oi'll have him. Oi'll catch him with the stuff on him one of these foine days,' proclaimed Matt after Len's lunch, a packet of sandwiches, vanished into thin air. 'Oi think the bloighter's havin' us on, teasin' us.'

It made sense. Pinching juicy peaches or even a lighter was one thing, but having designs on Len's meat paste sandwiches suggested more mischief than criminal dishonesty.

Despite a high level of vigilance, Matt and his men made no progress in identifying the miscreant and the crime wave grew. Night attacks became more frequent than ones during the day, and the fact that there was no forcing of locks or windows anywhere confirmed our suspicions that a keeper with a key was behind it all. When the real malevolence began, it all seemed to be aimed at the unfortunate Len.

'This—this imbecile, this kleptomaniac has a grudge against me,' he moaned bitterly to me one day, as we wrestled with a baby chimp that needed his polio jab. 'Vindictiveness, that's all it is. It can only be a keeper who thinks I've done wrong by him.'

'Why, what's he done now?' I asked.

Len drew in a great breath and then spat out the words with ripe indignation. 'Crapped in my tea!'

'I'm sorry, I don't understand.'

'Crapped—defecated—in my tea!'

Trying to keep a straight face, I asked 'What, how, when?'

'This morning, at eleven o'clock. I brewed up in the ape house instead of going to the cafeteria, poured a cup for me and one for Harold.' Harold was the patriarch of the orangutans at Belle Vue, a red-haired potentate with a figure like a Sumo wrestler, who relished a mug of sweet, milky tea. 'I took Harold his, came back to my room, picked up my cup and there it was, floating on the surface.'

I cleared my throat. 'Could it not have been, say, chimpanzee or orang excrement?' The great apes generally are enthusiastic and skilled throwers of faecal matter. Some, such as an orang at Rhenen Zoo in Holland or a male chimp at Dudley, are so adept at inswingers and so accurate, even when bowling backwards, that it beats me why they have not been snapped up by the MCC cricket team or transferred for a fat fee to the New York Yankees.

Len sniffed. 'It could not,' he said. 'No apes were loose. The cup and the table it was on are twenty feet or more away from the nearest animals, which are separated from the passageway leading to my room by a brick wall anyway, and the stainless steel drawers that are set in the wall for passing food through were closed. The only animal that could have had access to my tea was a human!'

'I suppose it could have been a chimp stool that he picked up and dropped in,' I ventured.

'Still a dirty, filthy, perverted sense of humour,' Len scowled.

The next day the invisible thief and defiler of teacups, if they were one and the same person, struck again. This time it was another batch of Len's sandwiches, not stolen but left crowned with a noisome offering. To add insult to injury his daily newspaper had been removed. '*Daily Mirror* gone and crap on my lunch,' Len roared at Matt and me as we tried not to laugh.

As usual there had been no sign of the villain, but interestingly the deed had been done while Len was feeding his animals elsewhere in the house with the outside door to the passageway leading to his room securely locked. Len was also quite certain that the catch had been dropped on the Yale lock when he closed it. Even if the culprit had a key to the house, it would have been useless with the catch down. The only logical answer, if Len was right, was that the villain had been in the house all the time.

I decided to look again at the scene of the crime. Len's room was a bare, smooth-walled place with an empty isolation cage against one wall and a single door. High on the wall facing the door was a window that flapped back on runners, leaving an opening too small for a human to climb through. The only furniture was a small sink with a gas ring, and the table. I looked around. Just possibly someone could throw objects from the outside up and over the window when it was open, but aiming would be impossible. I looked up at the ceiling and at the large, galvanised central heating duct which ran across the width of the room. Then I noticed something. The vent for warm air was a slotted grille in the duct, and it was situated directly over the table.

The great ape house's revolutionary system of channelling warm air to all the exhibits through the galvanised ducting had proved very successful until it was found that thick growths of mould had begun to sprout on the inside of the metal tube, encouraged by the warm, moist air. I had been consulted with an eye to possible health hazards from fungus spores being inhaled by the animals, and had managed to solve the problem by getting Len to spray a non-toxic fungicide into the airstream once a week. I recalled climbing up on a chair and looking into the mould-caked ducting through a manhole. Sure enough, every few yards there was a manhole covered by a disc of metal that was secured by two wing-nuts. The manhole in Len's room was firmly sealed. I walked back down the passageway and looked up at the ducting. Another manhole, sealed. Then another, its covering plate slightly askew and leaving a gap at one edge. Halfway down the passage was one manhole where the cover was completely off. I looked up at a round black hole from which a draught of warm air blew gently down.

'Get a torch, Len,' I said. 'I'm going to have a look up there.'

When at last a torch was found, Matt produced a step-ladder and I climbed up to the hole. There was just enough room for me to get my head and one arm in. I switched on the torch and shone it down to my left. An empty black tunnel, dusty but no longer choked with mould, stretched down to the end of the house. Wriggling round, I pointed the torch down the length of ducting extending over Len's room.

The torch beam ran along more sheets of grimy black

metal, then suddenly it was shining on a colourful, twinkling tableau at the far end, a cross between Fagin's den and Aladdin's cave. There, blinking in the beam of light, caught red-handed with surprise and apprehension written all over their faces, skulked the two missing De Brazza monkeys. They crouched on a bed of paper, shredded cheroots, dried vegetable peel and nutshells, surrounded by fruit of every kind, some fresh, some half-eaten. Bags of nuts, dog biscuits, potato chips and bars of stolen chocolate were near at hand. Amid the debris the polished metal of a lighter and a fountain pen glinted.

'Gotcha!' I said quietly, and climbing grinning down the step-ladder.

'Who's up there? Let me get at 'em,' shouted Len, rushing forward to take my place. There was a silence, then his wrath turned to chuckles as he came face to face with his perse-cutors at last.

The episode drew to a swift close. The De Brazzas were injected by dart-pistol with phencyclidine, a quick-acting anaesthetic, and when they were unconscious I raked them back to the manhole using a shepherd's crook lashed to the end of a long pole. Matt hauled the two dreaming felons back to their quarters in the monkey house, while Len cleared out the den in the ducting. The total weight of the cache of food and other items was seventy-eight pounds.

I was surprised that Len, while sitting in his room, had not heard any noises in the duct above him; heavily-built speci-mens like De Brazzas would surely have made a racket moving around on the thin metal floor of their hideaway. But the senior keeper had noticed nothing apart from the gentle scurry of mice, a sound to which he had long been accus-tomed. We could only assume that the monkeys, like prison-ers of war on the run, had lain motionless amid their booty as long as the 'enemy' was present below. It was surely acciden-tal that they had fouled Len's tea and sandwiches in obeying calls of nature close to the air vent. But what had happened when there were no humans about, particularly at night? They must have dropped from the manhole, moved up the passageway to Len's room and left the house through the gap in his permanently flapped-back window. From there it would be easy to enter almost any other building in the zoo through holes, skylights or broken windows. De Brazzas have a distinguished, aristocratic countenance and, loping over the flower beds with armfuls of edible swag, they would have been the nearest thing in the monkey world to Raffles and Bunny.

Three

It might have been a scene from a film about the Green Berets: I was John Wayne with an M16 carbine crouched at the open door of a helicopter gunship as it whirled low over the bush. Not quite, but I was hanging from my straps with the down-draught from the helicopter rotor arms blowing cold around me and my eye jammed to the sights of a rifle. I had drawn a shaky bead on something on the sunbaked ground forty feet below.

'Right ho, Doc, let her have it!' shouted the pilot, levelling the chopper out.

I squeezed the trigger gently. There was an almost inaudible crack and a spot of blue suddenly appeared on the offside haunch of the zebra mare galloping flat out through grass dark with our insect-like shadow and pressed flat by our rushing wind.

'Got her!' I bellowed, and we curved abruptly so that my doorway was full of the rich blue of the African sky studded with a scatter of vultures turning idly like paper mobiles suspended from a ceiling and keeping an eye on the flash of our red strobe lights. Although it was high noon, we had four strobes working; vultures dozed off after lunch, it seemed, as they sailed on the thermals, and the idea of intense flashes of light from the helicopter was to interrupt their morbid reveries and protect us from collision.

A minute later we settled down onto the scrubland in a cloud of yellow dust. Not far away the zebra mare was buckling at the knees, nostrils flared, eyes unseeing. Tidily she collapsed and rolled onto her side. Louie, the pilot, was already giving directions over the radio that would bring the boys in the truck over to us, while I ducked under the slowing rotor blades and ran with my tool-box towards the zebra.

Not a war film, not jet-set hunting even, at least not of the killing sort. I was in East Africa, on the Kenya-Tanzania border about fifty miles south-east of Arusha, collecting a group of zebras for Mr van den Baars, a Dutch animal dealer and one of my best customers. Instead of the pole and lasso handling from a pursuing truck, we were trying out the more sophisticated technique of air-to-ground missiles: blue-tufted flying syringes fired by compressed air from a dart-rifle and loaded with etorphine, a powerful, reversible anaesthetic.

It had been a very successful week, with thirty zebra captured, no deaths, no fractures, no men injured and only eight flying syringes, worth around ten pounds each, lost through misses. It had also been a helluva good time, with cold beer at the Nairobi Hilton every evening and slivers of roast lamb eaten before sunrise with Masai herdsmen after we had put the helicopter down beside one of their lonely circular corrals of thorns. Back home, the hills round Rochdale were showing their first sprinkling of December snow.

When the truck rolled up quarter of an hour later, the sleeping zebra was lifted easily by half a dozen cheerful Africans into a wooden crate. Just before dropping the slide to shut her in, I injected a syringeful of antidote into her jugular vein. She would be on her feet within minutes. Later in the day the whole bag of zebra would be on their way via Nairobi to quarantine in Mombasa, and after a couple of months there, they would make the three-week journey by sea round the Cape to Rotterdam. The mare was the last of the consignment.

Louie, a young white Kenyan with red hair and beard and a skin like burnished bronze, sat in the shade of his chopper with a grin on his face. He squinted after the dust cloud that was the wagon bouncing its way back to Nairobi and unscrewed a bottle of pomegranate juice.

'Well, Dave,' he said, with the rather old-fashioned turn of phrase to which I had become accustomed, 'I fancy all is hunky-dory. A spiffing week, I'd say.' For someone who was considered one of the toughest bush pilots in East Africa and had survived two serious crashes during the Mau Mau troubles, Louie talked like an Etonian officer cadet. 'What do you want to do for the rest of the day?' he went on, passing me the bottle. 'Care for a spin towards Meru? We might get a peek at some of those poacher johnnies.'

Elephant poaching was rife. We had dropped down a few days earlier beside the bloated corpse of a big bull that had died slowly from a gut shot. His tusks had been hacked from him while he lay dying and would by now be on their way to the Nairobi dealers who would turn them into souvenirs for genteel blue-rinsed ladies on package tours from the Home Counties, Connecticut or Cologne. Yes, I would dearly like to come across poachers in action, even though it was costing my client eighty pounds an hour to keep the helicopter in the air, and even though the poachers were reputed to be hard cases who would exchange fire with police and game wardens and pump rifle slugs at whirly-birds like ours that intruded on their rapacious forays.

'Top hole. Let's get the old girl wound up,' said Louie happily when I agreed.

The engine thumped into life, and soon we were scything through the air, our skids almost touching the tops of the acacia trees. There was not much life about: a small cluster of elephants sheltering from the midday sun, a lone warthog scooting angrily from a mudbank as we went milling by, a clay-red Masai in a ragged shawl leaning against the trunk of a baobab with the elegance of a Roman senator.

'I can remember when the game hereabouts was thick as locusts,' shouted Louie, 'but look at it now. Over-hunting, poaching, indiscriminate burning of tree cover. It's a bally shame.'

I looked down at a rare trio of whiskery wildebeest. Only a decade ago they would have been like lemmings around here at this season of the year. All at once we passed over a handful of zebras trotting apprehensively beneath our shadow.

'Some poppets among that lot,' bellowed my pilot. 'Still, we've got our quota.' He pulled the helicopter round into a tight circle and we ran back to look at the zebras head-on.

The lead stallion had had enough of this uncomfortable aerial attention. He wheeled about and broke into a fast gallop, the rest of the herd keeping up with him. There were ten altogether, including three young foals. We followed, hovering, as they raced along. I could not hear the pounding of their hooves but they were raising plenty of dust. There were trees ahead, leafless, twisted skeletons of acacia killed by a grass fire. As the zebras charged towards the trees they split into two groups, one passing the gnarled white trunks on the right, the other on the left. Once past the trees, they re-united into a compact band—except for one of the foals. From our seats in our floating plastic bubble, thirty yards behind them, we saw it gallop full tilt towards one of the acacias. It was twenty feet from the tree, going straight as an arrow. Ten, eight, still flat out. The machinery above us drowned the sound of the thwack. There must have been one, for the young zebra slammed hard and unswerving into the bleached wood and fell instantly as if pole-axed.

'Land!' I yelled, but Louie was already closing the throttle. He touched down light as a feather. The zebra herd had disappeared as we both ran across to the little body lying beneath the tree.

I knelt down and put my hand flat on the foal's chest. It was alive, for I could feel the heart thumping under my palm. I raised its head. Its nose was bleeding. I pressed cautiously over the head bones, but there was no detectable fracture. It was a youngster of around three weeks, concussed, out for the count.

'Darn queer how it ran slap bang into the tree,' mused Louie.

I lifted an eyelid to test the corneal reflex. Then I lifted the other.

'Damnation, just look at that!' I exclaimed, pointing to the eyes. 'There's your answer.'

Louie bent close as I indicated the blue-white spots deep within each of the eyeballs. They were true cataracts. The baby zebra was as blind as a bat.

The foal blinked and shook its head feebly. It was coming round.

'What are we going to do with the little blighter?' asked Louie.

At that moment I was not at all sure of the answer. 'Get my gear, please,' I said.

Louie loped back to the helicopter for the workman's tool-box in which I carry a full set of emergency equipment when on safari—whether in Africa or on English moorland. I gave the foal an injection of valium and betamethasone. We sat on the baking ground, watching as it wobbled into a sitting position.

What to do? That was indeed a poser. It was amazing that the animal had survived so long. I assumed that they were congenital cataracts, present at birth. The foal's dam must have taken good care of it, keeping a watchful eye to see that it did not stray too far from her side. It must have used touch and smell to feed, and hearing to move when the others did. But its future in the bush was predictable and sure to be brief. Taken by a hunting dog, hyena or lion, drowned at a waterhole, breaking its neck by falling into a dry river bed; one of those or something similar was the foal's certain fate today, tomorrow—soon, anyway. To be young and sightless when death came out of the long savanna grass or the red mud or the parched rock: life in the bush is devoid of pity and only the fittest survive.

Louie and I both knew this, but we were involved now, and we also knew we had to make a decision on the wild animal's behalf. Let it go? Maybe it would be found again by the herd. Kill it? I had a bottle of barbiturate in the box. I looked again at the unseeing eyes. A sunbeam caught one of the pupils and it narrowed fractionally. There was a faint light reflex, then, which meant that a normal retina probably lay behind the opaque lens.

'What are we going to do?' repeated Louie, looking concerned.

I made up my mind. 'Take it back with us,' I replied.

'Super idea.' Louie brightened at once and helped me carry the drunken-looking foal to the helicopter. 'But what are you going to do with him, old boy?'

That I was not so clear about. Get him back to Nairobi first of all. Then what? He could be artificially reared easily enough on cow's milk diluted with lime water and sweetened with lactose: I had done it several times at zoos in England. Maybe John Seago, the Nairobi animal catcher and a man with a deep feeling for all kinds of living things and infinite patience, would take the foal on. But the eyes, they would not clear spontaneously. What about them?

'Call up the Seago organisation,' I shouted when we were in the air. 'See if they're prepared to foster it after an operation.'

Louie got busy on the radio. When I was in general practice I had taken a special interest in ophthalmology, done a post-graduate course in eye surgery at Manchester Royal Infirmary and extracted a number of cataractous eye lenses from domestic dogs. I had never tackled a single case in a zoo animal.

'Seago and his partner are away for the next few weeks on a catching expedition,' Louie informed me after a while. 'What about keeping it at my place?'

I thought about it as we whirled towards the outskirts of Nairobi. Maybe van den Baars would accept the youngster if the operation went well. Louie had a big farm with lots of good loose-boxes. I decided that if the Dutch dealer would agree to have the foal added to his shipment, I would operate and the little animal could go down to Mombasa after a week or two. I would only be in Kenya for another fourteen days, so I would have to get cracking immediately. After I left, maybe one of the local veterinarians would keep an eye on the patient—if the surgery was successful. There were a lot of 'ifs', particularly in removing the lenses from an animal's eyes.

Back at base, the truck had not yet arrived. The zebras caught earlier in the week were munching alfalfa inside high wooden corrals. While Louie arranged the quartering of the foal in a cool loose-box at his farm, I went to phone van den Baars. As I had anticipated, the bluff Dutchman was pleased with the success of our helicopter hunt and readily agreed to take a chance on the little fellow. Now I could make arrangements for the operation, although the prospect made my spine tingle with a mixture of fear and excitement.

When I went back to the loose-box, a young Kikuyu with buck teeth and a smile from ear to ear was leaning over the half-door, looking at the foal. The animal was on its feet and wandering dreamily about.

'Jambo, Doctor,' said the African. 'I am Augustine. Mr Louie says I am to help look after the young one.'

'Have you taken care of young stock before, Augustine?'

'Yessir. Waterbuck, impala, Tommies, leopards, many things.'

'You'll do excellently. Now please make up a feed for it like this.' I gave him instructions and he went off for the ingredients and feeding bottle at a jog.

I took Augustine's place at the half-door, and watched the little zebra walk smack into a wall. He was moving so slowly he came to no harm, but it was clear that I would have to operate within forty-eight hours. First I wanted him to get over his shaking-up in the bush, and I also needed the time to dilate his pupils as much as possible with atropine ointment to give me a wide opening to approach the lenses. Augustine bottled the milk mixture into the foal with firm yet gentle expertise. It looked as if the baby—we decided to call him Tatu, Swahili for 'three', because he had three black spots on his forehead and was three weeks old—had found a capable foster parent.

Louie and I drove into the city. Although I had my pack of basic surgical instruments in my tool-box, they were not suitable for eye work. I needed special scalpels, forceps, needles and silk thread among other things. First stop was the main hospital, where I explained my problem to the consultant ophthalmologist. A pawky Scotsman with a broad Glaswegian accent, he had been an MO with the old King's African Rifles.

' 'Fraid there'd be the dickens of a row if I was caught lending out the theatre equipment,' said the surgeon, 'but what I can do is let ye use my old field kit. It's a bit antiquated but ye should be all right.'

He produced his set of instruments. They were collector's items: ivory-handled, thin-bladed cataract knives, loops and hooks for teasing out lenses, and tiny needle-holders. All matching, they lay in padded velvet within a brass-inlaid mahogany box.

'Take them and welcome. Hope ye're successful,' he said. 'After all, we Glesga graduates must stick together, mustn't we?' The surgeon insisted on our having a dram with him and talking about our Scottish alma mater before we left.

Next I called on a veterinarian who had a sizeable horse practice around Nairobi. He willingly agreed to watch over Tatu's post-operative care when I went on my way the week after next.

All was arranged. Now all I needed was a large helping of luck—and no nasty surprises lurking in a zebra's eye to

31

booby-trap me on what was, as far as I could tell, the first cataract operation on the species.

Two days later, Tatu was strong, lively and highly strung. His pupils were nicely dilated. I decided to operate in the cool of the day before the flies clocked on. With Augustine and Louie each holding one end of him, I slowly injected a dose of xylazine solution into his jugular. After three minutes Tatu was sleeping soundly and I dropped local anaesthetic copiously into each eye. When I was satisfied that all sensation had been dulled to nothing, we lifted the foal onto a table set up outside his loose-box. The light from a pink and silver sky was good.

Many folk imagine the eye to be a terribly frail organ that must be handled like a soap bubble. In fact it is a tough and resourceful piece of equipment that can be tackled surgically with the same basic techniques of cutting and stitching—needle and scissor work identical to that of the seamstress—which are employed on humbler areas of the body.

One cut opened the transparent and remarkably thick cornea along one-third of its circumference. Now for the tricky bit. The lens lies behind the pupil, suspended on tough strands of rubbery jelly. First I had to get a grip on the lens, a task rather like grasping a miniature greasy pig. I managed it with the help of a small rubber bulb and a metal pipe which stuck to the lens by suction pressure. Now to free the lens. I wiggled it very gently. It did not want to break free from its strands, so I would have to try dissolving the attachments with an enzyme. I injected a little of the chemical around the lens with a blunt needle, then waited for five minutes which seemed like five hours. Then the wiggling again. Marvellous! The enzyme had done its work, the lens came free and I lifted it out of the eye on the end of my suction tube.

Anxiously, I looked into the completely bloodless wound

in the eye. I was relieved to see that the thick jelly behind the lens had not tried to follow the lens out—a crucial matter. Now all that was left was to stitch the corneal incision with silk. The collapsed front of the eyeball would quickly fill up with water again if I made a watertight seal. In twenty minutes it was done. Dr Stewart-Scott, the Manchester surgeon who had let me attend his cataract operations on human patients, would have finished it in a quarter of the time. Still, I was as pleased as Punch. One eye done with no signs of trouble, now for the other.

We gently turned Tatu over and I began all over again. Augustine watched, wide-eyed. Louie dropped sterile saline into the foal's eye from a bottle every half-minute. It was beginning to warm up; I could not have the eye drying on me. The second eye went as well as the first had done. An hour and a half after I had knocked him out, Tatu was cataract-free.

'Whizzo, old boy,' crowed Louie as I plastered antibiotic cream into both eyes before we carried the unconscious foal back into the loose-box.

'Okay, okay, okay,' chuckled Augustine.

'Let's wait and see how he looks tomorrow before we start getting excited,' I said. 'Meanwhile keep him in the dark.'

Next day it was raining heavily when I went to look at Tatu's eyes. Augustine was standing outside the loose-box looking drenched and very miserable.

'Good morning, Doctor,' he said as I came up to him. 'Before you go in'—he cast his eyes down and I saw that there were tears as well as rain running down his face—'I have unfortunate news.'

My stomach turned over. The foal must be dead—post-operative collapse of some kind. Yet xylazine was normally so safe and reliable.

'What is it?' I asked, not daring to open the half-door.

The African kept his head down and spoke softly. 'I think, Doctor, that all was in vain. The cataract is back, worse than before in both eyes. I have seen it when I fed him this morning.'

Partially relieved, I flung open the half-door and looked inside. Tatu was standing quietly in a corner. 'Grab him quickly before he can hit anything,' I told Augustine.

The African went in silently and seized the foal around the neck. When he had backed its rump into a corner I went in and took out my pencil torch. The narrow beam of light played over the foal's eyes. True enough, they were blue-white again, all over; it was impossible to see the depths of the eyes. There was no sign of blood and the eyeballs had plumped up to their original shape. First class!

I slapped Augustine hard on the back. 'Don't alarm yourself, my friend,' I said. 'That's not the cataract back. Without lenses you can't get cataracts. The haziness of the cornea is quite natural after it's been interfered with. It will clear gradually over the next week or so.'

Augustine looked up at me and the ear-to-ear grin reappeared. More tears—of relief—trickled down his cheeks.

'Now go and get dried,' I ordered.

As the days passed, Augustine fed the foal, put cream in his eyes and generally fussed over him. The animal was taming surprisingly quickly. Each day I looked at the patient, and slowly the opacity of the cornea began to clear without any sign of infection or other complication. By the fifth day I got my first glimpse of the deepest part of the eye, the retina. It looked good, but I kept the pupils dilated with atropine and would not let the zebra be exposed to anything but the dimmest light. The acid test would come when I stopped the atropine and took out the stitches on the tenth day. Until then I had the other animals to blood sample and see loaded for Mombasa, and arrangements to make for a visit to Israel on the way home that van den Baars had just requested.

'What are you going to do if it failed?' said Louie, as we sat drinking Beck's the evening before I was due to take out the stitches. It was worrying him, too. I did not know what to say. I asked the bartender for an olive or two and he obliged by bringing a couple and adding them to my beer. Fishing them out, I looked at Louie and answered, 'Put him down, of course.'

Just before sun-up the next day the air was heavy with the perfume of frangipani blossom. Jays were quarrelling in the hibiscus shrubs around Louie's farm. The stupendous African sky dwarfed the land, pressing down on the flat brown buildings, the ochre soil, the close horizon. Augustine brought Tatu out onto the hard ground. I could not take chances nipping the sutures out of his eyeballs, so I gave him a knock-out injection of etorphine. When he was unconscious I squinted into his eyes through my ophthalmoscope. The interior of both eyes looked fine; I could trace the winding paths of the retinal blood vessels. The pupil constricted slightly as the light from the instrument hit the back of the eye—very good! There was still a fuzzy line of blue-grey where the eyes had been cut, but that should soon vanish after the stitches were gone. With forceps and scissors I picked up the knots of silk, cut them and pulled the sutures out. A shot of antidote and Tatu was back on his feet in five minutes.

Now for the test. There was an empty corral nearby. 'Put him in there,' I said to Augustine. 'Let him go and we'll watch.'

The little foal was pushed through the gate, then Louie, Augustine and I sat on top of the fence anxiously observing his movements. Tatu moved slowly around the enclosure. There were adult zebras next door. He could hear and smell them, and he seemed to be looking in their direction. When I called out loudly, he turned his head towards the sound. He was looking at me, wasn't he? Or was it just reaction to the noise? Tatu skipped a few steps, then he stood still, little nostrils distended, sniffing the morning air.

Suddenly something happened which was predictable but

which I had utterly forgotten about: the first fiery ray of the rising sun cleared the ground to the east. It flashed through the limpid air, a bolt of gold which spread over Tatu's left side. Then, to my spellbound delight, the little foal turned his head to look at the flash. He blinked, dazzled.

'He can see, he can see!' cried Augustine.

Louie whooped and whooped, while I scrambled exultantly down the fence, missed my footing in my haste and slipped, spraining an ankle badly. Augustine was still yelling, 'He can see,' as I limped into the corral and went cautiously towards the foal to make sure that we were not kidding ourselves.

Tatu dodged out of my way, pranced towards the fence and quite definitely checked when he came within two feet of the wood. Then he turned nimbly away. I was convinced —Tatu could see. Probably his vision was only fuzzy, for without a lens the eye cannot focus and in the wild he would still be greatly handicapped, but in a zoo or safari park he would be as good as the next little zebra.

For the first and only time in my life so far I had champagne for breakfast. Louie cracked a bottle of Mumm and by nine o'clock we were definitely tipsy.

With Tatu's eyes looking good, I prepared to leave Kenya for Israel. Louie arranged for Augustine to go with the foal down to Mombasa when the time came and to stay with him until he was shipped. On board ship there would be an experienced man from van den Baars' organisation to take over.

'See you in Rotterdam, young feller,' I said, as I took one last look at the zebra and waved my ophthalmoscope in front of him. He did not answer with words of course, but he said all I wanted to know by following my moving hand with his large, brown, shining eyes.

Judaism, like Christianity, sees Jehovah as mainly concerned with the pesky behaviour of one of the non-arboreal primates that He knocked together on one of His off days. There are few references in the Old Testament to charity towards other species, and Hebrew theology dwells more on the ritual slaughter and butchery of lower creatures. But animals are involved in other aspects of man's concern to keep himself and everyone around him in God's good books—whether they like it or not.

The El Al plane from Nairobi took me into Tel Aviv. Van den Baars wanted me to do some tests on a quartet of Somali wild asses which were in quarantine near Elat on the Red Sea, and which were suspected of carrying swamp fever microbes. It took only a few days, and when I had finished I went by road on the spectacular route past Sodom, the Fortress of Masada, through the rolling Judaean hills to the Old City of Jerusalem where I had lunch of stuffed pigeon in the shadow of the golden-domed Mosque of Omar, and finally back to brash Tel Aviv to pay a call on my old friend Dr Abram, director of the zoo. Tel Aviv's city centre animal park is small and sadly in need of renovation, but the inmates thrive remarkably well.

On my first visit, a couple of years earlier, Dr Abram had proudly shown me his new-born baby Indian elephant and the second crop of flamingo chicks to be hatched within twelve months from the same parents.

'Everything in the garden looks rosy,' I said as we walked round. 'You must be very pleased.'

Abram smiled wryly. 'Yes and no,' he answered. 'You know it is Passover now, when the rules of kosher are even stricter than normal for the observant Jew?'

I knew all right. I had been craving in vain some of the delicious pitta bread baked everywhere in Israel except during the Passover, but had had to make do with piles of insipid matzo biscuits, and I had become accustomed when asking for wine in a café to being hustled into some tiny back room and served the taboo beverage in speak-easy secrecy.

'Well,' Abram went on, 'Israel is a theocracy where the

Rabbinate possess real power, and I'm having some bother with them.'

'How?' I knew the director to be a kind and tolerant man with liberal religious views.

'As you know, I feed my herbivores a balanced diet containing bread and broken biscuits together with grain, legumes and fresh greenery. It's high in protein and you can see that the animals fatten and reproduce splendidly on it.'

'So what's the problem?'

'Someone has given me away, and I've had a high-powered deputation from the Rabbinate in my office. They have said that all leavened products must be withdrawn from the animals' diets forthwith or they'll see that the zoo is closed.'

'No bread or non-kosher cereal ingredients, then?'

'That's what they say. I've fought the edict, but they have a spy in the gardens each day going round looking in the food troughs. They've put pressure on my keepers, too, not to feed the stock. Not a scrap of bread or hametz, forbidden food, must be on the place, and I must sign a certificate agreeing to be a good boy in future and to observe all the Passover kosher rules for my herbivores. My diets must be changed; they leave that to me.'

Dr Abram and I spent several hours re-adjusting the feeding programme to available unleavened alternatives that would nourish the stock as well as their previous menus but would not shock the temperamental stomach and intestinal bacteria of the animals, producing diarrhoea or even worse. Rabbis know nothing of the subtle and deadly disease, bowel oedema, that can kill pigs suddenly when the tiniest alterations to their diet are made; similar ailments can wipe out zoo animals.

We completed our Passover diet for the zoo and Abram prepared to put it into action. Next day he pointed out a bearded, black-dressed individual who was moving methodically from pen to pen, peering into the feed troughs and ocasionally leaning over to rub a handful of the provender through his fingers.

'There goes the shochet, the official sent by the Rabbinate to see that the Cretan goats and the camels and the elephant aren't upsetting Yahveh.'

Yahveh was good to us. Only a few of the animals developed mild 'rabbinical diarrhoea' as we named it. The rabbis kept a careful watch on the zoo for years after that, with meticulous daily inspections during the holy season. Finally the religious authorities put Dr Abram on trust, although still at the start of each Passover he has to sign an affidavit in which he swears to bring up his wild beasts like good Jewish boys. Oy vey!

Four

My new life had its minor compensations; for one thing, night calls became few and far between. Zoo animals are locked up in the evening and rarely looked at during the next twelve hours. Unless an already sick individual needs attention or an important birth is anticipated, ailments and accidents that happen in the hours of darkness are not discovered until the keepers clock on at eight in the morning. General practice had been teeming with dogs run over just as the pubs closed, cats that threw fits in the early hours and woke a startled household and, of course, farm visits. Nature seems to choose the quiet depths of the night for nudging calves and foals out of their submarine slumbers in the womb and into a journey that sometimes goes badly wrong. At such times farmers or stable lads tend to be around, for their experience and intuitive stockmanship somehow enables them to smell trouble and to sense the imminence of birth. Among zoo keepers, despite their passion for and deep interest in the species under their care, such intimate closeness with their animals is the exception.

As a result, my glummest hour of the day now became that between 7.30 and 8.30 am. It is still so. As like as not, a shrill telephone bell at this hour heralds tidings of a warm corpse discovered when the house was opened up. If I can finish off my scrambled eggs and coffee and launch a sally at the *Daily Telegraph* crossword without the phone putting paid to these bastions of my day, you can be absolutely certain that, apart from an ancient monkey or emaciated snake that has long been on the critical list, the birds and beasts at zoological collections dotted all over Europe have passed a peaceful night without anybody of importance shuffling off his brutish coil.

It was a dreaded breakfast phone call, one bitter January morning, which summoned me urgently to Belle Vue. The twenty giraffes in the quarantine premises were in trouble, and four of them were doing the most sinister thing a giraffe can do: lying down and not getting up either because they could not or would not. It was the simplest but deadliest of symptoms, and Matt Kelly had often told me when I was a student, 'Boyo, if a giraffe goes down it never gets up!' I knew that he was not entirely right, for I had seen giraffes recover after being down, but he was as near right as made no difference.

Although the giraffes with problems on this occasion did not actually belong to Belle Vue, they were the zoo's responsibility. They were new arrivals into the country and were being quarantined there in two red-walled blockhouses. Once the giraffes had finished the quarantine period, the dealer who had rented the accommodation and other facilities from the zoo would sell the animals to collections all over Great Britain. They had arrived in Manchester on a foggy October day, having been in the heat of Mombasa three weeks before. No-one in their right mind brings African fauna into Britain after September, but the cut-price East German freighter booked to carry them had been delayed for weeks in setting sail from East Africa. It had been gross folly on someone's part to consider loading the animals on the delayed vessel but, as usual where commercial interests are involved, time is big money. To over-winter the giraffes in Africa would entail considerable expense and so someone gambled—with the dumb animals' lives. The journey had been made even longer by unscheduled stops at ports on Africa's west coast, and the animals' feed ran short. The giraffes slimmed considerably en route and lost some of their protective layers of fat.

I drove up to the quarantine area and joined Ray Legge, the zoo director, and Matt in one of the blockhouses. Two giraffes were lying on the straw, surrounded by a forest of legs. Their companions stood looking lugubriously down at them. It was freezing hard outside and little warmer inside; there had been a power cut during the early morning and the temperature in the house had plummeted. The walls were thin and provided meagre insulation, so when the hot-air blowers failed, the contained heat leaked rapidly away. The picture was the same in the other blockhouse, where another couple of animals lay limply on the ground.

I examined the recumbent giraffes. They looked sleepy, with drooping upper eyelids, their pulses were abnormally slow, their ears flopped like spaniels' and they made no effort to rise. Some of the standing giraffes also had unusually limp eyelids and ears. The temperatures of the ones on the ground were way below normal at the mid-nineties Fahrenheit. While I cautiously worked over my patients I kept a wary eye open for the flailing kick of one of the nervous beasts who towered above me, silently supervising the examination. The three of us made all our movements slowly and talked softly; if the standing animals panicked and began to mill around in the confined space, I would be pounded into the ground in an instant.

There was no evidence of infection, and I had no doubt that I was handling my first cases of hypothermia—chilling, or exposure—in giraffes. Manchester's winter frosts and bitter winds had gripped these unacclimatised creatures. If only they had had an English summer to give them time to adjust, to grow longer coats, to store up fat.

'What do you think?' asked Ray anxiously. 'The emergency blowers are being brought over this minute. Is there anything else to be done?'

In general practice, I had brought round cows dragged out of icy reservoirs by vigorous, commonsense treatment. I had once given a prescription to an owner of a horse that was found half-buried in a snowdrift so that she could get a bottle of whisky from the local pub outside licensed hours and pour it down the animal's throat. The pub's landlord had accepted the prescription. I decided to try the methods that had proved successful in domesticated animals, since there seemed no reason why they should not work just as well on giraffes. 'Blankets, sacks, more straw, some clean yard brushes, two bottles of good rum from the bar,' I ordered. 'While you're getting that, I'll give some injections.'

The droopiness and slow hearts of the animals worried me. Circulation seemed to be failing and the extremities were icy. I took some bottles of millophyline and Pastrum out of my bag. These circulatory stimulants should make a difference, and to get maximum effect I would shoot them straight into a vein.

Finding the jugulars of giraffes is dead easy when they are lying down. I knelt by the first animal's chest and curled myself up to avoid sideways lunges of its head. The giraffe did not seem to notice the needle and soon the stimulant liquids had all swirled away into its bloodstream. I kept a hand on its pulse and listened to the mighty heart through my stethoscope. After a few seconds, when the drugs first came into contact with the heart muscle, I felt and heard the pumping action increase in speed and volume, but the effect seemed to fade rapidly.

As I completed the injections, Matt and Ray arrived with the equipment I had asked for.

'Right,' I said. 'Now pour some of the rum over the legs and hindquarters and start brushing it in vigorously with the brushes. Make sure your movements are all upwards towards the heart.'

Matt shook his head sadly as he splashed the rich liquor over the first animal. 'Can oi have a pull too, Doctor?' he asked.

'Yes—when they're on their feet and not before,' I answered with a grin.

They both worked away at the rough massage while I set about giving inner warmth to the nearest giraffe. Holding the animal's muzzle under one arm was not difficult; it seemed too weak to struggle. With my other hand I carefully pushed the neck of the other rum bottle between its lips, through the gap separating its front and molar teeth, and let the alcohol slip over the back of its tongue. When a quarter of a bottle had disappeared I moved on to the next patient. Although I kept checking circulation, there was little sign of improvement. The giraffes retained their bleary, morning-after-the-night-before expressions. I gave them more shots of stimulant, and once again there was a short-lived boost in the circulation.

My vague worry was now a distinct feeling of apprehension. When Ray and Matt had worked up a good sweat brushing the animals' legs, we covered the recumbent beasts with a loose sprinkling of straw and then laid blankets and sacks over the top. The air spaces supported by the straw between the giraffes' skin and the blankets would make a warm, insulating layer. If these animals reacted like bullocks, they would be chirpy and warm as toast in no time—*if* they reacted like bullocks.

We went for a cup of coffee in Ray's bungalow and discussed ways of combating future power failures. An hour later I returned to the giraffes and was horrified to find that there were now three animals down in the first blockhouse and five in the other. The ones I had already treated were worse, if anything, and the newly prostrate beasts were showing the identical signs of failing circulation and drowsiness. By now I was thoroughly alarmed, Ray was white as a sheet with worry and Matt was muttering colourful Irish imprecations under his breath.

'It's like oi've told ye,' opined the head keeper, nodding grimly. 'Giraffes never get up!'

The two of them set to work rubbing and brushing with further supplies of rum, while I tried anti-shock drugs, filling giant, 60-cc syringes with cortisone and anti-histamine solutions and jabbing clammy buttocks. The air blowers, reinforced by portable heaters, were pumping hot air into the buildings in gusts that swirled about us. Surely, if only the giraffes would hang in there for a little while longer, they would feel the rosy glow of vitality.

Not so. As we stood and watched, first one and then another adopted a posture of the head and neck that I knew to be a near-precursor of death. Curling their necks round and tucking them into their sides, they gazed with half-shut eyes at their rear ends. By pulling we could straighten an animal out again, but as soon as we released our grip, it insisted on returning to the curled-up position. I was almost desperate, but I had a few shots left in my locker. I sent for glucose powder, dissolved it half a pound at a time in hot water and bottled it into the giraffes as another source of calories. When that failed I transfused dextrose solution into the jugular, using Matt and Ray standing on chairs, their arms outstretched painfully high above their heads for long periods, as holders for the slow-dripping bottles. At least no more animals were going down, but the eight prostrate giraffes started to fade into semi-consciousness. As a last frantic resort I attempted to heat them up centrally by pumping water warmed to just above blood heat into the bowels through a stirrup pump and a greased rubber hose inserted as far as possible into the anus.

No matter what we did, the eight giraffes were slipping inexorably away. Nothing had the slightest effect. One animal quietly died, then a second and before long a third. Night came and then another morning and the three of us worked on without sleep, moving from one blockhouse to the other, going through the motions of rubbing, drenching and injecting but knowing that all was in vain. That afternoon the last of the recumbent giraffes died. Not one of them showed an iota of pathological abnormality when I wearily tackled the huge task of autopsying them, alone in a cold and windy yard. The twelve remaining animals were given supplements of glucose in their drinking water; it was the best I could do.

Exhausted and demoralised, I set out at last for home. My drugs, all our efforts, had proved utterly impotent and eight giraffes out of twenty had been lost. Even those that had collapsed whilst I was on the premises had eluded me. I was playing in the big league of animal medicine now, I thought, and it looked like I wasn't up to the standard of the game. I had taken on a bunch of big boys from overseas—and lost.

During the next few days I was not called out anywhere. I had plenty of time to sit in my favourite room of the Jacobean farmhouse that was our home. It had windows piercing the thick stone walls on three sides and overlooking a raised garden where rhododendrons and roses crowded round a little pool which I had installed and stocked with frogs and ramshorn snails. Sprawled on the couch, I would immerse myself in the baroque music of J. S. Bach, Telemann and Couperin which, combined with the peaceful surroundings, was an unfailing washer-away of depression.

The room was my think-tank, too, and there I ruminated for a long time over the shambles of the giraffes. As far as I could learn, no-one had reported dealing with hypothermia in the species before. I was puzzled by the lack of response to normally effective stimulant techniques: it was as if the circulation system of these animals, which we knew to be specially adapted to forcing blood up and down long legs and necks, passed a point of no return and collapsed remarkably quickly.

Such physiological considerations were not the only ones which troubled me. There was a gnawing sense of guilt on several levels. First, I had to face the fact that my treatment had met with complete lack of success. Had I missed something in the diagnosis? Or in the therapy? Then at another level I pondered over my position as someone working for an organisation that did daft and irresponsible things like letting giraffes get cold. I had not personally given the OK to load the animals onto the boat in Mombasa, nor had I selected the blockhouses as quarters for the new arrivals, nor had I played any part in installing the vulnerable heating system, but I was part of the business, a supporter of the machine that made cash out of captive animals. At yet another level I questioned once again, as I had done a thousand times and still do every day, whether I as a human being had any right to assist in any way in the bringing of wild creatures forcibly out of their rightful habitats. I was glib with plausible justifications: education, scientific study, conservation, enrichment of the lives of those who cannot afford to travel to the Serengeti or Galapagos. But such sophistries neglected the moral argument, and that was the one that tugged and still tugs. My brother the warthog? Yes, that did ring a bell deep inside me. Yet is seemed at the time, as indeed I suspect it still does, too easy to let Handel's glorious trumpets and mighty organs drown such uncomfortable thoughts.

I decided to use some of the long hours when the telephone did not ring in improving my command of some foreign languages. Already I had had awkward moments of mutual incomprehension when speaking, sometimes on urgent emergency matters, to clients and veterinarians overseas. There was the Italian with the private zoo who had a smattering of English and, I was convinced, a much-thumbed copy of *Roget's Thesaurus* instead of a dictionary, into which he delved with reckless enthusiasm before sending me one of his express cables. 'SUCCOUR PLEASE,' one ran. 'AM HAVING MANDRILL WITH PYROMANIA OF MELANCHOLY. I IMPORTUNE APPROVAL.' For a moment I toyed with the idea of a big blue-faced mandrill (a type of baboon) which, to the despair of his analyst, had taken to playing with matches after a fit of depression. But why was his owner so keen that I

47

should give my blessing to the fire-raising ape? It took several hours of head-scratching and a final telephone call to Naples to discover that the request for assistance was meant to be 'HELP PLEASE. HAVE MANDRILL WITH INFLAMED SPLEEN. REQUEST RECOMMENDATION.'

Many of the people contacting me from abroad spoke some English and, with the shreds of my School Certificate French and German, we got by. Even so, it could not have sounded very elegant to my foreign clients when in a serious medical discussion I had to use Rabelaisian synonyms—the sort which in a dictionary are followed by the severe epithet, '(vulg.)'—for key anatomical or physiological terms because of my poor command of the language. It just would not do; I had to achieve a basic working knowledge of French, German and Spanish together with all the most useful veterinary phrases. I got down to it seriously after a memorable visit to Duisberg Zoo in Germany, where I lectured to a group of keepers on the breathing system of whales and dolphins. In my mixture of English and German I talked about the amazing sensitivity of the blow-hole that lets air in and keeps water out, even in stormy seas, and about how the organ opens and closes apparently automatically when the animals sleep. It was the raised eyebrows of the zoo director and the helpless mirth of his staff as I repeatedly referred to the animals' blow-holes that eventually made me twig. I thought I had used the correct word for the hole in the creatures' heads—*blassloch*—whereas in fact I had consistently referred to the *assloch*, a more lowly orifice elsewhere in the anatomy.

The most illuminating demonstration of the value of even a limited knowledge of languages occurred later that year, when I went to the first conference of the newly formed European Association for Aquatic Mammals which was being held at the Dutch seaside resort of Harderwijk, a little town that boasts one of the finest Marinelands outside the United States. When the first day's papers had been delivered and discussed, I repaired along with a group of other veterinarians, zoo directors, dolphin trainers and marine scientists to a local hostelry for the most important function of any conference: swapping gossip and talking 'shop' over a few litres of Amstel beer. In our corner of the bar were the director of Whipsnade Zoo, Victor Manton; a veterinarian from the US Navy Undersea Warfare research division, John Allen; the professor of anatomy at Cambridge, Richard Harrison; and Peter Grayson, later to succeed Raymond Legge as director of Belle Vue Zoo.

We had been jawing away for an hour or so when Peter whispered something in my ear. 'Have you got any drugs with you?' he asked.

Normally I never travel abroad to see a case without making sure that certain important anaesthetics, tranquillisers and other drugs which might be impossible to locate outside Britain are with me. So, should I or some other specimen of homo sapiens develop a headache, get bitten or suffer, say, the Kurdistan Collywobbles, I can usually root about under my socks and find a pill or a potion labelled 'For Treatment of Rhinoceros' or 'Gorilla: 3 drops daily in fruit juice', which makes life bearable again. On this occasion, however, I was not carrying even so much as an aspirin.

'Sorry, old boy,' I replied as our beer mugs were refilled again. 'Why, what's wrong?' It was difficult making myself heard above the jolly din.

'Got a pain, really bad,' Peter answered with a grimace.

'Where?'

'In my . . . in my urethra.'

The others noticed Peter's anguished features and asked what was up. He repeated his trouble and naturally everybody fell about laughing. Ribald remarks were made as to possible diagnoses and causes and no-one seemed inclined to treat the poor fellow's complaint as being in any way serious.

'But it's awful, bloody awful,' shouted Peter, clutching his groin. 'I'm not joking. If you haven't got any drugs, could you give me a prescription or something then, David? I'll see if I can find a chemist. I must do something!'

Still loath to take Peter seriously, I agreed to write a note for some Penbritin capsules on the back of a beer mat, but warned him that it might not be acceptable in Holland. To the cheers of the rest of us, Peter dashed out clutching the prescription.

It was over an hour later that he re-appeared, relaxed and no longer wearing an agonised expression.

'You look better,' I said. 'Did you get the Penbritin?'

'No,' Peter replied, 'but I nearly got arrested!'

He went on to tell us what had happened as he hurried through the twilight-dim streets of Harderwijk, looking for a chemist to fill his prescription. With the pain in his water-works almost unbearable, he had at last spotted a shop with bottles in the window and a sign over the door that read 'Droguerie'. Dashing in, he thrust the prescription into the hands of a young lady in a white coat standing behind the counter. She turned the beer mat over, muttered in Dutch and looked distinctly nonplussed.

'Penbritin. Pen-bri-tin cap-sules,' groaned Peter. It was plain that the girl spoke no English. He tried another tack. 'Pain. Got pain down here. Bad.' He gesticulated towards his groin.

The girl was getting a trifle agitated, Peter noticed. She called out and was presently joined by another white-coated female who, equally puzzled, looked at the paper mat and then at the Englishman pointing miserably towards his trousers. Peter was at the end of his tether. He felt that at any moment his bladder would burst. Why didn't they do something? There was no doubt in his mind: 'droguerie' sounded so like 'druggery', it must be the Dutch for 'pharmacy' to anyone with a glimmer of intelligence but no working Dutch.

Then he had an idea. Producing a pencil and taking the beer mat back from the shop assistant, he hurriedly drew the outlines of the human male genito-urinary organs and added a large arrow pointing to the source of the agony. He handed the beer mat back and said with great feeling, 'Pain. Have you got anything to take away pain?'

The girls' eyes bulged as they stared at the masterpiece. They began to fidget and talk rapidly to each other.

Perhaps, Peter thought, there was some confusion about the subject of his diagram and the girls had interpreted his squiggle wrongly: it did look rather like a plan of the motor-racing circuit at Zandvoort. Impatiently, he grabbed the beer mat, slapped it once again on the counter and pulled out his pencil. This time there would be no doubt. He carefully sketched in some anatomical details, shaded the thing to give it perspective and then thrust the paper under the girls' noses and waved it about. 'There,' he shouted, and jabbed with a finger at the spot where the figleaf should have been.

This latest effort produced an unmistakable reaction. With shrill squeaks the two girls lurched back from the counter, grabbed at one another for support and bundled themselves through a door leading into a back office. Moments later a man in a white coat appeared, red-faced and angry. He leaned over the counter and grabbed Peter tightly by the lapels of his jacket.

'Now, mister,' he said, 'English, eh? What the hell do you think you're doing? Looking for a burlesque show?'

Still holding firmly on to Peter's lapels, the man rattled on about how his shop was not a house of ill repute, his two assistants were good-living, God-fearing provincial girls, and how beery foreign day-trippers should confine themselves to the red-light district of Amsterdam. When Peter at last got an indignant word in, the truth on both sides came out: drogueries in Holland are cosmetics shops that do not deal in any medicines whatsoever, and the maidens recovering in the back room were beauticians.

The shop-owner was soon reassured that Peter really was in pain and in search of help. 'Go down the street and look for the sign "Apoteek"—apothecary—and good luck,' he said, smoothing my friend's creased jacket and leading him to the door.

The pain was now almost unbearable and to cap it all, when Peter eventually found the chemist's shop, it was closed. The poor chap dragged himself back to the bar where we sat, but before joining us staggered into the men's room to see if he could spot anything visibly wrong with his nether parts. Suddenly there was a 'ping' and the fierce pain literally vanished. He had passed a tiny bladder stone which had lodged in his urethra, causing obstruction and intense agony.

'I'd have given my eye teeth to be able to speak a word or two of Dutch,' said Peter as we listened to his story between further litres of beer and fits of helpless hysterics. 'Damned useful things, foreign languages.'

A polar bear mother brings her three-month-old twins out into the morning air. Not long after this photograph was taken, the Belle Vue polar bears started turning chocolate-brown. (*Syndication International*)

For my money the most spectacular species of monkey in the world – a De Brazza and her baby. The sagacious expression so typical of these beautiful creatures is just what one might expect of truants who have the wit to 'hole-up' in the warm-air ducting of their monkey house. (*John Doidge*)

With his sight almost back to normal, Tatu became much more difficult to handle and examine. (*Tony Evans*)

My early losses with giraffes produced intense anxiety in me whenever the call to another sick member of the species came in. As new methods of treatment and safer anaesthetics were developed, my confidence began to return. Regular health examinations and close contact with the new group at Windsor helped. (*UPI/Tony Evans*)

Killer whales show more good humour and playfulness than their name suggests ... at least in captivity. Here Paul Legge, a trainer at Marineland Côte d'Azur, surf-boards on an eighteen-foot male. (*Press Agency (Yorkshire) Ltd*)

On a bitterly cold morning we prepared to see what happened if I tried to inject Cuddles with 'flu vaccine while he floated free in the water. (*Press Agency (Yorkshire) Ltd*)

Five

I missed the end of that Harderwijk conference, because Shelagh phoned my hotel the next evening with news of an accident at Belle Vue. Pedro, the smallest of the zoo's bull giraffes, had been wounded in the neck. He was eating and drinking all right, but dribbles of food and water were running out of the wound when he did so. I took a taxi to Schiphol airport and caught the next plane back to Manchester.

It was past midnight when I met Matt Kelly, the stocky little Irish head keeper, outside the darkened giraffe house. 'Looks nasty to me,' he said, clicking his teeth. 'We'll have to be careful goin' and puttin' the loights on.'

When zoo animals are put down for the night, they expect to be left undisturbed. Suddenly breaking the routine by switching on lights and making a noise can startle the resting or often snoring inhabitants, with disastrous results in that confined space both to panicking animals and to any humans who happen to be in their way. After 'lights out' you go back into an animal house very carefully.

We went up to the door. Before opening it, Matt began to talk just loud enough to be heard inside. Gradually he increased the volume, whistled a bit, tapped on the woodwork and finally turned the knob. Very slowly pushing the door open a crack, he addressed the animals pulling themselves to their feet and flaring their nostrils in the blackness. 'There, there. How're ye doin', me beauties? Oi'm sorry to be disturbin' ye.' He moved a hand to the light switches, put on one bulb, paused, then lit another, paused and lit a third.

We moved unhurriedly into the house, both billing and cooing softly towards the knots of zebra, giraffe and wildebeest that stood alertly, all with eyes upon us and ears pricked, ready to panic. After a few moments inspecting us, the animals relaxed: there was no mistaking the familiar, friendly tones of the head keeper.

Pedro, the giraffe, was standing in a corner. He seemed unconcerned about the ugly, six-inch long tear, caked with blood, in the left side of his neck.

'How did it happen, Matt?' I asked, as Pedro wandered over to the railings, craned over and curled a rough grey tongue round a twist of my hair to give my scalp a painful tug.

'We're not too sure, but it looks as if he got his muzzle jammed in one of them water bowls up high on the wall, panicked and threw himself about and crashed against the iron hay-rack. It came away from the wall and a bracket went through his throat.'

Matt pulled an apple out of his coat pocket and offered it to the giraffe, who took it willingly. Pedro chewed it, drooling saliva down onto us, and swallowed. We watched the sinuous waves of the gullet muscles carrying the mashed-up apple towards the stomach. As the waves reached the neck wound, a pink finger of foam welled out of the bloody hole and then, to my horror, soggy white pieces of apple pulp flecked with pale green slivers of peel emerged from the wound and dropped onto the straw-covered floor.

'Bejasus!' exclaimed Matt.

There was no doubt about it. Pedro had punctured his gullet, a rare and serious injury, particularly in an animal like a giraffe.

There was nothing to be done that night apart from shooting a couple of dart-syringes containing penicillin into his buttocks. The formidable prospect of trying to close the wound would have to wait until daylight. I drove home to Rochdale with my head full of questions. How to lay hands on the big beast in a place that was smooth walls on three sides and iron bars on the fourth? What type of anaesthetic to use on the most notoriously unpredictable of zoological patients? The operation itself: how badly damaged was the gullet? Repairing such a wound might present problems never encountered in the day-to-day cobbling together of skin and muscle injuries. Giraffe again, I thought. One of the most difficult of all zoo species to treat, and one which seemed lately to be needing a lot of my help—such help as I could give. At least things were busy, but the cases were rough.

'Well, you can always go back to speying cats and vaccinating poodles,' Shelagh said provocatively next morning as I worried over the turn of events.

'Don't be daft,' I retorted, stabbing at a fried egg that was not looking for trouble.

As I arrived at Belle Vue I was no nearer finding the answers which had haunted me all night. Matt was already in the giraffe house, looking worriedly at Pedro, whose appearance had altered distinctly in the past six hours.

'Would ye look at that, Doctor,' said the head keeper, pointing. 'He's gettin' fatter somehow.'

Sure enough, Pedro did look plumper. It was not that he was bloated with air or excess food in his belly, but he seemed simply to have enlarged. There was no question that his neck, chest and forelegs were fatter. Ominously, the giraffe had stopped eating and was looking depressed and miserable. Sticky froth had made a trail down his neck from the puncture wound.

'I'll need to examine him, Matt,' I said, 'but how?' There was at that time no proven reliable anaesthetic for giraffes, no swinging gate or funnel-shaped 'crush'.

'What d'ye want to do exactly?' Matt asked.

'First, I'd like to feel him to see why he's so much bigger than last night, then if possible get a finger into that neck wound.'

'It's goin' to be tricky. Let's try a door and some straw

bales.' He shouted to a bunch of keepers, 'Lift the elephant house door off its hinges, and look sharp about it!' The elephants were already outside for the day and had no need of their night-house door.

After a few minutes the keepers tottered into the giraffe house, straining and sweating under the weight of the massive, iron-studded door which must have weighed five or six hundredweight. The idea now was to take it into the giraffes' quarters, having moved out all the animals except Pedro, and then gradually press him against a wall by using the door as a portable barrier.

All went well at first. The door was introduced quietly and slowly. Pedro began to pace about nervously as the men under Matt's command advanced cautiously, carrying the door in an upright position. At least if the giraffe lashed out with one of his feet to deliver the powerful blows that can brain a charging lion, the solid wood should afford the keepers some protection. Gently cornered at last and unable to turn round, Pedro began to 'stargaze'—holding his head up so that his chin pointed directly at the ceiling—a sign of profound mental agitation. I told the men not to press the door actually onto the animal, for under such circumstances anything could happen. Pedro might try to climb the wall, jump amazingly upwards on four legs like a spring lamb, throw a limb over the door or even, seemingly, try to fly. Such remarkable displays always ended in torn muscles, fractures or even worse.

Matt piled up some bales of straw on our side of the door and I gingerly climbed up them. Now I was high enough to put my arm over the top of the door and do a bit of prodding around. 'Coosh now, coosh,' I murmured, the words that Pennine farmers would use when approaching a prickly-tempered cow. I lightly stroked Pedro's neck. Niggled, he swung his head to and fro and then lunged down awkwardly, trying to butt me with the hard pegs on his head. 'Coosh, coosh, boy.'

Pedro became accustomed to my touch on his skin, which flickered and jumped beneath my fingers. I prodded carefully. Scrunch! Scrunch! It was just like pressing shredded cellophane—I could hear as well as feel the crackling beneath the skin. This was not fat, nor was it the soggy fluid of dropsy. It was gas, gas collecting in thousands of bubbles under the animal's hide and puffing him up like the Michelin man. If the gas was being produced by bacteria that had entered through the wound, Pedro really was in trouble. Gas gangrene is usually lethal and runs a quick course, but somehow he did not look poorly enough for that. I looked at the neck wound from a few inches away and listened intently. As Pedro moved his head about I could hear the faintest sucking sound. A bubble of serum would appear at the hole, swell, shrink and vanish. That was it: movement of the neck was drawing air in through the wound, which acted as a valve. Once inside, the air was gradually working its way through the subcutaneous tissue. Another day or two of this and Pedro could be like a zeppelin right down to his hind feet.

The operation to repair the gullet and close the overlying tissues would put a stop to all that. As long as I continued to provide an antibiotic 'umbrella', the air under the skin would be absorbed by the blood capillaries and harmlessly dispersed. Ready for trouble, I moved my fingers up towards the wound. I touched the crusted blood, then, ever so delicately, pushed my index finger into the ragged hole. Pedro swayed about. I swayed with him, letting my hand ride with his neck. I felt my finger pass through a thin layer of split muscle and slip on the smooth lining of the gullet. The gap in its wall was as big as a plum.

I turned my head to look at Matt. 'There's a bloody great...' I began but then all hell let loose. Pedro had had enough. Kicking mightily sideways with a fore leg and a hind leg in concert, he connected with the door with a crash that shook the building. The heavy slab of wood fell away from him, taking me and my pile of straw bales with it. The men buckled under the tumbling mass and collapsed to the ground. A yelling, struggling heap of keepers, plus one startled veterinarian, saw the great door come toppling down onto them. Only Matt Kelly had managed to skip out of the way. Luckily the straw bales in which we were tangled took much of the impact and saved us from being utterly flattened.

Unconfined once more, Pedro stalked haughtily from his corner and actually walked over the door beneath which we were sandwiched. The momentary addition of his weight resulted in a broken collar bone and a bloody nose for one of the keepers, and made my ear swell up like a tomato. When we emerged from our press we found Matt hopping about in a mixture of amusement and agitation like a red-faced leprechaun.

As our wounded were borne off I explained the situation and told Matt to prepare for an operation. At that time few attempts had been made to anaesthetise giraffe, and those who had tried it had found grave difficulties in coping with the tall beast: its peculiar circulation system seemed to distribute anaesthetics in an unpredictable way. Slowly induced anaesthesia resulted in dizziness, panic and awful accidents, while fast knock-out shots were dangerous, tricky to administer and brought the animal crashing straight down from its height of seventeen or eighteen feet. In the rare cases where the operation was completed satisfactorily, a giraffe might well refuse to get up on its feet ever again and there was the strange business of individuals which developed grotesquely twisted necks for some reason. Zoo vets had one recurring nightmare: that a giraffe might need surgery.

Even chiropody was a headache. In captivity giraffe hoofs sometimes grow long and curl upwards, but the difficulty was doing anything to remedy the situation. I had had some success putting the patient into a specially built travelling box, removing the bottom plank on one side and working through the slot, but it was a dangerous technique. The horn, particularly in dry weather, can be hard as iron. A hoof-knife as used on sheep or cattle was useless, and there was not room to apply a blacksmith's hoof-clippers with the foot planted firmly on the ground and maybe a ton or more of weight resting on it. It was a painless operation but the giraffe usually resented his tootsies being fiddled about with, so it was difficult to decide which was best: to sweat away with a saw, waiting for the inevitable, lightning-fast kick to shatter the metal blade; to chip with a chisel and mallet and risk a broken arm or the chisel smashed into one's teeth; or to use a fast, electric portable saw and maybe amputate the giraffe's ankle when it suddenly struck. Just before leaving my old practice, though, I had used an injection of ace-promazine, a sedative made for farm and domestic animals, on an old bull giraffe at Dudley Zoo that had had terribly overgrown feet for years. It had worked well. The drug had left the animal standing but droopy-eyed, relaxed and uncaring. There had been no problems in darting the bull or cutting the horn and there seemed to be no after-effects to the acepromazine.

I had not wanted to use the drug just to examine Pedro, but for the operation on his throat I reckoned that the best and safest thing to do was to use acepromazine, put the patient behind the door again and then numb the operation site with plenty of local anaesthetic.

Even with the decision about the anaesthetic resolved, there were still the surgical problems. Left untreated or simply dressed with ointments or plasters, the hole would never heal as saliva and food passing through the orifice would encourage the formation of a permanent link, a fistula, between the gullet and the outside of the neck. I would have to close the gullet with special stitches that rolled the wound edges inwards, so that the mucous membrane lining the tube could knit together, and I must not cause an obstruction to swallowing by narrowing the tube too much. I had opened ostrich gullets in the past in search of metal foreign bodies which they had swallowed and which we had located with army-issue mine detectors, but I had never had to operate on a mammal's gullet. Even in dogs it is rarely necessary—gullets get blocked sometimes, but they normally emerge from accidents unscathed. The rest, closing the muscle and skin, and thus putting an end to the air-sucking, would be simple.

The first step was to give the sedative. As usual, I worked out the dose by taking the average of three estimates of his weight, mine, Matt's and the senior giraffe keeper's. Then I assembled one of the aluminium flying darts with its ingenious, explosive-activated plunger and selected a needle appropriate for the buttocks of an adult giraffe. Finally I charged the dart with the calculated volume of acepromazine, a beautiful golden-coloured liquid. There should be just enough to make this giraffe as peaceable and amenable as the one at Dudley.

With a soft 'phut', hardly loud enough to startle the animal, the dart flew from my gas pistol and homed perfectly into the giraffe's rump. So fast and surely do these devices travel that there is far less sensation for the recipient than there would be if a hypodermic needle were punched in manually. Pedro seemed unaware that he had been slipped a Mickey Finn.

I looked at my watch. Usually the first signs of drowsiness appear after five minutes or so. We all waited.

Six minutes went by. The giraffe started to droop his upper eyelids, instead of his normal alert expression he looked rather dumb, and his muscles visibly relaxed.

'Get the door, lads,' I said, 'and approach him nice and easy.'

As I spoke, Pedro gave a great sigh, keeled over as if struck by invisible lightning, and crashed onto the thick straw. I was stunned. The giraffe lay flat out, legs flailing and eyes rolling wildly.

Matt and I dashed over, and I put my ear to his chest, listening to the slow thud of the mighty heart.

'Get up, Pedro, get up!' yelled Matt, slapping the animal ineffectually on the flanks, his teeth grinding with tension.

I felt the pulse in the giraffe's femoral artery. It was soft and weakening.

'Come on, everyone. Prop him up on his brisket. Two of you hold his head up!' I shouted, and the keepers crowded round. 'Head up at all costs,' I repeated, and rummaged in my bag for syringes and needles.

Thoughts whirled through my mind. Certainly I had taken the correct drug from the correct bottle. Dose? We had all agreed that he weighed around sixteen hundredweight, and I had given 5 cc, a low to moderate amount. I looked at the dart to check. Yes, it was a 5-cc dart and could not have held more. It could only be a side-effect of the acepromazine: heart failure had been reported occasionally in domestic animals, and it was recognised that one effect of the chemical was to lower the blood pressure.

As Matt and his men pushed the now unconscious giraffe into some semblance of a normal sitting position, with the head propped on one fellow's shoulders, I drew a quantity of noradrenaline into my syringe, fast. I bent to pick up a skin swab and heard Matt's words as if in a dream.

'He's gone, Doctor. He's gone,' he said quietly.

I went over to the giraffe, cold sweat breaking out under my shirt. I gently touched the cornea of one eye. I jammed my head against the warm chest and listened. Matt was right. Pedro had died. Just like that. The acepromazine had over-expanded the blood vessels, Pedro's blood pressure had plummeted and his vital brain cells had been starved of circulating oxygen. 'Damnation,' muttered Matt. The men all stood back and let the giraffe's body slip onto its side.

'Unpredictable things, giraffes. Bloody terrible to treat,' I said. It sounded like an apology.

No-one said anything further as we collected our gear. Matt left silently to phone the knackerman.

I drove home in despair. Only a fool would take on the agony of zoo medicine, I thought. Pigs, cats, cows we understand; giraffes can only bring heartache.

Shelagh knew what had happened with one look at my face when I entered the house. She also knew that it was best to stick the lunch in the oven; I would not be eating. I went to my office to sit and think, go over all the possibilities, to try to get an inkling of what had gone wrong. The thought that one day there might, there would, be another giraffe was like iced water in my brain.

Shelagh brought me a cup of tea. 'Come on,' she said. 'The cup that cheers. By the way, there's been a veterinary student on the phone a couple of times. He wants to know something about lobsters. His name's Greenwood, Andrew Greenwood.'

'You can tell him what he can do with his lobsters, love,' I replied, and stared unseeing out of the window. The gangling, long-necked creature that the ancients had called a camel-leopard, *Giraffa camelopardalis*, was becoming my jinx.

On the way to Harderwijk for the conference which Pedro's accident interrupted, my old friend Mr van den Baars had invited me to Rotterdam to look over a mixed bunch of animals belonging to him which had just arrived from East Africa. One of his keepers took me round the live cargo: giraffes, antelopes, a hippo and zebras.

'You should be interested in this one,' the keeper said, pointing to one slatted crate. 'It's a young zebra.'

My heart leapt as I put my face to a slot in the woodwork and looked inside. A beautiful, nine-month-old zebra colt was looking directly towards me with his ears pricked forwards and his eyes glistening like cobs of coal. There were three spots on his forehead. It was Tatu!

I was ecstatic. Tatu had survived. Blind and concussed in

the heat of the bush eight months before, he was now a stroppy individual with glancing, arrogant eyes on his way to a zoo in Poland.

'Spirited little devil,' said the attendant. 'He kicks and bites as soon as look at you.'

'But does he look?' I asked. 'You've not seen him bump into things or miss objects, have you?'

'Definitely not,' came the emphatic reply. 'See this blue dent in my wrist? That's where he grabbed me a couple of weeks ago when I was mucking out. He saw all right.'

I was content. No doubt Tatu could have done better with a pair of bifocals or even contact lenses if such things had existed for wild animals, but he was biting folk accurately enough. That was just what I wanted to hear.

Pedro's death drove all thoughts of Tatu from my mind, and it was only some days later that I remembered to tell Shelagh about my reunion with the young zebra. She was thrilled.

'What's for dinner?' I asked when I had finished my tale.

'Can't you smell it?' Shelagh replied.

It was true there was a strong fishy smell about. 'Herrings!' I said, my mouth beginning to water in anticipation of baked rollmops with mashed potato and mustard sauce.

Shelagh shook her head. 'Wrong. It's mackerel today'.

'Fine by me.'

'And it's mackerel tomorrow, and the day after and Friday, Saturday, Sunday . . .'

'Whoa! Hold on!' I interrupted. 'What are you going on about?'

'Mackerel—twenty stone of it. It arrived on the front doorstep this morning, sent by Pentland Hick of Flamingo Park. He wants you to check its quality. He's bought a killer whale in Seattle and hopes to fly it over in two or three weeks, so he's been talking to merchants at Billingsgate about fish supplies. Oh, and that student, Andrew Greenwood, has been on about his lobsters again.'

Never mind lobsters—a killer whale! Determined to make his Flamingo Park Zoo in Yorkshire the finest in England, Hick had built one of the country's first dolphinaria and had become fascinated by the potentialities of the cetaceans— whales, dolphins, porpoises and the like. Harderwijk in Holland had had the first European killer a few months previously, but it had not survived long before dying, it was said, of a brain haemorrhage. Now with any luck I was actually going to touch one of the most awesome marine mammals, probably handle its medical problems.

A frisson of excitement ran down my spine as I thought about it. Since my first contact with Flamingo Park, capturing an escaped nilgai antelope for them, I had gradually seen more and more of Hick's growing empire of animals. I telephoned him immediately.

'Yes,' he said in his deceptively soft and sleepy voice, 'I'd like you to go to Seattle next month. Bring back a killer whale. Think about it. Check everything. Talk to the Americans by phone. But remember'—his voice took on the menacing tones of the Godfather—'nothing, but nothing, must go wrong, David.'

My contemplation of this momentous news was interrupted by Shelagh's more mundane but highly pressing problems as owner of 280 pounds of mackerel, a fish renowned for its lack of keeping quality. It was all over the kitchen, ousting my beer bottles from the refrigerator and filling the sinks. My daughters, Stephanie and Lindsey, peered somewhat mournfully from behind a stack of fish boxes which we had to climb over to get out of the kitchen.

'Lancastrians don't seem to eat mackerel,' Shelagh complained. 'I've managed to give away about ten pounds to the Schofields, old Fred the other side and even a pair to the postman, but look at the rest! I'm not going to waste them by dumping them in the dustbin, but what are we going to do with them before the house stinks of rotting fish?'

For the moment, though, they were beautiful fresh fish,

youngsters about seven inches long. I inspected a selection, checking gills, eyes, skin, oil content, smell, parasite load, muscle firmness; they were perfect. It seemed safe to order this for the new whale, but just in case there were invisible bugs in the fish I took samples from half a dozen for bacteriological culture and for analysis for heavy metals, an increasing worry as the seas become polluted by man and his industries.

That evening I was to be found bearing unsolicited fishy gifts wrapped in newspaper to friends and even mere nodding acquaintances all over Rochdale, and for the next week my enthusiasm for the hobby of cooking was put to the test as I experimented with the mackerel.

On the Sunday night, as I called the family to the supper table, Stephanie asked apprehensively, 'It's not mackerel again, is it, Dad? How have you done it this time? We've had it boiled, with white wine sauce, barbecued, as kedgeree.'

'And don't forget when we had it in cider, and with cucumber, and with tomato,' chimed in Lindsey, who was also approaching the table with less than her usual enthusiasm.

Shelagh pointed at the cat. 'Even poor old Lupin doesn't look like he could face a mackerel again for ten years.'

I knew I had plumbed the depths for this evening's meal but put a brave face on it. 'Tonight,' I declared gaily, 'my pièce de résistance—curried mackerel.'

With the groans of the family in my ears as I retreated to the kitchen to bring in the dishes, I began to doubt a killer whale's famed intelligence; after all, he would swallow a hundredweight of this stuff, day in and day out for years—and raw, without benefit of my sauces!

Before I had time to make serious preparations for my visit to America, I was summoned by the manager of the Garden of Eden, a sleazy night-club in Manchester, to sort out one of the alligators which had a 'funny tail'. My only previous contact with the establishment had been to treat an eye condition in the phython who was the working partner of Miss Seksi, the striptease dancer there:* I had never actually set foot inside the place and could not imagine what alligators were doing in such surroundings. Props in some exotic, erotic burlesque sketch—Tarzan and nude Jane, maybe? Perhaps they made alligator steak flambé out of them. After all, people rave over the rather indifferent soup made from that other enchanting reptile, the turtle—a dish which Shelagh insisted we never ate because of the cruel way the gentle animals are killed to titillate the palates of gourmets far away.

Reptiles form one of the most difficult and neglected areas of zoo medicine, and there are not the funds or the scientific facilities available for much research into the special problems of a group of animals that are rarely worth more than a few pounds apiece. So the more reptile practice I got, the better: as a student I had watched Matt Kelly first slip a leather or rope noose round an alligator's jaws, thus putting the more lethal end out of action, then jump boldly onto the thrashing muscular tail and eventually force the reptile over onto its back. With the beast in that position Matt had begun to stroke it gently and repeatedly in a straight line down the middle of its body, beginning at the point of the jaw and going right down the underbelly to the vent. After six or seven passes of this kind, the animal had become immobile and perfectly relaxed in a hypnotic trance. As a mere nuisance of a student I had not been allowed to participate in or get too close to these mysteries, but this Garden of Eden case might be my big chance. I had seen it all and was sure I was up to it, even if my alligator patient was a fine nine-footer like the ones at Belle Vue which had laid eggs in captivity—the first to do so in any European zoo. Noose, jump onto the tail, whip over and begin the Svengali bit.

*See *Doctor in the Zoo*

Taylor the Zoovet will emerge with flying colours this morning, I thought, as I pulled up outside the night-club.

There was no mention of alligators among the collection of curling photographs of fishnet-covered flesh on the billboard by the entrance, a small black door set in a grimy wall in a back street, but I could not help musing on the cosmopolitan spice in a zoo vet's life that is rare in the general-practice world of say, a James Herriot.

Nothing inside the dimly lit basement room recalled in the slightest the first Garden of Eden, unless it was a reek of original sin. There was not even a plastic apple tree. The place was tatty, smelling sourly of stale beer, yesterday's cigars and cheap perfume. Groups of small tables, with crumb-dusty, wine-stained covers and guttered candles stuck in empty Sauternes bottles, surrounded a minute dance floor. The whole garden of delights was illuminated coldly by blue fluorescent strip-lights which made the dandruff on the manager's jacket sparkle like snowflakes as he led me to my patient. Around the edge of the dance floor there was a narrow, water-filled channel perhaps twelve inches wide and six inches deep. The water was turbid and oily. Floating on the surface were cigarette butts, bits of cork and other scraps of debris.

'He's in there,' said the manager. 'There's three of 'em altogether. Quite a gimmick, don't you think?'

I scanned the grey water. Sure enough, three pairs of green-gold eyes just broke the surface. Yes, the Garden of Eden had alligators, each about one foot long and as lean as hazel twigs—not quite the monsters I had hoped for.

'That's the one, I think,' said the manager, pointing towards one of the three. 'They don't have names. There's something wrong with his tail. I wouldn't have troubled you myself but one of those bloody Eytie waiters seems to have got attached to the little perishers and said he'd report us if we didn't do something. I mean, I could understand if it was a dog or something, but well . . .' He sniffed disdainfully.

I plunged my hand into the channel and brought out the small alligator by the base of his tail. Four inches of his length was tail and half of that was brown, lifeless and rotting. It had obviously been gangrenous for weeks.

'What do you feed the alligators on?' I asked. Not only was the creature rather small, but the death of tissue without sign of infection, particularly on an extremity such as a tail, might well suggest something lacking in the diet. And the creature was rather small.

'What do you mean, feed them?' replied the manager.

I thought back. Perhaps I had phrased my question awkwardly. No, it seemed to make reasonable sense. 'What do you feed the alligators on?' I repeated. 'What food do you give them?'

The manager seemed perplexed. 'Food?' he mumbled. 'We don't exactly feed them at all. That's up to our customers.'

'What do you mean by that?' I felt the first stirrings of understanding and anger.

'Well, you know. The customers, the punters. They feed the little fellows. That's part of the gimmick—dancing with crocs all round you, throwing 'em bits to eat. Thrills the ladies no end. We're the only club in the North with the idea.' He smirked proudly.

'But what do the customers give the alligators?' I persisted. 'And how much?'

'Well, that'd be difficult to say. Prawns from the prawn cocktails, bits of steak, cheese of course, bits of melon—we do have quite a name for our Ogen melons filled with port wine you know, you ought to come some time and bring the missus—oh, and of course they get potato crisps and peas and scraps of lettuce.'

'Is that all they get in the way of food?' I asked, tight-lipped.

'Well, yes. But the people at the tables closest to the dance floor throw plenty in. They like to move 'em round a bit.

Trouble is, they do throw fag ends in as well. Never seen 'em eat those, though.'

'Have you ever seen them eat anything that's thrown in?' I looked at the carpet of decaying food remains and filth that lay on the bottom of the channel.

The manager reflected for a moment or two. 'Can't say I ever have, to be honest. Being so near the band puts 'em off, I suppose. Maybe they eat after closing. That's it—they're nocturnal, aren't they?'

'What do you think they normally eat in the wild?'

The manager frowned, then sniggered. 'Wogs, I imagine, natives, black boys, eh?' He gave me a jolly poke in the ribs. 'No, seriously, I reckon when they can't get human flesh they, well, they, er, graze on weed or chew reeds or something. Anyway, our food's very mixed, and the vegetables are good. They must get better fed here than up some mud creek among the fuzzy-wuzzies.'

Despite having to keep myself from punching this unlikely paradigm of zoological erudition in the eye, I was eager to hear more. 'How long have the alligators been here?' I inquired, gritting my teeth.

'Three years, about. They've grown a bit.'

'How big were they when you bought them, then?'

'Oh, about nine or ten inches, I'd say.'

It was appalling. The little reptiles had grown only two or three inches in three years. The reason was plain: eating little and very rarely, in cool water and a confined space, cold-blooded creatures like alligators grow barely at all. These should have been eight times their actual size. The wonder was that they were alive at all.

I inspected the tail of the little alligator closely. It was my first such case but I felt sure that the basic cause of the disease was vitamin B_6 deficiency. What was more, the bones of all three reptiles seemed unusually soft and pliable, so there was the complication of rickets too. The whole mess was one of gross neglect and malnutrition.

The manager paled when I asked him to hold the alligator while I amputated the gangrenous portion of its tail. 'Oooh! I couldn't possibly,' he said. 'Can't bear to touch the slimy beasts. Can't stand blood, really I can't. So sorry.' He edged away, muttering something about accounts to attend to and wine to order.

As it was the middle of the morning there was no-one else around. I took off my jacket and slipped the alligator inside head first, leaving just the tail protruding. Holding the wriggling reptile through the sleeve with one hand, I managed to inject a ring of local anaesthetic around its tail. Giving time for the anaesthetic to act, I prepared scalpel, suture needles and nylon thread. Meanwhile the alligator, alarmed at the prospect of imminent surgery, disappeared completely down my jacket sleeve. When I was ready, I pushed my hand down to feel for my little patient. As my fingers reached him, he bit down hard and painfully, seizing two of my fingers in a miniature gin-trap of spiky teeth. In agony, I withdrew my hand, bringing with it the tenaciously engaged alligator. I did not want to break the little fellow's teeth so I slowly used the blunt end of a scalpel in my other hand to prise open his mouth and release my punctured digits. That done, I wired his jaws securely together with an encircling strand or two of nylon.

At last the operation could begin, but without any helper I had to hold the animal, cut and stitch. The problem began when the tail had been amputated, a fraction closer to the body than the line where the rotting tissue ended, and I was attempting to suture the wound neatly. How was I to tie knots in the nylon? The slightest relaxation of my grip on the alligator's body and he prepared to scuttle off. I turned him upside down on the nearest table and stroked his tummy in the style of Kelly, the croc mesmerist. He seemed to like the tickling sensation and lay still. When I thought he had gone properly into a trance, I released my hold on him. Quick as a flash, he flipped onto his feet and fled over the dirty tablecloth. I cursed the Garden of Eden and its fallen angels. Retrieving my bolting patient, I held him up to my mouth with one hand. I would have to use my teeth. I passed the needle and nylon thread through the edges of the scaly skin with my other hand, caught and held them between my teeth while I slipped a knot round with my bleeding fingers. Right under my nose, the soggy rear end of the alligator smelt distinctly unpleasant. Slowly, one by one, I 'toothed' surgical knots across the tail stump until it was completely sealed. Then I gave all three alligators stiff shots of vitamins and liquid minerals.

My final job was to deal with the manager and I went to his office.

'I've operated on the alligator,' I told him, 'but the Garden of Eden is a bloody disgrace. You've kept those animals for three years in abominable conditions and with no provision for proper diet or care.'

The manager stood up abruptly from behind his desk with a look I imagine he normally reserved for clients requiring the attentions of his bouncer. There was no bouncer at hand.

I continued, 'You know nothing at all about these creatures, you've been neglectful and cruel and you're not fit to keep tame bluebottles!'

'Now look here, young fellow, I don't know who you think you are, but . . .'

'I give you one week to donate those alligators to the zoo, otherwise I blow the whistle. *Manchester Evening News*, police, Cruelty to Animals Act, the lot—you get my point?'

The word 'police' seemed to quieten the manager down immediately. 'Yes, er, quite, quite,' he said. 'Now how about a drop of short stuff before you go?'

'Thank you, no. But please remember my advice about your donation to the zoo.' I had made him make an offer he could not refuse.

Sure enough, the manager did remember, for three days later the local newspaper carried a publicity shot of Miss

Seksi, she of the python and the striptease, presenting Belle Vue with the trio.

'"Do take care of them, we're so fond of them," said Miss Seksi,' read the blurb beneath the photograph.

The three alligators from the Garden of Eden were named Adam, Eve and Abel by Clive, Belle Vue's reptile keeper, and under his care they began to grow long and fat. When Belle Vue closed in 1977 they were all around eight feet long and they went off to sunnier climes in the new Zoo de la Casa de Campo, Madrid, where I still see them.

Six

There were only three more days before I was due to fly out to Seattle to see how the Americans went about shipping the killer whale. It was breakfast-time again when Shelagh answered the phone and said it was Matt from Belle Vue. My appetite vanished as I pushed back my chair to take the receiver.

'What now?' I asked tersely, steeling myself for further catastrophes. Not more giraffe problems, I prayed.

'A woipe out. Not a survoivor,' came the Irishman's voice. Yet he sounded remarkably cheerful for a bearer of sad tidings.

'How many of what?' I barked.

'Oh, the lot. Around three dozen, they say.'

The man must have cracked under the shock, I thought. He was quite clearly chuckling.

'Three dozen dead what?' I bellowed.

Matt paused for maximum dramatic effect and then said quietly, 'Fleas, Doctor, the whole bally lot of 'em, the performin' fleas.'

Belle Vue possessed the last surviving example of that Victorian curiosity, the flea circus. In a small round kiosk in the centre of the zoo, the flea trainer would crouch over a miniature ring set on a table-top and put a troupe of shiny brown fleas through their repertoire. The circle of paying customers huddled round him would see two of the minute creatures fence with swords made out of fuse-wire, another couple pull Lilliputian chariots and a supposedly female star do a high-wire act along a filament of cotton whilst clasping a diminutive parasol. The fleas worked well. They submitted gamely to being harnessed with the aid of a magnifying glass and tweezers, they pushed and pulled and lifted in demonstrations of their relatively enormous strength, and the show went on. It was not actually true to say that the fleas were trained; they did what they were supposed to do quite naturally. Put a well-fed flea on a thread and he (or she) will walk along it. Give him a little parasol to grab and he will grab it for sure in one pair of legs and still walk happily along on the remaining two pairs. Place two fleas face to face, give them each a bit of fuse-wire and they will wave the useless things in front of them (what else should a flea find to do with fuse-wire?), looking for all the world like a pair of miniature Errol Flynns.

If that makes it sound too simple, let me hasten to point out the pitfalls before you tell your boss what he can do with his job, shake the cat in search of an off-the-peg and out-of-work company of artistes and take a one-way ticket to Broadway. First, there are fleas and fleas. To put it another way, there are Thespian fleas, fleas that have greasepaint and the roar of the crowd in their yellow blood, that are invigorated by the limelight, that dream dreams of playing Hamlet or Macbeth, and then there are the common herd, the fleas lacking in pizzazz. It goes without saying that flea circuses depend on a plentiful supply of the former variety, plentiful because of the brevity, if brilliance, of their lives and because of the tendency, so well known among flighty show-biz types, to be unreliable, miss rehearsals, elope. Experience has shown that only *Pulex irritans*, the human flea, has got what it takes to make the grade in flea circuses.

The second necessity, common to all performers whether they be Laurence Olivier or a six-legged blood-sucker one-eighth of an inch long, is nourishment, and where Lord O. might make do with a cold cutlet or fish and chips, fleas demand meals of blood. Human fleas prefer human blood and take other brews with reluctance. The provider of the meals, usually by baring his forearm, is the long-suffering trainer who owns the flea circus.

Now I come to the bit that will bring tears to the eyes of every dedicated animal conservationist: along with the blue whale, the Javan rhinoceros and the okapi, the human flea faces the sombre possibility of extinction, at least in the West. The plain fact that the species is becoming increasingly difficult to find is no doubt the principal reason why flea circuses, those bizarre backwaters of show business, are no longer around. The decline of *Pulex irritans* was brought on by increased standards of hygiene in the human population and especially by the universal use of DDT and other pesticides and fly-sprays around the house. What applies to the human flea, however, does not seem to have worried unduly the hundred or more other species of flea that make their homes on almost all kinds of mammals and birds throughout the world. They thrive, but the trouble is that their histrionic abilities are said to be abysmal.

'The feller runnin' the flea circus is as sick as a parrot,' Matt was saying. 'Some joker squirted Flit in the room where he keeps his insects. He thinks it was his woife after they'd had a bit of a barney. Anyway, he comes in this morning and foinds the lot with their legs in the air, croaked.' He chuckled louder than ever.

'Can't he get replacements easily enough?' I asked. My knowledge of the flea business at that time was zero. I assumed that a quick dash down to the nearest Salvation Army doss-house would have a full complement of performers on cue for the afternoon performance.

'No chance,' said Matt. 'Human fleas are loike gold nowadays. His last batch he had sent in from a scientist in Wales at two pounds apiece. But apparently that source has petered out.'

'And they must be human fleas?'

'So he says. It's traditional. Apparently if they're content and well fed they'll march about and not indulge in too much jumpin'. Other fleas object to marchin'.'

'Surely some other species of animal flea would do as a substitute, at least temporarily?'

'Well, that's whoiy oi'm ringin' you. The flea circus man doubts it'll work but he thinks it's worth a go. Perhaps some of the zoo animals have their own fleas on them, fleas mebbe with a little bit of talent. Dog and cat fleas he says are an absolute dead loss. They clear off before you can say Finn McCool.'

'So?' I queried.

'Well, if you could spare half an hour, he'd be most obloiged if we could look through some of our animals.'

'To round up candidates for audition?'

'Correct, Doctor.'

I went to the zoo. Apart from the reptile house, where blood-sucking ticks on snakes and lizards were carefully controlled, our defence against external parasites was simply to powder, bath or spray any bird or mammal on which ticks or mites had begun to cause skin disease or itching. Newly arrived animals were inspected for fellow-travellers and dealt with as necessary. Fleas, of all the various types of creature that pass their days browsing beneath the fur or feathers of their hosts, are rarely seen.

Matt and the mournful flea trainer, whose name was Alf, met me and we set off round the gardens, carrying with us a handful of small, waxed pill-boxes. There was no question of picking over some of our beasts, and we passed by the big cats, the wolves, the gorillas and such. A selection of monkeys was clean as a whistle. (People often think that these creatures can be seen picking fleas from one another's coats but it is not so: what they see is mutual grooming, with the groomer taking skin scales and grains of salt from the other animal's body.) We parted the lush wool of the llamas and alpacas, grabbed a Barbary sheep or two and frisked an amazed group of kangaroos. They had not got a single flea among them. On we went, like the School Inspectors who came once a year and scratched around our heads in search of 'nits' when I was a little boy.

Then we made our first capture. A little black fellow fumbled his take-off leap from the belly fur of an Arctic fox and was collared by Matt. Soon we bagged a rather somnolent brace of bigger reddish ones which were napping on a parrot. Within a couple of hours we had almost twenty fleas of various sorts safely incarcerated in our pill-boxes. We went back to the flea circus kiosk to see them auditioned. When we were inside and securely battened down, Alf illuminated the table-top where all the action took place, set up his props and laid out the pill-boxes in front of him. Each box had been labelled with the name of the host species. If by any chance there was a minuscule Richard Burton waiting to be discovered in one of the containers, we needed to know where more like him might be obtained.

One by one the pill-boxes were opened and the inmates removed with tweezers. Alf first examined them through the magnifying glass. Some he thought were far too small, as apart from the difficulty of putting on the cotton harnesses, the audience would have difficulty seeing them. He tried the bigger ones in the ring. The first three of these, from a coatimundi, took one look at the Big Top and vanished, never to be seen again. The next, a solitary, mahogany-coloured individual plucked whilst still sucking brunch from the neck of an ostrich, was found to have expired in the pill-box. So it went on. Some jumped straight out of the ring, others keeled over, legs bicycling furiously in the air, when urged to walk. The few that Alf actually managed to encumber with parasol, fuse-wire or harness seemed to be struck with instant stage fright and froze up, feigning death.

'Just like I thought,' muttered Alf. 'We've always said in the profession that there's no substitute for yer grand old 'uman variety.' He shook his head sadly, recalling the gracious, flea-ridden days gone by.

My part in the attempt to save the death of another little bit of theatre ended there, and although Alf eventually obtained a small troupe from somewhere, the growing difficulties of supply did finally bring down the curtain on Britain's last flea circus.

The news of Alf's misfortune had got into the early edition of the evening paper, I found later that day, and before I had finished reading my copy, there was a phone call.

'My name's Andrew Greenwood,' said the voice. 'I'm a veterinary student at Cambridge. I live over the hills from you and read in the paper about the flea circus at Belle Vue. I wondered if I could be of any help.'

It was the chap who had been chasing me up about lobsters, I suddenly remembered.

'I've collected some of the biggest fleas in Britain, if you'd like them,' continued the voice earnestly. 'They're mole fleas, a quarter of an inch long. I'd be delighted to bring them along.'

The mole flea certainly is a giant of its kind, though still not as enormous as the pea-sized monster of a flea once seen in the nest of an American beaver.

'Thanks anyway,' I said, 'but I don't think we're in the market for any more fleas today.'

Less than a week later, I was sitting in a restaurant on the Seattle seafront, chewing whopping great pieces of broiled lobster and outsize oysters. Like so much American seafood, they looked delicious and were temptingly served, but had somehow outgrown their subtle, flavourful birthright, sacrificing delicacy and taste for sheer size. Oh for a Cornish lobster or a dozen Whitstable natives, I thought, as my jaws began to ache with the effort and I washed the rubbery chunks down with a dispiriting beverage that claimed to be wine and went under the enigmatic name of 'Cold Duck'.

Through the window I could see below me the round

metal pools of the Seattle Aquarium. Floating motionless in the one nearest to me, like an inflated plastic bath toy, eleven feet long with oil-smooth, jet-black skin and crisp, snow-white markings, was the young killer whale I had come for. He was a perfect specimen, about two-and-a-half years old, with the teeth at the front of his jaws only just beginning to push through the gums. I was stoking up for the two-day journey to Flamingo Park. He was fasting; whales and dolphins never travel on full stomachs.

Don Goldsberry and Ted Griffin, the two owners of the Aquarium, were the pioneers of killer whale catching. Using a mile of immensely heavy and unwieldy stainless steel netting, they trapped the powerful and sharp-witted whales in Puget Sound. Goldsberry, Griffin and their veterinarian, Bill Klontz, were the experts at what was a fairly new game. All I was supposed to do was watch and listen and learn.

The first of their killers had been given the Eskimo name of 'Namu'. Later animals were christened 'Shamu', 'Ramu' and so on. They had a few appropriate, noble-sounding suggestions for my little fellow.

'Sorry,' I said, 'Pentland Hick has already decided what he is to be called. His name is Cuddles.'

The Americans did not like it. I hated it. But Hick was a shrewd entrepreneur with an eye to publicity: 'A fierce hunter of the oceans with a soft and winsome name. It's a good gimmick that will catch the imagination of the media men,' he reasoned. He was right.

Goldsberry and Griffin gave me a long list of do's and don'ts concerning the whale, all of which I meticulously noted down. This was the gospel to be followed—any infringement and Cuddles would undoubtedly run into trouble. 'If his dorsal fin flops over he's short of sweet water'; 'Use a three-inch needle if you have to inject him'; 'The only safe vaccine is 5 cc of such and such'; 'A shot of penicillin before he travels is all he needs'; 'Eggs are bad for him'; 'Sugar and glucose aren't absorbed by his gut and may do

79

him harm'; 'If he falls ill give him a quart of Maalox and fly us over'.

It sounded daunting, but who was I to judge? The practical study of larger cetaceans in captivity may have been in its infancy in the United States, but it had not even been born in Britain. It was prudent to go along with the instructions that accompanied the goods, not least because Pentland Hick had paid fifteen thousand dollars for Cuddles and was in no mood to quibble. It would be two years or more before we realised that the Seattle team knew little more about the care and treatment of these complicated marine animals than we did.

Next day Cuddles' long journey began. A padded hammock with holes for his eyes, flippers and vent was slipped under him as he floated in three feet of water. He did not fight or complain as a crane picked him, dripping, out of the pool and lowered him gently into a framework of tubular steel in which the hammock was to be slung. At last I got a chance to touch him. It was a wonderful experience. As I leaned over the placid beast after clambering up the bars surrounding him, he exhaled with a soft roar. A blast of hot air, carrying a not unpleasant, cow-like smell, hit me in the face. I revelled in the sensuous delight of passing my fingers over the skin. It was polished, very finely grooved and had the consistency of hard india rubber. It was soft and cool under his axillas, like sheet-steel across the blade of his tail fluke and warm as toast on his forehead, or melon. I climbed down and looked through the holes in the hammock. I waggled the paddle-like flippers and tried to trace the outlines of the bones within, bones that are identical to those in the fingers of human beings. Then I peered close to one large round brown eye. It was streaming with transparent tears as thick as syrup. The eye with its pleated, chocolate-coloured iris rolled slightly and fixed on me. He was looking at me. I stroked the nearby flipper and whistled.

To my utter delight, the eye remained gazing at me and a

squeaky, high-pitched chirruping was squeezed out of the blow-hole on top of Cuddles' head. I whistled again. The whale chirp-chirped in turn. He was answering me. Cats answer back, Henry, my goat, willingly exchanges bleats, dogs do it and tigers have a lovely habit of replying to a low 'prrh-prrh' with a similar welcoming sound that never fails to excite me, but this was something unique and it touched me deeply. It was to become a regular feature of my relationship with Cuddles, but that first moment when I came eyeball to eyeball and conversed with a Lord of the Sea, as the Eskimos call these magnificent beasts, was one of the most moving of my life, a vivid instant of sentiment, not sentimentality. Quite inexplicably, a bond had been forged between the whale and me. Whales, and particularly this one, were going to be something extra-special from now on.

As a greenhorn with whales, I was allowed to help in coating every inch of Cuddles' body with thick lanolin grease. This would stop the delicate skin drying out and cracking. Next, towels were spread along his back and smoothed to get rid of air-bubbles that could 'burn' the skin during the long journey. After that, hundredweights of crushed ice were sprinkled on and around the whale. The entire framework was shrouded in plastic sheeting and a water-spraying system of pipes, pumps and electric batteries was set up. The animal would go all the way sticky, wet and cold to avoid the killer's principal enemy, the risk of internal overheating.

We set out for the airport by road, on the back of a long low-loader. In the freight hold of the TWA jet freighter purposely kept at 1°C to help keep the whale cool, it was no fun clambering over his framework for a solid twelve hours. Don Goldsberry, Ted Griffin and I had to keep a constant watch for 'bed-sores' that can end weeks later in death from toxic gangrene, for blobs of lanolin melting and running into the blow-hole, for shifting towels that could be sucked in by one powerful inhalation of the whale's breath. The water sprays had to be kept going, batteries replaced, the system cleared of blocking particles of faecal matter re-circulated with the water. Most important of all, the whale must be constantly reassured. Stroking his forehead, whistling to him or just talking nonsense into his pinhead-sized but highly sensitive ear—it did not matter what, as long as we kept doing it, hour after hour. I had brought my *Collected Poems* of John Betjeman with me, a constant companion on my travels, and I passed the time on my spells of duty at the head end by reading aloud from the book. Apart from the comforting murmur of my voice, I wonder if Cuddles got anything more from such Betjemania as the delightful, awful Miss Joan Hunter Dunn.

Arriving at London Airport, we passed smoothly through Customs, then came the inspection by the Government vet. He had never even seen a whale before and would not have been any the wiser if our boy had been lying there in the terminal stages of rabies complicated by bubonic plague. His main function, he said, was to count incoming animals. To my amazement, he climbed up onto the whale container, looked down and said, 'One'. This he wrote in his notebook before jumping down and bidding us good evening.

After a six-hour road journey up into the north-east of England, where Flamingo Park lies in the sleepy village of Kirkby Misperton, the whale was unloaded from his truck and hoisted above the floodlit figure-of-eight pool that was to be his new home. Gently he was lowered into the icy cold water where several of us were waiting in wet-suits to release him from his hammock. The cold water and my tiredness were forgotten as the canvas fell away. Heart in mouth I waited, bobbing by Cuddles' side. If he had become stiff and could not flex his tail flukes, if he sank out of control, or if he listed because of a congested lung, we would have little chance of manhandling his great bulk in the deep pool. I saw that the two Americans who were conducting the releasing operation were looking tense, too.

For a second Cuddles hung in the water. Lazily he raised his great tail. Its deceptively powerful upbeat thrust the water into foaming furrows and his torpedo body glided gently forwards into the centre of the pool. We paddled after him—not that he needed us, but with all the photographer's flash-bulbs popping we wanted to look useful. Goldsberry called for a mackerel and threw it a couple of yards ahead of the whale. It sank in a flickering spiral through the blue water. Instantly Cuddles saw it, blew out a broad plume of water droplets and dived. Half-turning gracefully ten feet down, he opened his mouth a mere inch or two, sucked and the mackerel shot in. To the cheers of the crowd Cuddles rose to the surface, floated vertically with his head well clear of the water and opened his jaws wide. For the first time I saw the salmon-pink expanse of Cuddles' unmistakable grin.

Half an hour later this untrained animal that had roamed the north Pacific only one month before, that had raided fishing nets, murdered great whales, out-run and out-thought sharks and sealions and dolphins, this grinning, cuddly Cuddles with the appealing chirrup, was seen to begin playing with a floating beach-ball.

During the following weeks the killer whale settled down admirably in his new home. Every few days I made the 200-mile round trip over the hills, through the cities of Leeds and York and across the fertile farmland of the vale of Pickering that stretches east to the coast, to see that all was going well. This usually entailed swimming with Cuddles in his pool of artificial sea water. In a wet-suit and face mask I inspected his ventral surface under water; it would be several months before he was trained to roll over on command so that his tummy could be viewed and prodded from dry land. Underwater, too, I had a chance of catching for parasite analysis a sample of his elusive, near-liquid faecal matter before it dispersed irretrievably in his wake. Even so humble a task as collecting droppings from these remarkable creatures presented quite special complications, as the whale, ever curious about the submarine antics of this ungainly caricature of a drunken walrus, buffeted me with his rounded nose.

Giving injections was another poser. Asian 'flu swept through the human population of Britain shortly after Cuddles' arrival and, on learning that Sea World in San Diego had evidence that the influenza virus could attack cetaceans, I had to think of some way of jabbing Cuddles with the current strains of 'flu vaccine. In the early days we had no special slinging device for 'dry-docking' the whale, and emptying the 300,000-gallon pool except for serious emergencies just was not on. For one thing, artificial sea water is expensive to make up. For another, the local river authority did not take kindly to so vast a quantity of brine passing via the drains into their waterways. The salt injured freshwater river life and could poison vegetation along the banks. I had already seen the effect of brine discharge into a stream near the Marineland on the Côte d'Azur: every one of the three dozen majestic palm trees in the gardens of villas running down to the stream was dead as a dodo in a couple of weeks and had to be given fake crowns of branches cut from other trees. The villa owners played hell. On top of these problems, pools like the one at Flamingo Park, built in sandy soil with a high water table, often object to being emptied by collapsing inwards when the enormous outward pressure of their contents is removed.

Cuddles had behaved like a playful, amenable child so far. He doted on humans, craved their attention and was impeccably well-mannered. Pondering the problem of the 'flu vaccination, I decided to try simply swimming up to him in the water and slapping a needle in. I was a dab hand at doing this sort of thing with large land animals. Take an elephant: thump his buttocks hard with your clenched fist one, two, three times so that he knows you are there and is accustomed to what is, to him, a friendly pat on his inch-thick skin. Then, O wily elephant doctor, still keeping up the regular rhythm, with the fourth thump flick forward the wide-bore hypodermic needle that you have concealed in the palm of your hand. Slap goes your fist for the fifth time and the needle zooms to the hilt right through the tough grey leather. The elephant does not feel a thing and consequently has no nasty memories to never forget. This technique is used on horses, cattle and pigs by James Herriots all over the world.

I looked at the whale contentedly basking on the surface after a snack of twenty pounds of mackerel and I reckoned there was a good chance of doing it the same way with him. The press were going to take pictures of the novel inoculation, and I came forth from the dressing room looking like Dustin Hoffman in *The Graduate*. Apart from the frogman outfit I carried a disinfectant aerosol in one hand and a syringe fitted with a ten-inch needle in the other. With the panache of a commando off to plant limpet mines on the *Tirpitz*, I somersaulted backwards into the pool. This flashy entrance was then followed by a more feeble dog-paddle towards my prey. As I arrived at Cuddles' glistening hull, steam was rising from his forehead where it was drying while he basked. He tolerantly rolled a liquid brown eye at me and gave me the salmon-pink grin. The sloping rows of conical white teeth sparkled.

I selected a spot on the top of the killer's back at the base of the dorsal fin. Supporting myself by throwing one arm over his loins, I sprayed the area with disinfectant and then threw the can away from me. Cuddles was most intrigued. Only his big eye moved, following my every movement.

I balanced myself in the water and raised the syringe and needle high in the air. Cuddles watched it go. Then with my free hand I slapped at the disinfected spot. One, two, three. 'What *is* the lad up to?' I could imagine the whale musing good-humouredly. Four, five—down came the syringe, straight as an arrow, and at exactly the same instant I had the impression that someone had dropped an atom bomb on the *Tirpitz*, prematurely aborting my mission. The pool water beneath me seemed to levitate itself. I was in no doubt that the entire three million pounds of liquid was unexpectedly on its way up towards the ceiling. Certainly I was proceeding in the opposite direction. Somehow I had been transported into a giant washing machine. Arms and legs flailing, I was sucked down, tumbled, rolled, swept and swirled in a maelstrom of foaming water. What looked like a nuclear submarine with a full-open throttle was tearing round me. My lungs were bursting. I had swallowed what felt like a hogshead of salt water du maison. My syringe and needle had vanished, and my shins had received an excruciating blow from something that could only have been Neptune's iron trident.

A half-drowned veterinarian was hauled miserably over the edge of the pool and lay, puking salt water, in a very un-commando-like fashion at the feet of the pressmen, who found it all very interesting.

Apparently, as soon as the needle had touched the whale. he had launched himself forward with full, fast beats of his flukes. The entire muscle strength of a cetacean's body is concentrated on the focal point at the hinge of the tail. The energy contained in this highly efficient propeller is enough to storm-toss incredible volumes of water in the twinkling of an eye. I had been the centre of such an instant storm and the painful bruising of my shins had been caused by the tip of a flipper grazing by.

Half an hour and a stiff shot of brandy later, I felt ready to try again. I was loath to use the dart-gun, since its longest needle measured only three inches and anyway I was afraid that the wide bore might carry unsterile water into the tissues. I would not have been able to disinfect the skin and there was the problem of retrieving the spent flying syringe.

The question of needle length interested me. It was generally assumed that a long one that could reach beyond the thick blubber layer was essential: everyone talked as if the blubber was inert stuff, without blood vessels that could pick up and circulate drugs and vaccines. But even fatty tissue must have blood to remain alive, and I decided to try a foolproof but shallow injection method on Cuddles. I telephoned a friend at a Leeds University dental clinic, and a car was sent over with what I wanted: the needle-less gun that fires liquids at high velocity into human gums or skin. It was the instrument being developed for mass vaccination against cholera, typhoid, polio and so on.

The dose of vaccine for a killer whale was my next problem. With most vaccines it is by no means true or safe to give, say, six times the amount of vaccine to an individual who weighs six times the average for any particular dosage. Vaccines do not work like that. Nevertheless it was possible to use too small a dose—in Seattle Cuddles had been given what was thought to be an adequate shot of a vaccine against germs of the lockjaw family, but tests I had done on his blood when he first arrived showed virtually no antibodies to lockjaw circulating in his system. He was not protected as everyone thought. In the end, I decided to give Cuddles three times the human dose of 'flu vaccine and then take blood after a couple of weeks, by when, I hoped, a dry dock would be ready. I would check the level of 'flu antibodies and give bigger booster shots if necessary.

The intrepid frogman re-entered the water carrying the vaccine-gun. Once more Cuddles was resting and gave no sign as I approached that only a couple of hours before I had tried to harpoon him and had been summarily demolished. Again he grinned disarmingly. A trainer on the pool-side threw a mackerel into the gaping jaw. Cuddles sucked it down with smooth ease and ogled me. I raised the gun and drew in a big breath. If the typhoon struck, I was determined to keep my mouth shut this time, no matter what.

I pulled the trigger. There was a sharp crack. I got ready for drowning.

Cuddles grinned benevolently again and did not move an inch. He was vaccinated and had not felt a thing. Now all I had to do was wait and hope that the inoculation was effective.

I was quite pleased as I struggled out of the pool for the second time that day. One way or another, I had injected my first real live killer. By the time I had showered, admired the blue and red protuberances on my shins and got into warm clothing once more, everyone had gone from the dolphinarium except one fellow. He stood at the water's edge, looking down intently at the whale, a camera slung from his neck and his pockets bristling with notebooks. I took him to be the last of the press, or possibly the usual late arriver from the local rag who always gets upset when you politely explain, 'No, it isn't possible to do it all again just for you. No, not even mocking it up. No, even though I appreciate how bloody-minded your editor's going to be if you return without the hoped for pictures of Dr Taylor being eaten by a killer whale or stomped by a rhinoceros.'

'Get what you want?' I asked the mousey-haired young man with the faintest resemblance to Robert Redford.

'Oh yes, very much so,' came the reply. 'By the way, I'm Andrew Greenwood. I spoke to you a few months back. Lobsters, fleas—remember?'

'Come and have a spot of lunch and tell me all about your lobsters,' I said.

Andrew barely touched the meal, he spent so much time enthusing over his determination to practise with zoo animals once he had qualified from Cambridge.

'How did you know I was working on the whale today?' I asked.

He grinned. 'I drop a keeper in the bird section a packet of fags every week or two to keep me informed.'

His chutzpah appealed to me. 'And the lobsters?'

Earnestly, he explained. 'You may well know of the significance of lobster blood serum in identifying a certain type of haemophilia in humans. It's a very rare condition, and only about eight cases have been reported so far, but Manchester Royal Infirmary are working on a test for the disease. That test relies on a supply of lobster serum.'

'Quite. To detect the missing clotting factor in the human blood,' I said, nodding sagely but not knowing the faintest thing about the rôle in such obscure areas of medicine of a crustacean that until then had been useful to me only when coated with a mixture of cream, parmesan cheese, white wine and garlic, and lightly broiled.

The intent young student appeared to think that I knew all about the matter. 'So I've been asked to supply the laboratory at Manchester with lobster serum and I came to you, Dr Taylor, for advice on taking blood from lobsters.'

It was flattering, of course, but I had no idea where to begin finding veins on such an armour-plated creature.

'I'm afraid I can't help you,' I confessed. 'Lobsters don't fall sick very often these days.' (In fact, within a couple of years Reg Bloom, a zoologist friend, started flying plane-loads of Canadian lobsters over the Atlantic to stock his 'lobster farm' at Clacton, and I discovered then that the species can be expected to feel poorly with monotonous regularity.)

Andrew Greenwood seemed disappointed that I could not shed any light on how to persuade the shellfish to enrol as blood donors, but I had the feeling that he was not the type to let it rest at that. When we parted he asked if he could contact me and keep me informed of his progress.

'There must be a way of sampling a lobster without doing it like the Dutch scientists do—simply chopping off a claw and letting the poor thing bleed into a jar,' he said.

I liked that. Andrew seemed a promising sort of bloke.

I was further impressed when, three or four weeks later, he proudly appeared at my home in Rochdale carrying a little tube of pale blue liquid. He had studied the architecture of the crusty old lobster and had found a particular soft spot where a needle can be inserted and blood drawn off easily without hurting or damaging the lowly creature in any way. It was his unusual début in the world of wild animal surgery.

Seven

From the vast room's high ceiling, tattered strips of red velvet wallpaper hung down in rows like Tibetan prayer flags. In the centre of the floor stood a full-length billiard table lit by hooded lights and with a small Capuchin monkey curled up asleep on the green baize over the spot reserved for the blue ball. The air was heavy with an aroma of mothballs, Cologne water, Capuchin monkey and sheer age. A velvet-covered sofa was drawn up before the deep, broad hearth where a cheap electric fire's single bar glowed dully amid gently waving cobwebs.

On the sofa reclined Mrs Crabbe. A Singer sewing machine and a large pile of Tetley teabags were on a card table nearby. She had been neatly stitching two lines across the middle of each teabag and then separating the halves with a snip of her scissors when we arrived. Renowned in the town for 'having nowt to learn about making brass go a long way', Mrs Crabbe was worth half a million and found it easy to stay that way. Two stools, low and wooden like milking stools, were placed before her and slightly to one side to avoid blocking the feeble heat from the fire. On one sat Dr Aspinall, Doctor of Medicine, humans for the treatment of, and on the other sat I, Doctor of Veterinary Medicine, physician to the countless other living things on this planet that Dr Aspinall was not concerned with. Dr Aspinall and I both held a liqueur glass brimming with a thick yellow liquid. Mrs Crabbe had a firm grasp on a tumbler filled with the same stuff. Dr Aspinall and I sat in silence, glumly sipping the sickly Advocaat from time to time. Mrs Crabbe gulped large mouthfuls at frequent intervals while giving us an imperious dressing-down.

Over eighty, small and wiry, with hennaed hair and a face thickly powdered with what looked like flour, the old lady was not having any nonsense. It was the first time Aspinall or I had met her, but like every Rochdalian we had heard much about the history of this remarkable woman. Widow of the Crabbe who expanded the Crabbe cotton textile mills into the largest family concern west of the Pennines, she had chased over the moors on foot, following the Rochdale Hunt, until well into her seventies; with one swipe of a lacrosse stick she had broken the arm of a canvasser who had imprudently distributed Labour Party leaflets to her gardeners; and she had literally closed down a Methodist chapel of which she was the patroness and main financial support when the new young minister had professed a belief in evolution. Since her spouse had abruptly expired while doing the hokey-kokey at a Masonic function twenty years before, Mrs Crabbe had soldiered on in the great black stone house, served faithfully by a small staff, the youngest of whom, referred to as 't' gardener's lad', could not have been more than ten years younger than his mistress. Time creaked along in the house set on the moor edge above the chimneys of the family mills that filled the narrow valley below with smoke. House and inhabitants were slowly grinding to a halt. Essentials were attended to. Non-essentials were not. The brass knobs and knockers bearing the ornate 'C' were crusty with verdigris, the Victorian wood and ironwork were dull. The kitchen, which six nights a week had handled the victualling of a gaggle of mill owners, Conservative Party notables, parsons and their wives, lay cold and dank, its shelves empty but for Weetabix and Ovaltine. The garden, once trim and spruce, was regaining a wild beauty and making for the moorland. The cellar, though, was full—not, as in years gone by, with crusted port and well-bred clarets but with rack upon rack of Advocaat. Mrs Crabbe doted, depended, survived upon egg-flip. Therein lay the problem, for both Dr Aspinall and myself.

It was actually by pure coincidence that the doctor and I had driven up to the house at precisely the same moment. We had parked our cars on the circle of cobbles through which a forest of vigorous weeds was thrusting six inches high, greeted one another—Aspinall had stitched me up once and I had treated some of his sheep-farmer patients who had picked up orf virus from their flocks—and knocked on the imposing front door.

'D'ye think we've been called to see the same patient?' Aspinall chuckled as we waited.

'Hope not,' I said. 'Apparently the old lady's got a monkey. What are you here for?'

'Mrs Crabbe herself.' He sighed heavily. 'This is my first visit. She's a private patient, just switched to us from Landau's practice. I can't say I'm over-enthusiastic. She's a bit of a tartar by all accounts. She led Dr Landau a hell of a dance and would never take his advice.'

The door opened at last with much groaning of hinges to reveal a bad-tempered crone in high button-boots. She showed us into the room where Mrs Crabbe was treadling furiously away at the suturing of teabags. The whirring of the machine continued until the old lady had bisected several rows of bags to her satisfaction, then she stretched out on the sofa, protectively nestling two bottles of Advocaat in the crook of one arm and surveying us unblinkingly over the tilted brim of her glass. Breaking the ice, I suggested that I wait outside while Dr Aspinall did his stuff. I had already spotted my patient slumbering soundly on the billiard table.

Mrs Crabbe emptied the glass, looked from one to the other of us dolefully, slowly passed a furry tongue across thin lips and then reached for one of her bottles. Without speaking she leaned sideways, felt under the sofa and produced two liqueur glasses. These she filled before replenishing her own glass. Eventually she addressed us in loud and plummy tones.

'Sit down there, both of you. Take a glass. And listen.'

We did as we were told.

'Let me make myself clear,' she continued. 'Ethel, my housekeeper, let you in at the front door. You came to the *front door*.' She uttered the words 'front door' like Edith Evans as Lady Bracknell referring to 'a *handbag*' in *The Importance of Being Earnest*. 'The front door is never opened. I want that clearly understood. In future please remember to use the tradesmen's entrance.'

Dr Aspinall and I cowered on our stools. Mrs Crabbe downed half her tumbler and made a gargling noise.

'Now then.' The old lady's plumminess was sounding distinctly over-ripe. 'I take it you are the two doctors. Are you going to look first at Thoth?' She turned her head briefly towards the sleeping monkey.

'I'm here to see you, Mrs Crabbe,' said Aspinall bravely. 'I'm Dr Aspinall, your new doctor. I've come to give you a check-up and . . .'

'Who's that, then?' interrupted Mrs Crabbe, pointing accusingly towards me and snatching a deep swig that emptied the tumbler.

'Er—I'm the vet. To see the monkey. You rang, I believe.' I smiled reassuringly.

She kept her pointing finger firmly in position and frowned intently. Her dark, deep-sunken eyes bored into me. 'You're Dr Aspinall then. What do you know about monkeys?'

Aspinall groaned and put down his glass. 'Mrs Crabbe, if I might explain, Dr Taylor is here to see your monkey and I'm here to . . .'

Mrs Crabbe's imperious finger swung instantly round, aiming at the unfortunate Aspinall. 'Ah, I see,' she interrupted effortlessly. 'You're his assistant. Quite right. Good. Must have the best for poor Thoth there. Now you may examine him. But don't hurt him, mind. You, Dr

Taylor'—she was speaking to my companion—'hold him gently. Watch what Dr Aspinall does. I've heard he's got quite a way with monkeys.'

I looked at the doctor and he stared helplessly at me. It was perfectly plain that the old battleaxe was suffering from a combination of the passage of time and a surfeit of egg-flip. I raised my eyebrows and bit on the edge of my liqueur glass. With a sharp crack a crescent of glass broke off the rim and dropped from my lips onto the carpet.

'Really, Dr Landau!' barked Mrs Crabbe. 'That's Waterford. Fifteen and sixpence if I'm not mistaken. I shall deduct it from your bill at the end of the quarter.'

Dear God, I thought as I dabbed my bleeding lip with my handkerchief, quarters! What I needed was clients who paid cash or at least promptly after receiving one of Shelagh's monthly accounts.

Aspinall shrugged and rolled his eyes. I tried once more. 'But you sent for the doctor yourself,' I explained. 'Wouldn't it be better if Dr Aspinall—he—your own human doctor examined you elsewhere while I attended to the monkey, to Thoth?'

The old lady grunted indignantly. 'Certainly not. Examined by your assistant, Doctor? What are things coming to? No, sir. You must see to my poor Thoth first, then you can take a look at me and see about my little problem.'

'But, Mrs Crabbe, he is your doctor.'

'Doctor? Doctor? Is he or isn't he a veterinarian, qualified to work with monkeys?'

'No, madam, he isn't, but . . .'

'Quite so.' She squeezed out a stern smile. 'I don't mind him assisting you, Dr Aspinall, while he learns, but I couldn't possibly allow him to treat Thoth alone.'

'I'm the veterinarian, Dr Taylor,' I half-shouted in exasperation.

'Of course you are, Doctor,' she said quietly. 'That's why I called you. And I've every faith in you.'

'Tell you what—why don't you look at the monkey and get that part over with?' Aspinall sounded strangely faint. He stood up and stared intently at the peeling ceiling.

I walked over to the billiard table and looked down at the monkey. 'What's been worrying you about Thoth, Mrs Crabbe?' I asked.

'It's his teeth, Doctor. They seem to be giving him a bit of trouble. He drools and holds his face and is easily offended.'

'Offended?'

'Yes. For example, old Fairbanks, my solicitor, looked at Thoth in a wrong sort of way the other day and Thoth bit his ear.'

'How long have you had him, Mrs Crabbe?'

'Oh, at least forty-five years.'

I gasped. Forty-five years was a sensationally long life-span for a Capuchin monkey.

'Forty-five years for sure?' I asked.

'At least. Possibly longer. He was ever such a smart young fellow when my late husband was in short trousers. I remember his father before him.'

'He was bred round here, you mean?'

Mrs Crabbe slopped a thick stream of Advocaat into the tumbler again. Taking a mouthful, she closed her eyes and seemed to be thinking deeply. 'I think not, Doctor,' she said eventually. 'His family originated in Rhodesia or Nyasaland or somewhere like that.'

'Thoth? He's a South American species, not African, Mrs Crabbe.'

'What are you talking about, Doctor? Old Fairbanks' parents lived in Bulawayo as near as I can recall. Fine stock.'

A muffled choking noise came from the direction of my medical colleague. I dared not look round at him.

'How long have you had Thoth, Mrs Crabbe?' I persevered.

'Nearly ten years now. He's never had a day's illness. You may wake him up if you like.'

I tickled the little creature at the back of his head and, remembering Fairbanks' luck, put on an expression of which the monkey would approve when he opened his eyes. He awoke immediately and glared at me. Then, baring his teeth, he crawled off awkwardly and stuck both legs in a corner pocket. I looked at him carefully. He was an ugly specimen, with a swollen, punch-drunk boxer's face and lips bulging over an upper jaw that seemed too big for his mouth. No, ugly was not a fair word to use. His whole face was deformed. There was no symmetry to it and all the features were askew. Its bones were lumpy and seemed to be trying to press out through the skin.

I approached the Capuchin warily and put out a hand. He pulled himself out of the pocket and shuffled on his knees across the green surface of the table. Now I could see that not only his face but the whole of his puny body was totally deformed. With grotesquely bowed limbs and sunken ribs, this monkey was a hunchback, a miniature Quasimodo. I went after him, grabbed him swiftly behind the neck and with one hand swept his arms behind him into a full nelson. He gibbered infuriatedly but was not able to reach me with his teeth. Gently I put him down onto the floor and released him. The distorted little body dragged itself like a wounded beetle across the dusty carpet. It was not walking. Its feet were redundant. It was crawling, slithering, hauling itself along on elbows and knees.

'Has he always moved like this?' I asked, dismayed.

'Always,' came the reply. 'Why? Capuchin monkeys always walk like that, as you should know, Doctor. Have you ever seen a nicer specimen? It's just those teeth, those naughty peggy-wegs that bother him.'

Quite often I had come across owners, pet-shop dealers, folk who claimed to know a bit about monkeys, who really believed that Capuchins and other New World species such as woolly and spider monkeys naturally haul themselves about in this bizarre and pitiable manner. As a student I had heard zoo men declare that such a way of moving was a classic characteristic of a group of primates who spent their entire lives high in the forest canopy and whose legs as a result were as obsolescent as the human appendix.

I picked the monkey up again, immobilised him in the full nelson and lifted his upper lip. Mrs Crabbe was quite right: Thoth had a mouthful of tooth problems. Looking in, I saw a scene of utter shambles as if a miniature grenade had exploded between the jaws and blasted every tooth out of its foundations. The teeth were there OK but apart from that everything was most definitely not OK. There were teeth growing down from the middle of the roof of the mouth, under the tongue, in clusters one on top of another, three or four abreast struggling to occupy a socket meant for a single one. There were teeth doing their own thing—growing upside down with their roots just visible and their crowns buried deep in the gum, some pointing in towards the tongue, others taking the opposite direction and burrowing into the cheeks.

'Look at this, Doctor,' I said. Aspinall was still studying the ceiling.

'Yes, young man,' said Mrs Crabbe. 'Go and give Dr Taylor a hand and learn something. You'll never be much of a monkey vet if you moon about like that.'

As if in a trance the doctor quietly obeyed.

'SAPD—South American Primate Disease, worst case I've ever seen,' I whispered. 'Malnutrition essentially. Head bones soften while the teeth are developing, letting them drift off into any old place. Ribs cave in. I'm surprised he's not dead long ago with pneumonia. I'll probably find half a dozen pathological fractures in his limbs if I X-ray him.'

The doctor nodded. A more complex and dramatic disease, it nevertheless has some of the features of human rickets.

'What does Thoth eat?' I asked, although I had a pretty

98

shrewd idea—sugary junk with minimum protein and hardly a vitamin.

Mrs Crabbe was silent.

Right, I thought. 'Grapes, bananas, chocolates, sweeties, cakes, biscuits, apples, oranges, sugar lumps, tea, fruit drinks—that's the sort of thing he has, isn't it, Mrs Crabbe?' I inquired confidently.

'No, Dr Aspinall. Definitely not.' Mrs Crabbe's voice was distinctly plummier. 'Thoth has what I have. None of that rubbish you mention. He's got a very sweet tooth and I see he gets plenty of nourishment.'

'What exactly, Mrs Crabbe?' There seemed to be a bleat of desperation in my voice.

'Good wholesome food.'

'Yes, but what exactly? In the wild these monkeys get very high levels of protein including animal protein, minerals and a massive daily intake of vitamin D_3. Does he get meat, chicken, vitamins, cereals as well as vegetables?'

'He gets eggs.'

'That's good. What else?'

'Eggs.'

'And?'

'Eggs in the most nourishing form.'

Light dawned. Of course—the Advocaat.

'Does he drink the egg-flip, Mrs Crabbe?' I asked.

'Of course. I do. It's what keeps me as fit as I am. So does Thoth. It has eggs—there's a whole meal in eggs, Doctor—sugar for energy and grape spirit. It's first-rate stuff.'

'What else does he get, Mrs Crabbe?'

'What else? Nothing else. What else would one need, sir? Advocaat's a perfect diet. Tell me any other monkey you know that's so well cared for. Advocaat's not cheap, you know.'

I lifted Thoth back onto the billiard table and returned to my stool. 'Mrs Crabbe,' I said, picking my words carefully, 'you're killing Thoth. Advocaat is an atrocious diet. He's a cripple because of it. He's deformed because of it. His chest is collapsing because of it.'

The old lady stared at me in stunned amazement.

I went on, 'I can't undo all the damage you've done, but with a little luck I can help him. Maybe he'll walk again for the first time in years. But no more Advocaat for him, ever again. From now it's going to be meat, chicken, milk, nuts, cereals, fruit and daily vitamins and calcium. I want you to have a run built for him outside so that he can get direct sunlight with its ultra-violet light. As for medicine, I'm going to give him some stuff called Sterogyl—an ampoule now and another in three weeks. You understand?'

Mrs Crabbe poured herself another tumbler of the yellow cream and glowered at me. Then she muttered acidly, 'Very well, Dr Aspinall, but I hope you know what you're doing. However, I have decided that I do not need you to examine me. I'll do very well, thank you.' She fussed pettishly with the hem of her dress.

'But there's your doctor.' I pointed at Aspinall. It was starting again.

'I will certainly not be handled by your assistant, Doctor.'

Admitting defeat in the battle of words, I took an ampoule of Sterogyl out of my bag, broke it and poured the alcoholic solution of vitamin D down Thoth's mouth. A connoisseur of booze, he seemed to relish the change of liquor.

'That's me done,' I said. 'Now I'll leave you with Dr Aspinall. I can assure you he's an excellent doctor.' I made for the door.

'Come back,' boomed the plummy voice as I put my hand on the knob. 'Very well then, have your way with a poor old lady. Get on with your examination. After all, Thoth seemed to like you. But please ask this animal doctor friend of yours to leave the room while I undress.'

I turned the door-knob and kept going.

Three weeks later I revisited the black stone house. There

was no sign of Dr Aspinall this time. Again I banged on the front door. After four or five minutes I heard someone come to the door, the letter box was flapped open and the housekeeper's tetchy voice told me to find the tradesmen's entrance. It was a sunny day and I was in a good mood so I walked round to the back of the house.

In the billiard room something dark brown and chirruping darted about the floor. It was Thoth. Mrs Crabbe, reclining on the sofa, greeted me with a charming smile and asked me to sit next to her. There was no sign of Advocaat bottles anywhere.

'Dr Landau, how nice to see you,' she murmured, taking me by the hand. 'Now do please have a little of this.' She reached under the sofa as before and pulled out a bottle of dark red liquid. Two glasses followed, a sherry size for me and the tumbler for her. She poured out the Buckfast Tonic Wine.

'Not drinking Advocaat, I see,' I said, toasting her.

'Oh dear me no, not since that nice Dr Taylor was here the other week. He gave me a thorough examination and said that I was short of protein, vitamins, roughage and heaven knows what else in my diet. He made me have steak and fish every day. Vitamin pills, too. I feel marvellous. I might even consider getting married again.' She gave me a roguish wink. 'Yes, Dr Taylor said that having the Advocaat and not much else to eat was giving me these dizzy spells and cracked lips. Anyway, I mustn't go on about me. You've come to see Thoth, haven't you, Dr Landau?'

Though still grossly mis-shapen, Thoth was indeed a different monkey. He was using his legs, walking and even running for short distances. He looked happier and more energetic. His pugilist's face had softened, the lumpy bones were not as prominent. The progressive collapse of his skeleton had been halted, though he would be scarred for life. It was a dramatic change that I had seen many times before in such cases. Now, with the jaws firmer and less likely to shatter as I pulled with my tooth forceps, I could begin sorting out the jumble of teeth in his mouth. Thoth was going to need at least three sessions of dental surgery under general anaesthetic.

'Isn't it absolutely wonderful, Doctor? said Mrs Crabbe. 'A miracle in three weeks. I'd never have believed it. But what about the toothache?'

I explained the next stages of treatment, gave the monkey another ampoule of Sterogyl and inquired how well Thoth had taken to his proper, teetotal diet.

'Have a close look at the billiard table, Dr Aspinall,' commanded Mrs Crabbe.

I looked. The six net pockets had been lined with pieces of newspaper. One had been filled with chopped hard-boiled egg, another with peanuts, a third with dates and raisins and so on. Each pocket contained some item of suitable food. One was even brimming with shiny, writhing mealworms, a fine Capuchin delicacy. A crystal bowl of milk stood on the pink spot and a matching piece containing vitaminised water was on the yellow spot.

'First-rate,' I said.

'Now before you go, Dr Taylor,' beamed Mrs Crabbe, 'just have a little drop more of this most wholesome wine and tell me what you think about this rheumatic joint of mine.'

She began unbuttoning her dress before I could say a word.

The balanced diet and the Sterogyl continued to transform Thoth. Under anaesthetic I extracted all the rogue teeth and left him with a small but adequate set. At last the time came for my final visit. Thoth now had his outside run built onto the billiard room. As far as I could see he was on the wagon, and seemed to relish his mixed diet and his new-found ability to exercise with gusto. He did not drool, showed no sign of pain in his mouth and was altogether more amiable. He had not drawn another drop of human blood and did not seem to care how you looked at him. Apart from his physical improvement, I assumed that his mind was enjoying a certain clarity of thought after ten years of toping; Thoth the easily offended had probably been the equivalent of the bellicose bar-fly.

Mrs Crabbe, on the other hand, had quickly dispensed with Dr Aspinall's diet and was subsisting on voluminous quantities of the tonic wine which, as she said, had the added spiritual dimension to its nutritive qualities of 'having the church behind it'. Naturally her dizzy spells had re-appeared.

'Thank you for everything, dear Dr Aspinall,' she said thickly when I told her that Thoth, though hardly a show specimen, should get along fine if she stuck to the diet. 'Now before you go, there's something I want you to have. Follow me.'

I followed her uncertain path through the corridors of the old house, up a wide staircase of orange marble where our steps raised puffs of dust and sent balls of fluff rolling like tumbleweed, and through rooms smelling like mushroom farms. Eventually we came to a small boxroom that was empty save for an enormous, rust-encrusted safe.

Rocking slightly on her heels, Mrs Crabbe brought forth a large key from her décolletage and with much difficulty found the keyhole.

'Now, Dr Landau,' she puffed. 'Please turn the handle for me and pull open the door.'

I twisted the heavy brass lever and heaved against the protesting stiffness of the old hinges. The door gradually yielded and came open.

Mrs Crabbe stepped forward and started sorting through a heap of trays and boxes. It was a stupendous sight: dull gold rings by the score; old-fashioned pendants and earrings heavy with succulent emeralds and rubies as big as damsons; dusty tiaras which burst into diamond flame as the old lady blew winey breath over them; the baubles of Freemasonry, the tie-pins, signet rings, seals, swizzle-sticks, cuff-links, loving cups, heirlooms of the Crabbes; silver presentation salvers from the mills; gold fobs from Victorian Crabbes; sapphire souvenirs from Edwardian cruises long forgotten.

'In here I have something specially for you, my dear Doctor,' she whispered as she rooted about.

It was as exciting as Christmas morning. What was she going to bestow on me? Some nugget, some pea-sized diamond of the first water that had belonged to old Crabbe? I could not see anything that was not worthy a tidy sum. How very unprofessional, a little voice chivvied inside me. How bloody marvellous, breathed another.

At last Mrs Crabbe appeared to have found what she was looking for. She withdrew a lumpy, brown paper bag, about the size of two clenched fists. 'There,' she said, giving me the bag, 'and thank you so much, Dr Landau. Please also thank your assistant, Dr Taylor.'

We retraced our steps with me clutching my present and my mind whirling. The bag weighed about one pound, I guessed, but its lumpy shape mystified me. Precious stones, gold dust, an assortment of jewellery, watches? I could hardly wait to get outside to my car and look inside. Anyway, I thought, as I shook hands at the door (tradesmen's entrance), from what I've seen of the safe's treasures, whatever it is it's bound to be fabulous.

Jumping into the car, I opened the bag and looked inside. Beneath a scrap of paper, on which was scribbled in pencil 'To Doctor Aspinall, the best vet in the world, with grateful thanks from Thoth', lay seven or eight plump, fresh tomatoes, undoubtedly not long picked from the green-houses behind the big black stone house.

'Where did you get these from?' asked Shelagh, as she sliced the tomatoes that evening and mixed them with slivers of raw mushrooms and onion to make my favourite salad.

'Well, love, in a nutshell,' I explained, 'from treating the monkey of an old lady who thinks I do wonders for her rheumatism and whose doctor is a dab hand at . . . oh, forget it—it's so confusing that I'm not quite sure who I am anyway.'

My wife gave me a curious look and kept on slicing. Stephanie and Lindsey, drawing at the kitchen table, looked at each other then raised their eyes to the heavens at this further evidence of the mysterious behaviour of grown-ups.

Dotty and befuddled Mrs Crabbe may have been, but she justified the townsfolk's opinion of her canny attention to all matters financial. Months later, when my bill was settled, she faithfully deducted exactly fifteen shillings and sixpence.

In those early months of 1970, I was happy to realise that my practice was becoming busier and busier. I had been on my own now for eighteen months, and it seemed that the venture might have turned the corner. Cuddles, the killer whale at Flamingo Park, occupied a good deal of my time and attention, of course: like any infant, he had teething pain as more of his ivory fangs came through his gums, but I soothed his mouth with vast quantities of babies' teething jelly held on by water-resistant denture paste. That winter was becoming quite eventful elsewhere, too, which was why I came to be sitting on a Derbyshire hillside one freezing afternoon, cradling my dart-rifle.

Whereas America has its Big-foot and the Himalayas their Yeti, not forgetting Scotland's own *Nessiteras rhombopteryx* as Sir Peter Scott so precipitately named her, the English have to make do with the more mundane monsters which are reported every six months or so in the newspapers and are usually identified as pumas or, less frequently, lions. Regularly these large felines are spotted by ostensibly sober members of the community in the suburbs of Birmingham or on the village green at Wormwood Magna. 'I was hoeing the radishes one evening when this mountain lion walked out of the privet hedge and jumped over the fence into next door's garden,' affirms a worthy citizen, or 'I glanced out of the loo window of the bingo hall and there was this puma mooching round the dustbins.' Occasionally in mud or snow, Footprints are Found, which the 'local naturalist' pronounces as those of no animal known to science. The constabulary wearily assure the townsfolk that they are checking all zoos and circuses in the vicinity just in case no-one noticed that one of the big cats had not shown up at roll call. The story hangs around in the papers for up to a week and then, no doubt tiring of the humdrum series of brief encounters with postmen, gardeners, schoolboys and late-night strollers, the beast clears off and lies low for a few months, to re-appear as sure as fate miles away.

I often marvel at the certainty with which folk whose knowledge of the jungle is limited to admiring the Town Hall palms will cry wolf (or tiger, or puma) when a twitching brown tail is spied vanishing into a thicket three hundred yards away. Sadly, lions no longer roam wild in England, bears and wolves became extinct more recently and, unlike the Scots, we cannot boast even one wild cat in our forests. The mystery pumas are almost invariably big dogs enhanced by the unreliability of the human eye, a fertile imagination, alcohol or fabrication.

The 'puma' which surfaced that January in Derbyshire, fifty miles south of Rochdale, was bothering the inhabitants of a little town set on a hillside criss-crossed with limestone walls. The beast had been seen by the schoolmaster, several farmers and various other people. It was exactly three feet to eight feet long, a minimum of four feet to six feet high at the shoulder and was variously black, dark brown, gingery and light yellow. It was known to have a long tail or none at all, showed no signs of timidity or shot off at the slightest sound, and ate remarkable quantities of other people's chickens, cats, pet rabbits, dustbin waste and garden-pond goldfish. I was asked to go over with a dart-rifle and join in a concerted hunt by police, RSPCA men, journalists and small boys.

Apart from the cold, the weather was good for puma

hunting. I was being paid well for a leisurely stroll over fine countryside, and was confident that I would end up by tea-time, when the exercise was due to end, feeling as fit as a fiddle and without having seen anything more wild than a hare. There are wild wallabies living and breeding success-fully in the Derbyshire heather; they are rarely spotted but I reckoned that the 'puma', if it existed at all, was probably one of them.

The local village constable organised the sweep of the countryside very efficiently. He had plotted the most recent sightings on a map and when I arrived was distributing walkie-talkies, maps and thermos flasks of tea. He lined us up and announced the Orders of the Day as if he was sending us in after Bonnie and Clyde. Off we set, and I soon found myself alone on the hillside, pushing through beds of drip-ping bracken with the wind making my cheeks tingle. When I was almost at the top of the main ridge and could look down at the streets of glistening grey slate roofs, I was told over the walkie-talkie to find a sheltered spot by one of the moorland walls and wait. The constable had deployed his posse in a circle enclosing hundreds of acres. I was the centre point of that circle and the order to beat inwards would now be given.

Squatting on a dry stone out of the wind, I passed the time outstaring the curious sheep that had gathered to inspect me. The object of our game was to see who blinked first. I could not see any of the other searchers although I could hear the constable chivvying his right flank, his left flank and his centre with the authority of Rommel making a dash for Tobruk. There was no doubt, I thought, that before long the complete bunch of hunters would find themselves on top of me, puma-less.

The sheep got bored with me and resumed grazing. Suddenly I heard my name called urgently over the walkie-talkie. I took in the astounding message that came crackling over the air in the excited voice of the village constable: 'Dr

Taylor, Dr Taylor, hold your position. Animal sighted coming in your direction.'

I looked hurriedly around and pressed in against the dry-stone wall. My heart began to beat rapidly with excitement. The beast existed and was on its way! I still could not see any of the men and there was no sign of the monster. I carefully checked that the safety catch on the dart-gun was securely in the 'off' position. When the man-eating minotaur or whatever it was breathed fire down my earhole I did not want a repetition of what had happened once when I was called to recapture an escaped axis deer in Sussex. After hours of painstaking stalking, its keepers had driven it so that it stood, a perfect target, only a few feet away from a special camouflaged hide in which I lurked, peering out through a tiny hole. I had aimed, pulled the trigger of the dart-gun and heard that depressing 'clunk' which means that the safety catch is on. Like lightning the deer had leapt off, startled by the 'clunk' and far too rapidly to let me put my mistake right by flicking the dratted catch. No axis deer had been retrieved that embarrassing day.

Now I was certain my gun was in fighting condition. There was a new compressed-air cylinder in the chamber, a syringe loaded with enough phencyclidine to clobber a grizzly bear was up the spout and the safety catch was most definitely off.

The walkie-talkie crackled again. 'Dr Taylor, Dr Taylor, keep down, keep down. Animal seen still coming your way, approximately quarter of a mile from you. Other side of your wall. Running at present time parallel to wall.'

If they had been able to identify the creature, no-one had bothered to tell me. I decided not to talk back in case it was frightened off. At this point, quite honestly, I felt a trifle apprehensive. I had tangled with big cats many times in zoos and in Africa, but under controlled conditions. Still, I thought, the poor whatever-it-was was probably scared to death. Escaped zoo big cats never enjoy life on the run and appear positively relieved once they are back in their own territory, among sights and sounds they know, with warm beds and regular meals.

The difficulty I faced now was knowing when to stand up and look over the wall. Too soon or too late could obviously be disastrous. The wall was too well built to have any chinks in it. The trusty constable solved the problem almost at once. 'Dr Taylor, Dr Taylor, animal now one hundred yards approximately to your left. Still running parallel to wall.'

He said nothing about speed or range from the wall. My mind raced. I would have only a few seconds in which to stand up, aim and fire after taking into account the wind, which might deflect the bulky dart, and the low temperature, which affected the gas pressure and consequently the maximum range of my weapon. Whatever it was, I would aim for the middle of the target. That would give me some latitude for error. I had fitted my shortest barbed needle, so that no matter what the creature or virtually where I hit it, there was the smallest risk of the needle entering a major body cavity. I would swing the gun round with the movement of the animal, assuming it was still running. I do not like using the dart-gun on moving targets, but that way I might have least risk of a bounce-off.

The nettle must be grasped at once. I stood up and rammed my rifle over the wall. Twenty feet away, slightly to my left and going at a steady pace, loped a tawny creature which at first sight looked dramatically like the Hound of the Baskervilles.

The beast that had been blamed in the locality for every sort of misdeed, with the possible exception of the spate of obscene phone calls that was also occupying the constable's busy life, was a long lanky Great Dane. Looking closer, I saw it was in terrible shape. Scurfy skin was stretched tight over its prominent skeleton, its sides were disfigured with numerous red scars and L-shaped wounds where wire and thorns had left their marks, the eyes were sunk and desperate and ropes of glutinous saliva speckled with soil hung from the slack lips. It was an animal that must have been out on the run for weeks if not months, and it was easy to see from the slight sway of its hindquarters that it was coming to the end of the road.

All the same, my sudden emergence like a jack-in-the-box produced a surge of alarm and determination in the dog. Its eyes bulged with the effort as it strained for more speed and veered away from me. I looked down the gun barrel, made my split-second assessment of wind and likely trajectory and fired. The dart flew strong and straight—straight over the back of the Great Dane. It thwacked impotently into a tussock fifteen yards away, the dog vanished over a rise in the ground and I shouted unrepeatable epithets at the re-gathering sheep. You never get a second chance in such cases.

It was a very subdued marksman who shortly afterwards explained to the constable and his troops what had happened. They took it very politely and we started another, rather half-hearted hunt. By late afternoon there had not even been another sighting of the dog and we were about to call it a day when an amazing piece of good news came up from the town: the Great Dane had dashed into a timber yard and someone had had the good sense to close the yard gates. It was holed up behind a pile of wood and was in a mean mood.

Somewhat cheered by this turn of events, I went down to the yard with the constable and some of his men. Distressed and terrified, the animal crouched behind a pile of wood, obviously prepared to go down fighting. It was snarling and snapping in earnest, and no-one dared go near it. There was no way I could find to get a shot at the dog other than from directly in front, but with the way it was barking and moving its head, and with its emaciated frame presenting no expanses of muscle from that angle, I was afraid that the dart might hit the head. Even hungry animals like this one are not

110

always easy to knock out by drugging meat, but I sent a boy to the nearest butcher's shop for a pound of pork sausages. When he came back with them I threw a couple to the dog, which swallowed them ravenously. Next I took a third sausage and carefully pressed it in the middle. The meat within the sausage skin compacted towards each end, leaving an inch of empty skin in the middle. Now, with a fine hypodermic needle passed through the sausage meat and into the empty space, I slowly injected a quantity of powerful narcotic. The sausage was now fixed and ready, with no smell and no taste. I tossed the Trojan Horse morsel to the wild-eyed dog. One gulp and it was gone. In eight minutes the poor creature was sound asleep and I could approach him to make a thorough examination which confirmed my earlier opinion. He must have been straying for a very long time and was suffering from malnutrition, multiple wounds, a grass awn embedded in the cornea of one eye and a tumour on the breast.

The owner was never traced but the story ended happily. Now no longer equipped with an operating room for domestic animals, I arranged with a colleague to hospitalise the wanderer, operate on his eye, remove the breast growth and generally tack him together. A good home was found for him by the RSPCA, and when I saw him a month later he had become plump, glossy and relaxed on an intensive diet of steak, eggs, fish and milk—but no more sausages. And the would-be 'puma' nearly licked my hand off.

Eight

The family sat at breakfast. I had just taken the first call of the day and it had produced an instant cloud over the grilled kippers and marmalade toast. 'Doesn't Daddy look grumpy all of a sudden?' piped Stephanie as I pushed away my plate.

'Grumpy as Rump . . . Rumpul . . . Rump . . .' Lindsey agreed, fumbling for the word.

'Rumpelstiltskin.' Stephanie's dark eyes bored into me as she leaned over and reached up to pat my head. 'What's up, Doc?' The girls chuckled happily.

Shelagh knew instinctively what was likely to have made my face so bleak. She frowned at the children and shook her head. 'What was it, love?' she asked quietly. 'Giraffe trouble?'

I nodded as I put on my coat and picked up the instrument bag from the cloakroom. 'Yes,' I said, 'at Flamingo Park. A young giraffe's been beaten up by an ostrich. It might be a broken leg.'

Shelagh knew what that meant. I raised my eyebrows and tried a smile. It felt an effort.

Giraffe surgery was really beginning to prey on my mind. Since the death of Pedro, I had noticed the quickening of my pulse when the phone rang and a voice brought tidings of sickness or accident in some member of this particular species. If the complaint seemed to be essentially a medical one—upset bowels after a Bank Holiday's over-indulgence in visitors' titbits, or skin disease—my heart rate returned quickly to normal and the knot in my stomach would melt away. It was the surgical side of this beast, the prospect of

112

having to knock out any more of these jinxes that was, I realised, making me lose my nerve. Sometimes I would wake in the small hours when nightmares crowd in the coiling dark, and sweat over the difficulties of struggling to be a giraffe-doctor. An animal half camel, half leopard? It almost seemed true—such freaks of nature could hardly be other than doom-laden.

I had seen the results of a furious attack by red-neck ostriches on zebras and giraffes before. Flailing their powerful legs, beaks agape and stubby wings jutting out like ragged flags, they had snapped limbs, broken skulls and staved in chests. This time the curator had talked of a six-month-old giraffe with a hind leg that dangled and would not bear weight. Dear God, let it be severe muscle bruising! If it was a femur broken, there was just a simple choice—surgery or death. I would not contemplate euthanasing the animal, so then there would be no choice. Please let it be bruising and crushing of muscles. I had some marvellous drugs in my bag for such conditions: cortisone, Novalgin, trypsin. They were all first-class, and could be administered without anaesthetic. By the time I turned into the gates of the park I had quite convinced myself that I was going to face a simple case of severe bruising.

One glance at the giraffe with its swinging hind leg quickly put me straight. I felt slightly sea-sick as I stood and watched the calf, a male, lurch gracefully on three legs. The femur—the thigh-bone—was broken, although the blow from the ostrich's horny foot had not left so much as a scratch on the skin surface.

Frank, the curator, was impatient for my decision. He had hand-reared the youngster himself when its mother had refused to stand for her offspring to suckle. 'What about it, then, Doctor?' he asked. 'Plaster of Paris?'

I shook my head slowly. 'No chance. If the break had been lower down the leg, maybe. That or fibreglass. But with high fractures in the femur there's too much ham muscle round

113

the site. The plaster can't hold the bone pieces firmly.'

'What then?' Frank sounded a fraction aggressive. He would not have agreed to euthanasia even if I had suggested it.

I took a deep breath; it seemed to ease the queasiness in my guts. 'I'll have to pin the leg with a vitallium spike. Maybe screw a plate on as well. I can't say more for sure till I open up the leg to look.'

Frank's tense body sagged in relief. He managed a tight smile. 'Great, Doctor.'

While Frank and his keepers prepared ropes, straw, water and all the other things necessary for surgery al fresco (it was a warm sunny day and I prefer to operate outside in the cleaner air whenever possible), I turned my attention to the old bugbear of anaesthetic. Should I pre-medicate with valium instead of acepromazine to avoid the blood pressure effects which had killed poor Pedro? Then what? A touch of xylazine as a tranquilliser with a final knock-out shot of etorphine, or etorphine alone? There was no chance of using tubocurarine or succinylcholine to relax the muscles completely; either would be too risky without gas and giraffes are terribly difficult to put onto a closed-circuit gas machine. I pondered. If the broken ends of bone had overlapped I would have to use brute force to re-position them. I settled for the valium, xylazine and etorphine cocktail.

When all was ready the giraffe, calm as a child's pony, was coaxed into a narrow, high-sided box. Before starting, I listened to its heart through my stethoscope. It was bounding but I could not detect any abnormalities. The animal accepted slivers of apple from Frank while I began the injections into its neck muscles. I worked like a zombie. There was just me and the giraffe and the box in the whole universe. I could hear nothing but the breathing of the animal, the tap of its hooves from time to time against the woodwork, the dull rush of blood in the centre of my head. I could see nothing but the long camouflaged neck and the

114

dark rivulet of blood that lay on the skin like a twist of thread where my needle had been.

After the valium the calf soon became droopy with half-closed eyes. The xylazine settled it down gently onto its knees in the straw. I still felt queasy, but the giraffe showed no sign of the fainting that had finished Pedro. Now to bring oblivion down onto the gentle creature and to begin the surgical equivalent of the furniture repairer's craft. The door of the box was lifted and I squeezed inside. The giraffe's colour was good. It was drooling saliva, I noticed, but there was no sign of the dangerous regurgitation of stomach contents that can sometimes drown an unconscious animal. I felt the pulse. It was reasonably regular and the volume was good. Quickly I injected a small dose of etorphine into the neck. Once flat out, the giraffe would be hauled out of the box by Frank's keepers and I could work in the open.

Again I put my stethoscope to the rib-cage. 'Lub-dup, lub-dup, lub-dup.' All sounded well. 'Lup-dup, lub-dup, lub-lub-dup.'

My hand clenched over the diaphragm head of the stethoscope. What was that again?

'Lub-dup, lub-lub-dup,' then 'Lub-lub-lub-lub-dup.' Pause. 'Lub-lub-dup.' I instantly began to pour out tacky sweat. One hand still on the stethoscope, I groped with the other beneath the animal's groin to take the pulse in the femoral artery. It was hard to find. The sound coming through my ivory ear-pieces seemed softer now. I pushed the diaphragm hard onto the animal's chest and checked its position over the heart. 'Lub-dup, lub-dup, lub-lub-lub-dup.' Pause. 'Lub-lub-lub-lub-dup.' Long pause. 'Lub-lub . . .'

Wildly I looked at the breathing. It was barely detectable. I took a deep breath, fought down the panic. 'My bag—quick,' I hissed to the curator who crouched behind me. 'He's collapsing.'

The words echoed round my head. All else was silence.

The keepers were hushed. It took me a few seconds to load a syringe with theophylline, a circulation booster, and another with cyprenorphine, the antidote to the etorphine. Thank God giraffes have jugulars like drainpipes, I thought, as the drugs shot into the bloodstream. Then I thought, why did I ever dabble in giraffes and such? The old times at the Rochdale surgery with a bitch for hysterectomy on the table—predictable, my assistant to help, my partner coming in to have a chat whilst we stitched up—oh, the fond remembrance of times past. 'Lub-dup, lub-lub . . . lub . . . lub . . . lu-u-b . . .'

I could not believe it. There was no more sound, at least no more heart sound. Just the distant squeak of the bowels, contracting after life had slipped away.

'I'm afraid he's dead,' I said bluntly. 'And I haven't got a bloody clue why.'

It would be nice in some ways to be able to run away from such disasters, to jump in the car and get the hell out of it, shake the dust off one's feet, have a whisky and talk tough about 'c'est la vie', 'you win some and you lose some', and 'when they gotta go, they gotta go'. But it can't be done. The indefinable sense of guilt must be expiated in the rites: the explaining, the analysing, the agonising, the excusing, first in public to the keepers, curators and directors then, more importantly, to oneself in bed at night. An autopsy forms part of the ritual and sometimes yields valuable information that might save future lives. I decided to do an immediate post-mortem on the young giraffe. The scalpel revealed white, dry areas of tissue scattered throughout many of the muscles of the body and most significantly in the thick muscular wall of the heart. It was quite unmistakable, but the first time I had come across it in a giraffe: 'white muscle disease', which I had often seen in calves and even wallabies and pelicans. The diseased heart had simply failed when the added stress of anaesthesia had been loaded onto it.

I suppose there are several points of similarity between a puma
(above) and a Great Dane (below). Large dogs such as this explain
the fairly frequent reported sightings of 'pumas' in Great Britain.
(*Zoological Society of London*/*Hans Reinhard* & *Bruce Coleman Ltd*)

When an onager looks as mean as this, he will follow up his fearsome squealing with teeth and hooves. (*Zoological Society of London*)

Rio Leon safari park, where an onager frightened me as much as any creature that I have ever had dealings with. Lions, zebras, lechwe and elephants roam the park set in a valley west of Barcelona. (*Rio Leon*)

The most practical way of getting to grips with a sick whale is to drain the water from its pool. Even in this position Cuddles could knock me off my feet with a sweep of his tail. (*Richard Reed*)

Surprisingly, this contraption which we built at Flamingo Park to haul Cuddles out of his pool for treatment worked perfectly from the very first. It saved draining his pool and he loved it so much that it was often difficult to get him to leave the sling. (*Press Agency (Yorkshire) Ltd*)

With no fog and strong weld-mesh between me and the tigers, darting this pair with enteritis vaccine was considerably less hair-raising than my surprise encounter at Stukenbrock. (*Tony Evans*)

It was little consolation for Frank as I explained the cause and gave my opinion that the animal's days had been numbered anyway. 'Irreversible change caused by a deficiency of a chemical called selenium in the fodder and herbage,' I said. 'I'll take some samples of soil and hay for analysis.'

So it turned out: there were barely two parts in ten million of selenium in the soil and even less in the fodder. Selenium is a rare element, named after the Greek word for 'moon' and of little interest to anyone except the occasional scientist. It is a by-product of copper refining, is used in the manufacture of photo-electric cells and is invariably ignored completely by schoolboys swotting for chemistry examinations. Selenium means as little to them as it does to, say, chimpanzees or giraffes. The difference is that to giraffes the presence or absence of the invisible element in the soil and herbage of their environment can be literally a matter of life or death. A mere five parts in ten million of the strange 'moonstone' would have been enough and perhaps there would be a giraffe walking around Flamingo Park today with a shiny pin in his mended leg.

That evening Shelagh listened as I fumed over this latest giraffe débâcle. The girls kept tactfully out of the way while I cursed the day I had ever decided to specialise in exotic animals.

'Not only do I feel I'm wasting my time, but I'm beginning to think that I'm a positive menace where giraffes are concerned. Cats and dogs, pigs and ponies—that's where I should be. They're more my measure. Bring back the budgies and the moggies.' My bitterness was without humour and almost the real thing.

'Do you really mean that?' Shelagh asked quietly after a moment's silence. She smiled gently and fixed me with unblinking green eyes.

'Er, no,' I said. 'No.' I tried in vain to adopt the air of a martyr.

117

'I'll get you a cup of tea while you work out a dose for supplementing the other giraffes with selenium,' said Shelagh, rising to her feet.

There was trouble back at Belle Vue that winter, too. It came not from the giraffes but from homo sapiens: Belle Vue's director, Ray Legge, was up to his neck with complaints from bothered visitors. The female chimpanzees were a perennial source of trouble, as they are at many zoos. When these animals are mature and come into season, the skin round the vulva becomes remarkably red and swollen. Biologically this phenomenon is a visual sexual signal to what must be rather slow-witted males, but you can be sure that it also triggers off a response from some animal-lover who visits the great ape house and decides to tackle the authorities about the matter.

On this occasion a worthy middle-aged lady teacher—of biology!—had stormed into the director's office demanding to know why something was not being done about the chimpanzee with the prolapse. The animal must have been in terrible pain, she declared in high dudgeon, and she as a woman as well as a teacher knew about such things. What was more, she was not leaving the office until the veterinarian appeared and did something. She then grabbed the office phone to put a call through to the RSPCA and was about to do likewise to the police, press and BBC until physically restrained from doing do by the director's secretary. A conversation was eventually arranged with me by telephone. It got rid of the good lady, but despite my lengthy explanations as to the nature of the swellings I got the impression that I had not calmed her down much.

'I cannot believe,' she said huffily at the end of our conversation, 'that so alarming, so . . . so . . . blatant a display could be part of the Creator's design. I warn you I shall take the matter up with my gynaecologist, Doctor.'

Well, I thought, even the Creator himself would have

difficulty persuading such folk that chimpanzees and their ways were made for chimpanzees, not for lady teachers and their gynaecologists.

Hot on the heels of that little fracas came a similar incident involving a camel that had calved happily enough and immediately after the birth could be seen in the paddock with the placenta still hanging from its behind. That really stirred up one old lady, who complained that it was utterly disgusting that children might witness such scenes of gory intimacy. I am afraid I give such people short shrift—no doubt they mean well, and I entirely accept that the visiting public has a duty to ensure that zoos maintain a good standard in the care of their animals, but I do not believe that animals mating, giving or having just given birth should necessarily be kept off exhibition. If seclusion would be good for the mother or baby, fine, but otherwise I am strongly for folk being able to watch such miraculous goings-on. The true appreciation of living things must involve real life in all its facets. It is rarely ugly, except where homo sapiens is involved; indeed it is generally beautiful and always edifying. Zoos particularly have a lot to gain by presenting animals as they really are, warts and all. Thank God animals are not intricate toys made of icing sugar or ormulu. Elephants smell, camels burp, predators kill, scavengers rake muck. The blood, the guts, the excrement, the new life and the old death all knit together into a flawless, balanced unity.

More trouble came when a Belle Vue keeper let an animal which should not have been on display out into its paddock and could not get it back again. It did no harm to the creature, in fact the fresh air and sunshine did it all the good in the world. The trouble, once again, was with the paying public. This time the outraged visitor went straight to the nearest telephone kiosk and rang the police. Before long the police called Ray Legge, the zoo director.

'We've had a complaint from a visitor to your zoo,' said

the constable. 'Sounds bloody horrific if it's true. They say you've got a young lion with shirt buttons stitched all over his ears. Is this right?'

'Yes, it is,' replied Ray.

'And could you explain what a lion is doing decorated with pearl buttons, sir? Have the vandals been at it again?'

Ray roared with laughter, as I did when he told me later. Both of us tried to imagine a couple of typical louts, the sort that cause such annoying trouble at city zoos all over the world, climbing over the wall one night after an energetic pub crawl. Full of Dutch courage and bravado, one suggests to the other that they indulge in a merry prank. Whereas normally this involves harassing, chasing or simply killing any animal they can find, preferably one of the gentler species such as wallabies or penguins, this time they decide to try something more spicy.

''Ere, Bert,' says one. 'Wot abaht givin' that lion over there a bit of the old 'ow's yer father?'

'Wotcha mean, 'Arry?' says the other.

'Well, you grab 'old of 'im, see, an' then I'll stitch some o' me shirt buttons on 'is lug'ole.'

'No sooner said than done, me old son,' says Bert, catching the snoozing lion by the tail and holding its jaws closed with finger and thumb.

Harry meanwhile snaps the pearl buttons off his beer-stained shirt front. Producing in a trice the needle and thread that Saturday night revellers always have to hand, he proceeds to attach the buttons deftly to the astonished lion's ear flap. Harry and Bert then stagger off home, leaving the button-bedecked lion to resume his rudely disturbed slumbers.

Happily, this dramatic fantasy of drunken prowess was not quite the explanation of why the lion was indeed sporting a number of ordinary pearly buttons stitched to one ear as he yawned in the pale winter twilight. Jambo, the lion in question, had been playing with his companions and the fun had involved rolling, tumbling and cuffing one another, claws retracted, about the head. One over-boisterous right hook had burst a blood vessel beneath the skin of Jambo's ear, and within minutes a giant blood-blister had developed, puffing out the curved leaf of the ear into something more like an outsize piece of ravioli. It was the first stage of the process which in humans leads to the formation of a 'cauli-flower ear': left alone the blood would clot, the clot would gradually be converted into scar tissue and shrink, and the ear would be crumpled up like a ball of waste paper. It was not painful or dangerous, but I had to do something about it for the sake of Jambo's looks, if only to keep the little old ladies at bay.

With Jambo dreaming happily under phencyclidine anaesthesia, topped up with drops of barbiturate from time to time, I made an S-shaped incision in the ear flap and removed all the clot lying between the skin and the central plate of cartilage. To avoid the ear simply filling up once more with blood, I needed to pin the skin down to the cartilage long enough for adhesions to fill any space where blood might accumulate. I therefore put in stitches all over the surface of the ear, but to avoid the risk of cutting and to distribute pressure efficiently, I incorporated a flat, sterilised button, supplied by Shelagh from her sewing box, with each stitch. It worked perfectly: Jambo's ear would be uncrum-pled and as good as new when I removed the buttons and stitches after ten days. Meanwhile I had suggested that he be kept in the big cat house to avoid the incredulous stares of the public and possible re-matches with his playful mates. My prediction about the visitors' reaction was proved right when a keeper lifted Jambo's slide door by mistake.

Of course, the matter ended with Ray Legge explaining all this to the police, but I suggested that in future the enclos-ures or houses of any animals under treatment and on show should carry notices explaining the position. I believe it is good that the public should be able to see that most zoo inmates receive medical care at least as good as that given to pet poodles and racehorses.

As for Jambo, who soon regained a matching set of respectable lion lugs, he would have been amazed at all the fuss.

I had a chance to get away from such bothersome incidents for a few days when February came round. The Association of Marine Mammal Veterinarians, of which I was a founder member, was holding its annual symposium in Miami. Off I went for the anticipated binge of scientific shop-talk and gossip from the close world of dolphin doctors. One of the snags of living in a cotton town in north-west England has always been that there is no-one within hundreds of miles with whom I can indulge in an occasional talk-fest on exotic beasts of the oceans. The symposiums were, and still are, a chance to wallow with others who shared a passion for walruses and whales and a deep curiosity as to what makes them tick.

If California, with its Sea World, Marineland of the Pacific and US Navy research units, is the Mecca of cetacean buffs, then Florida, home of Seaquarium and the major catching grounds for dolphins, is the Medina—and it is now only a hop away from London by non-stop jet. All the same, I was delayed checking in to the symposium by bad weather over the Atlantic. Lightning struck the 707 with a fearful bang, sending a blue ball of light straight down the centre aisle, and the plane had to land at Nassau for inspection. I felt like a limp lettuce when eventually I set thankful feet on US soil. I knew that by arriving late I would find that the best hotel rooms at the conference centre had already been allocated, that the restricted list of delegates wishing to visit some particularly interesting laboratory had been closed and that copies of papers to be given had been snaffled by folk who wanted multiple sets. As I walked into the hotel lobby, my only thought was for a large Jack Daniels to restore my confidence in aeroplanes.

Someone touched my arm. 'Dr Taylor, you're here at last.'

I turned round. It was the lobster-sampling student again, Andrew Greenwood.

'What on earth are you doing here?' I asked, astounded. Students are chronically impecunious by tradition, and Cambridge to Florida and back by air ain't potatoes.

'I leaned on my father,' he replied cheerfully. 'It seemed too important a programme to miss.'

I marvelled at this further evidence of the chap's tenacity.

He went on, 'I've organised everything for you—got you a super room overloooking the sea, collected a full set of papers plus some new microfilms that were in short supply, put your name down for the trip to the shark research place and made sure you're one of only six delegates invited to join a dive on a new sea-lab mini-sub.'

I was speechless. Not only did this young man pop out of the woodwork with surprising regularity, but he was beginning to act like a first-class, unpaid personal private secretary!

'How very kind of you,' I said faintly.

He beamed happily and picked up my bag. 'Oh, by the way, Dr Taylor, when you've had a shower, I've got a large bourbon and dry ginger waiting for you in the lounge.'

That conference went like clockwork. My batman, advisor, aide-de-camp and new-found apprentice did everything except fan me with a palm frond when the lecture hall got stuffy. Andrew and I became firm friends and I grew increasingly aware of his powerful intellectual approach to the wide world of animal medicine.

Back from Florida, I found a message waiting. It was my jinx again—giraffes. A fine female at Rio Leon Safari Park in Spain had suddenly dropped dead and I was wanted to fly out to do a post-mortem examination. I was beginning to get a complex about giraffes, although this one had at least had the grace to give up the ghost without me being anywhere within a thousand miles.

Rio Leon is delightfully set in a valley by the sea about fifty miles west of Barcelona. Its slopes were terraced centuries ago and are covered with olive, cherry and almond trees. On the ridge tops above the valley the wind murmurs unceasingly through conifer groves where occasional escaped baboons can be glimpsed, sleek and rounded as they gather cones and berries. On the valley floor, zebras, elands, elephants, rare lechwe antelopes and ostriches mingle amicably on sandy flats. The little village of Albiñana nearby has barely changed in nine centuries. It has narrow streets of earth and boulders, Roman wells in overgrown orangeries, and old ladies in black who serve you peppery snails and succulent roast hare and press olive oil as thick as treacle. The village grows juicy, pale green clumps of garlic that are the most heavenly and unsociable in the whole of Spain. Visits to the park are delights, marred by the fact that my purpose is always one concerned with disease or death.

The autopsy on the giraffe was quite straightforward. The cause of death was almost identical to that in the case of the Flamingo Park giraffe: heart attack brought on by a deficiency of selenium in the soil and vegetation. I ordered the immediate addition of tiny percentages of selenium to the food of all the creatures in the safari park.

The director, my good friend Rolf Rohwer, was now faced with the problem of replacing the female giraffe. There was one available, a young beauty, so they said, but it was some four hundred miles away at a safari park which was closing down west of Madrid.

'I want you to come and look at it with me,' said Rolf. 'If you give it a clean bill of health, we'll bring it back together with a couple of African elephants they're selling as well. I suppose you'll want to tranquillise the giraffe for loading.'

I bit my tongue, thinking of Pedro and of Flamingo Park, but said nothing.

Next day we set off for the park that had the animals for sale, about forty miles from Madrid. It was set in a sleepy, unremarkable region of peasant farms and silent forests, and was approached by a narrow road that seemed to wind forever through the hills. It was not difficult to imagine why it was folding up: it was way off the tourist beat and could not have been easy for day-tripping Madrilenos to find. Rolf and I found a handful of peasants looking after the stock that remained in the crumbling clusters of buildings and fenced reserves where wind and weeds were waging a war of attrition on the entrepreneur's faded dreams.

The visit began badly. On hearing I was el veterinario inglés, the caretakers asked us to look at a fox they had locked up in a wooden box, an adolescent with all the signs of canine distemper. Looking into the box through a grille in the lid, I gave that as my diagnosis and offered to leave them some drugs and hypodermics. It is always inexcusably slipshod to make glib, split-second diagnoses, for when one of the men lifted the box lid and brought out the fox by the scruff of its neck, I saw to my horror that the sad-faced animal he held aloft had only three and a half legs. The fox had lost part of a fore leg in a gin-trap, and the fly-covered stump was a mess.

'Que pena terrible!' I said. 'I am sorry, Señores, there is nothing to be done. I will kill the animal painlessly. I have an injection in my bag.'

I was turning to go to the car when the man holding the fox shook his head and walked, still carrying it, towards a low, lean-to shed. His companions gathered round. A piece of cord was produced from somewhere. Incredulously, I watched as one of the Spaniards fashioned a noose in the cord and slipped it over the fox's mask. Transfixed with thunderous anger, the blood leaving my face icy cold as it drained rapidly away, I saw the other end of the length of cord thrown over a beam. They were going to hang the suffering beast!

With real effort, for all my powers seemed to have been turned to frozen clay, I managed to force out the biggest shout I have ever shouted. 'Stop at once, you!' I screamed, with plenty of volume but weak content: in my anger I forgot even the simplest words of Spanish.

The men ignored me and strung the fox up. I found I could still not move my legs.

'Rolf!' I shouted. 'Tell the bastards to stop or I'll kill one. I mean it!'

Rolf, grim-faced, was already running across the sandy yard towards the lynching party. My legs began to work. I remembered at last how to speak and be understood, and remembered too that Rolf had once told me the most obscene word in the Castilian tongue. I bellowed it out repeatedly as I ran. 'Cut that———rope, you———!' The fox was twisting in choking agony as the men, scowling, took the weight of the creature and let it down.

I pushed in among them, white-faced and trembling. They stood silently and still as I cradled the semi-conscious animal in my arms and went into careful detail about their parents, their mothers' gynaecological histories and how the descendants of Philip II and El Cid had, by some process of reversed evolution, descended into two-legged piojos—lice. Instead of sticking a blade between my ribs, the rough countrymen dispersed, snarling incomprehensibly and spitting onto the sand. I injected the fox with a massive overdose of xylazine anaesthetic, the stuff I normally use for quietening bison and buffalo, and it died peacefully in my arms.

Not surprisingly, Rolf and I were unaccompanied as we set off to inspect the animals. There were lions, including the uncommon Atlas Mountain variety, living in a compound littered with heaps of stinking bones; Imperial Spanish eagles, a protected species that should not have been there at

126

all; and, in a large, undulating reserve, the most dangerous and unlikely animal I have ever met.

Before going into the reserve we scanned the terrain thoroughly with field-glasses. It was a tranquil place of pale sand slopes dotted with small clumps of locust trees. A trio of ostriches pecked about in the dust two hundred yards away, a Watusi cow was daydreaming in a shallow mud hole, and in the far distance a couple of wild horses of some sort, impossible to identify accurately, were standing nibbling one another's manes. With such creatures around there could not be a bunch of grizzly bears or tigers lurking in the bushes and we carried wooden sticks for use against animals such as male red-neck ostriches, which are more of a nuisance than a danger but get a kick out of stomping on you. As we walked into the reserve, a blackbuck darted up from behind a boulder and sprang silently away.

'We should have brought a bucket of corn,' Rolf murmured. 'Those fellows think it's feeding time.' He pointed towards the two horsey creatures, which were now staring at us. One began to move slowly towards us. At that distance it looked as big as a mouse.

I lifted the field-glasses as the approaching animal broke into a gentle trot. No, it was not a Przevalski's horse, it was a species of wild ass that I had chased over the water meadows of Holland, an onager. A pair of such beasts barely twelve hands high and nervous as Derby winners, had arranged a smelly dunking in a Dutch canal for me.*

Rolf took the glasses and squinted through them. 'He must be hungry,' he said. 'He's coming in at a fair old canter now.'

The onager was now growing much bigger and was more easily recognised. It had covered half the distance between us. I could see puffs of dust rising from its hooves as it came straight as an arrow over the rolling land.

*See *Doctor in the Zoo*

127

'It certainly is keen to meet us,' I said, uneasily noticing that the canter was now more of a full gallop. It was absolutely head-on towards us. We had stopped walking and were standing, watching.

'Look at those legs go,' Rolf drawled easily. A tanned, lean Coloradan who had been a professional hunter in East Africa, he had been charged by more tough customers—elephant, lion, buffalo—than I had had hot dinners. He watched the approach of the harmless little pony, as unflappable as if he had been back in Zambia at the right end of a Winchester Express. 'Darn me—see how he's got his ears back,' Rolf chuckled.

It was true, they were so flat as to be invisible. What was more, the onager's lips were drawn back. Its beeline course was unwavering. It was a hundred yards away, still in top gear, and the sun glinted off a perfect set of upper and lower incisor teeth. Forty yards to go. Both of us could see, and hear, those incisors gnashing. Now the onager began to make an ugly, pig-like, squealing noise. My uneasiness became plain, naked fear. Rolf suddenly swore: he had not tangled with wild asses before, but his hunter's instincts had seen enough of this jet-propelled little pony. 'For Chrissake jump!' he yelled.

I had never considered myself to be much of an athlete, yet a moment later I found myself in the narrow fork of a locust tree. The ground was ten feet below, and I was tangled in an undignified embrace with Rolf who had taken wing simultaneously and lighted on the same cramped refuge.

The onager had screeched to a halt. It stood on its hind legs at the base of our tree, pawing and biting furiously at the bark. There was no doubt about it, the maniacal creature that was baying like a demented banshee a few inches beneath our trouser bottoms was trying to climb up and join us. Hatred blazed in its face.

'Don't that beat all?' said Rolf, as we hugged one another for support. 'Tree'd by a doggone ass!'

In the distance I could see a knot of Spaniards, the would-be fox-lynchers, watching the drama with expressions of rapt delight: 'Estupendo, the loud-mouthed veterinario and the Americano with the Corona Corona between his teeth are about to be torn to pieces. Que maravilloso!'

'Clear off! Vaya!' I shouted at the onager.

In reply it strained up the trunk and whinnied with such venom that I was surprised not to see sparks amongst the steam belching from its gaping, red nostrils.

Rolf broke off a twig and threw it down at our attacker. It bounced off the onager's muzzle. This really provoked the beast. It did a remarkable standing leap with its hind feet, such as only a few highly trained circus horses can do, or so I thought. Not only did it rise bodily a further six inches up the tree, but its teeth actually glanced off my shoe heel.

Pulling my knees up to my chin and clinging on to Rolf for dear life, I tried to think things out reasonably. 'Ever read the book by that woman who thinks you can communicate with animals by breathing at them nose to nose?' I asked.

'You ain't gonna use my nose with that bastard,' Rolf replied, trying to keep hold of me while extricating his buttocks from spiky branches that had pierced his jeans and embedded themselves securely in his flesh. 'I'll get those goddammed Spaniards to come down and chase it away.' At the top of his voice he shouted in Spanish towards our distant audience. 'Venga! Get down here and get rid of this blasted horse!'

The men heard him, I am sure, but stayed where they were, sitting on a fence, slapping their thighs, scratching and grinning like monkeys.

I tried a stern look at the onager, right in the eyes, no blinking. It looked sternly back and bit off another apple-sized chunk of tree. 'Animals don't like to be stared at usually,' I said.

'Well for Chrissake stop staring at the critter then,'

groaned Rolf. 'Mebbe you're provoking the son of a bitch.'

'He'll get tired and go back to his mate in a minute if we're patient,' I said confidently.

Half an hour later, 'He still ain't tired,' replied my companion.

The onager was on patrol, circling the trunk of our tree. It marched steadily, never stopping, never more than a couple of feet away from our precarious perch. From time to time it would look up at its prey, give that horrible, frustrated squeal and lunge up at a juicy portion of one of us in the hopes that it might get just one little taste.

'I don't understand it,' I told Rolf. 'We haven't tried to get between him and his food or a mare in season. We haven't said any rude words in onagerese. We're just innocent passers by!'

'It ain't no use analysing,' growled Rolf. 'This bastard's just a man-hater, that's all.'

That seemed the only logical explanation. This was not the aggression even of a creature that has been cruelly treated in the past by humans. It had the chilling appearance of irrational, intrinsic hatred, the blind rage of a rabid animal that has turned into a deadly robot obeying the virus infesting its brain cells.

Rolf had the same thought simultaneously. 'Couldn't be rabies, could it?' he asked.

I went through the cobwebbed mental pigeonholes containing what I knew of rabies in equines. Rag-and-bonemen's ponies in Rochdale did not often chase folk up trees, and Britain has been effectively free of rabies since 1921. I had never seen rabies in horses of any species, but those who had wrote of it taking the 'furious' rather than the 'dumb', paralytic form. They had, I dimly recalled from lectures long ago at Glasgow University, spoken of excitement, mania, uncontrolled actions that were violent and dangerous, including blind charges, and frequently chewing of the animal's own skin. Rabies was reported from time to time in Spain.

The onager, rabid or not, was still as determined as ever to destroy us. Detestation of us fuelled every straining sinew and corded vein in its body. All the symptoms of rabies taught me as a student seemed to fit the beast below me, except the bit about uncontrolled actions. Rolf agreed that this demon pony seemed highly controlled and calculating. It knew what it was after and was trying damned hard to get it. The absence of robot-like movement gave me just enough confidence tentatively to rule out rabies.

'The one driving force in the animal seems to be that it wants to eat us,' I pointed out when another hour had passed without the slightest change in the situation. 'I wonder if it'd be happy with a limb as a diversion while we escape.'

Rolf laughed bitterly. 'What do you want me to do? Amputate one of your arms with my penknife and throw it down like a spare rib to a hound-dawg?'

I looked at Rolf's natty suède jacket and then at my old denim one. I made the choice. 'Try to break off that thick branch above your head,' I said.

With great difficulty, while I hugged his waist, he tugged and pulled and went red in the face. Suddenly the branch broke with a crack and we both rocked violently. Only just did we avoid toppling straight down into the gnashing fangs below.

I took my jacket off and stuffed the branch down one sleeve, then I slowly proffered the bit of 'me' down to the onager. I saw delight and triumph sparkle in its bloodshot eyes. The one in blue was coming down like a lamb to the slaughter! With a great lunge the wild ass seized the 'arm' in the jacket, tore it away from me and flung it with immense force to the ground. It then began to stamp, rip and gnaw at it with terifying ferocity. It was utterly absorbed in reducing the 'arm' to pulp. Postage-stamp-sized pieces of denim began to flutter around. Rolf whispered just the one word, 'Go!' We dropped down from the tree and somehow ran like the wind on aching, numbed legs for the gate in the fencing. I was scared as hell, more scared than any escaped circus lion, elephant with raging toothache or tiger coming round prematurely from an anaesthetic had ever made me feel.

Miraculously we made the gate, crashed through and collapsed on the ground as it slammed behind us. At that instant, five hundred pounds of squealing, thwarted onager hurtled into the wire mesh beside us. The fence bulged alarmingly, some metal strands 'pinged' as they parted but mercifully held. After a valiant attempt to leap over the top at us, the onager returned to the remains of my jacket and its wooden arm and took up the furious attack again. We picked ourselves up and limped stiffly away. As we passed the grinning group of Spaniards, Rolf said something terse and explicit that wiped the grins from their faces.

We decided to buy the two elephants and the giraffe; when the weather was warmer we would move them by road to Rio Leon. We also made some enquiries about the onager, which turned out to be well-known as a fearsome scourge of homo sapiens, with two near-kills to its credit among the park workers. There was no chance of its being sold and we were told that it would have to be put down.

'When they do euthanase it, ask them to use a heart shot,' I said to Rolf. 'I'd very much like a look at its brain if that could be arranged.'

Weeks later Rolf took the trouble to acquire the brain of the dead onager and put it into a tub of formaldehyde for my next visit. When I eventually had a chance of examining it, I found a tapeworm cyst as big as, and bearing a close resemblance to, a table-tennis ball embedded in one side of the brain's frontal lobes. The onager had been a sort of robot after all—tragically controlled by a parasite picked up maybe years before when grazing. A blade of grass must have borne a tiny beetle which contained within its minuscule muscles the microscopic larva that would one day drive a wild ass mad and give a friend and me a very rough couple of hours.

Nine

Cuddles the killer whale had by this time settled down wonderfully at Flamingo Park. The 'flu vaccine worked and no booster shots were needed. He was devoted to the American girl whale-trainer, Jerry Watmore, who had come over from the USA to school him, and he was eating like a horse. A whale sling that could be run over the pool on massive steel beams had proved a success, and Cuddles had swum into it at our first attempt. Blood sampling and health inspections were easy and quick, and the only problem was to persuade the whale to back off out of the sling when the examination or whatever was over. He loved this giant doctor's couch, and never showed any of the 'once jabbed, twice shy' wariness of chimpanzees, who remember always their first encounter with nefarious individuals like me who chuckle heartily, bear gifts of grapes and then treacherously produce the syringe that had been hidden behind their backs. Cuddles was the perfect patient, provided you did not try to stick needles into him while he was swimming free in his own environment. Killer whales I have met since have behaved quite differently when faced with their medical advisor.

I fussed over every little ailment, real or imagined, that beset Cuddles. Slight cracking of the skin in the corners of his mouth? I had read of scurvy, the disease that was once the bane of mariners, cropping up in whales, so I trebled his daily dose of vitamin C. A small spongy wart on his dorsal fin? Into the sling, a shot of local anaesthetic and off it came. A slight iron-deficiency anaemia appeared a few weeks after his arrival, caused by some of the natural blood in mackerel being lost as we thawed out the whale's meals of deep-frozen fish. I boosted his iron pill supplement and the anaemia cleared; I was beginning to get the 'feel' of this animal. Every time I visited I swam with him for a few minutes. He adored having his tummy scratched and lightly kicked by my flippered feet as he hugged me between his flippers.

One day, Cuddles' keeper noticed that the whale's dorsal fin was bleeding. It had been unblemished the night before, but now, at 8.30 in the morning, it was oozing blood from a small group of what looked like ulcers. I was soon on my way over the hills in response to yet another breakfast-time phone call.

Once at the park, I arranged for the whale sling to be run out and Cuddles slipped in without a murmur. A few cranks on the winch handles and he was clear of the water. I walked out along the catwalk and inspected the skin disease. They were not strictly ulcers, more like ragged little wounds on the leading edge of the triangular black sail that is so characteristic of male killer whales. They did not seem to be infected and I had no idea what they were. I smeared them with neomycin ointment, plastered thick lanolin and denture-fixing paste on top, and coaxed him back into the pool.

Next day, more of the skin damage had appeared. It was all in roughly the same place, and the base of the dorsal fin was beginning to look rather ugly. Under a magnifying glass, the splits in the skin could be seen to be quite deep. Their ragged appearance was vaguely familiar, but I could not place exactly what they reminded me of. Over the next few days the skin disease worsened. One curious fact was that the bleeding area did not expand at all by day, but extended noticeably during each night.

'Any chance of vandals, or keepers with a grudge of some sort doing him mischief?' Pentland Hick asked me.

Mutilation of animals, sometimes by outwardly normal keepers, was not unknown to us, but the dolphinarium was securely locked up at night and it had high walls. Nevertheless, I asked for a dolphin trainer to sleep in a hammock slung near the whale pool for a few nights to see whether that might help. It did not. The damage to Cuddles' dorsal fin progressed steadily and the dolphin trainer was adamant that no-one had entered the dolphinarium.

My concern over what had begun as a relatively small if mysterious skin problem was by now considerable. Phone calls to the marinelands of America produced no concrete suggestions from their veterinarians and I simply kept on applying my antibiotic ointment and hoping that something would turn up. Laboratory tests had revealed nothing significant.

Andrew Greenwood's bush telegraph, fuelled by packets of cigarettes, had once again worked perfectly. Whenever I drove into the park to review the latest developments in the mysterious Case of the Bleeding Dorsal, a puzzle that was proving anything but elementary, there would be Andrew already at the pool-side, eager to play the role of Dr Watson.

We talked about the puzzle one day over tea in the cafeteria. 'I'm intrigued by the nocturnal aspects of the darned thing,' I said. 'It extends when he's floating and dozing during the wee small hours, but never in broad daylight.'

'What about setting up a surveillance system?' Andrew suggested.

'To survey what? Microbes dancing about in the moonlight? Little water sprites paddling out to the whale in fairy canoes and hacking at his fin with elfin axes?'

We both smiled. Suddenly I had an idea—maybe surveillance was not such a bad idea. 'We'll try it, Andrew,' I said. 'I'm going to phone the Green Howards.'

This reference to one of Yorkshire's most famous army regiments mystified the student. 'To do what? Hire a howitzer to blow up the water sprites with?'

136

It took several phone calls before the Army public relations people oiled the wheels and arranged what I wanted. A squad of soldiers would come out that evening with infra-red searchlights of the type being fitted at that time to some battle tanks, and some sets of night binoculars. I was going to light up the dreaming Cuddles in his pool with 'black' light and observe him through the hours of darkness. Maybe he was doing something odd like rubbing the fin against the piping or pool edge. With this system and warm clothing, plus flasks of strong coffee laced with rum, we might get a clue to the cause of the trouble.

The soldiers and their officer duly arrived and set up the equipment. As darkness fell, we took our places high in the rows of seating around the pool. Besides the military contingent and me, there was the ubiquitous Andrew, who seemed to carry in his little sports car clothing, equipment, victuals and all sorts of paraphernalia for impromptu exploits such as this.

It was a dark, moonless night. After the novelty of looking through the night-glasses and seeing the pool and its inmate sharply displayed in ghostly, lime-green light, the vigil became a cold and cheerless affair. No talking was allowed. We passed the night-glasses silently from one to another, took gulps of the coffee when the cold began to bite and cursed that no-one had thought to bring cushions for the hard wooden seating that was numbing our bottoms.

At 2 am, just when I was regretting having thought of so daft a piece of time-wasting, I was hit hard in the ribs by the army officer, who was holding the glasses at the time. He thrust them into my hands. I lifted them and looked.

Cuddles was where he had been since early evening, and at first I could see nothing that I had not seen before. Water, pool-side, whale—the usual lime-green scene. But wait! There was something new. Two luminous blobs had appeared on the pool-side, small, green like all the rest, but moving. They stopped briefly, changed places, merged into

137

one, separated and then moved slowly on. It was like something out of a badly out-of-focus horror movie. Fascinated, I watched the little ghostly forms go down onto the platform, approach the water's edge and stop. Then the blobs moved again: with graceful hops they sprang onto the whale's forehead and began to move up past his blow-hole. Cuddles gave no sign of movement.

When the blobs reached the dorsal I had had enough. 'House lights on!' I shouted. Andrew flicked a switch and the pool was flooded in powerful visible light.

'Good God,' Andrew muttered.

Two startled brown rats turned their heads towards us as they crouched on the broad expanse of the whale's back. In a twinkling they had scurried back to shore and disappeared down a floor drain.

I had heard of other zoo animals being chewed alive by rats, but usually they were sick or dying creatures. An amphibious assault on a fit and floating whale by such bold buccaneers was something else. Whether their vampire-like visits had irritated Cuddles or whether he had been as unconcerned about them as he was about needle pricks, I will never know.

The blobs had been unmasked. The next day we called in the vermin-control people, Cuddles' skin wounds healed and there were no further attacks from the drains.

For once, an early-morning telephone call brought glad tidings—my first hippopotamus birth. Fifi, the bucolic old female at Belle Vue had sprung a surprise and borne a lusty little 'horse of the Nile' during the night. I forgot utterly the planned luxury of a morning spent pottering in the garden and snatched a handful of buttered toast to munch as I drove down to the zoo. All new-born animals give me a marvellous thrill, and I wanted to see my first brand new hippo before he or she had a chance to become blasé with this sad old world of ours, while it still blinked brightly in the artificial Africa that men had built for it to end its days in, in the middle of a smoky, grey city.

The baby was a beauty. Only fools compare the physical features of animals and debate the relative charms of wombats and warthogs. The impala cannot be judged against the bullfrog, nor the sloth against the lyre bird. Apart from man, who sorts out the minority of his kind that can be expected to pass muster at beauty contests and similar sad gatherings, it is a universal truth that there are no ugly animals. The Vietnamese pot-bellied pig produces piglets that I consider utterly charming and close behind, for my money, come baby hippos. This one was plump and in showroom condition. The mother looked watchfully proud and had an udder whose teats bore globules of colostrum. Matt Kelly and I agreed: everything seemed absolutely OK. I arranged for Mum to get extra rations of food and half a cupful of cod-liver oil each day and told Matt to inform me if the complete afterbirth was not expelled within thirty-six hours.

Two days later Matt called me. 'Afterbirth came away OK,' he said. 'Mother seems foine. But oi'm not too sure about the little feller.'

I went to look. I agreed with Matt. The baby was not as perky and plump as it should have been at three days old. It looked listless and unhappy, though the keeper was adamant that it had been suckling vigorously on several occasions. Cautiously Matt and I tried to grab the baby for a thorough examination. Not a hope—the mother hippo was not having any such shenanigans and sent us hurriedly back over the barrier by charging with the speed and nimbleness of which these lumbering, tank-like creatures are capable.

'The best I can suggest is a dart injection of the baby,' I told Matt. 'I don't want to knock out Mum just to get at the little one.'

I do not like the old-fashioned guess-agnosis with zoo animals, but on this occasion I felt a flying syringe full of vitamins would be a good idea. It was easily done, though the mother indignantly pulled the emptied dart out of her baby's rump and chomped it up between her enormous teeth. I lose twenty-five pounds' worth of dart syringes every month that way.

The next day the baby was distinctly fading. Our initial exuberation had turned to despair. The baby was not feeding as frequently, although its mother was brimming with milk. It wobbled slightly on its feet. It slept more than I liked, and Matt noticed something else: the urine it passed was the colour of dark coffee. 'Looks like changed blood,' I said unhappily. 'My bet is a severe cystitis—inflammation of the bladder.'

While I went to fix another flying dart containing a dose of ampicillin, I asked Matt to try to dab up a spot or two of the baby hippo's urine, using a long pole with an absorbent tissue tied to the end. Despite defensive action by the mother, Matt got some of the brown liquid. To my surprise, tests showed no blood in it. But if the deep, murky colour was not caused by blood, what on earth could it be? I gave myself the benefit of the doubt and darted in the anti-cystitis antibiotic anyway.

'Ye know, Doctor,' Matt said, as we stared glumly into the pen, 'the little feller's not passed a motion yet.'

There was no simple way of administering a laxative, and surely the natural action of the mother's colostrom would produce droppings before long. Anyway, with a sickly baby hippo I would prefer constipation to debilitating, dehydrating diarrhoea.

The ampicillin had not the slightest effect. After a further three days, with the baby steadily deteriorating, I took more samples of the black and muddy urine. Still the blood tests read negative. I was puzzled but switched my antibiotic attack and brought in the expensive but powerful chemical called gentamycin. I might as well have been darting the baby with lemonade for all the good it did. It looked as if I would have to neutralise the mother with an anaesthetic and haul out the baby for a thorough going-over, but before I could go ahead with the plan, Matt phoned me with the worst possible news: the baby had died suddenly. It was heart-breaking.

'Get the little fellow's body out,' I instructed. 'I'll come over and do an autopsy.'

But when I arrived at Belle Vue no little corpse was lying ready in the post-mortem room. 'Can't get at it,' explained Matt dejectedly. 'She'll kill anyone who troies to go near it.'

I went to look. The bereaved female stood guard over the leathery little heap in the straw that was her first-born. Keepers with boards, brush handles or even thick doors lifted off their hinges were driven mercilessly back by the determined animal. No-one, but no-one, was going anywhere near her baby. I threw her tranquilliser powder in hollowed-out loaves of bread; she would not eat. We tried raking the body out with hooked poles; she broke the poles effortlessly with great snaps of her jaws. I darted her with valium; she drooped her eyelids but remained on guard, wheeling her hind legs whenever one of us tried to creep up behind her. Matt tried to lure her into other quarters with fruit and fresh vegetables; she never even looked in his direction. The day came to a close with us defeated and the hippo still standing four-square over the lifeless infant.

'She's stood over the baby all noight,' Matt told me next day. 'She won't eat, drink or go into the pool. Oi've tried lettin' the bull in with her. She went for him like a mad thing, took a lump as big as yer fist out of his cheek and now he's sulkin' scared in the river house.'

It would have to be anaesthetic. But suppose as she went under the effects of the drug she staggered into the water? It would take all day to drain her pool. No, I was not justified in darting any one of my hippopotamus anaesthetics with deep water so close to where she stood.

The hippopotamus and elephant house at Belle Vue has an old gallery running along the back of the animal pens. I looked up at it. Suppose we went up there with a rope and fished for the corpse? We tried it. It was a long drop. Matt fashioned a lasso out of thick cord and, leaning over the edge of the gallery that was caked with almost a hundred years of bird droppings, slowly lowered the loop down towards the little hippo. The mother did not once look up, but as soon as the cord dangled close to her head, she snapped at it with loud clumping noises of her teeth. Each time Matt nearly had the cord in place round the baby's muzzle, the mother's jaws swept the lasso away. The head keeper was red in the face and grinding his teeth in frustration. Suddenly, as he lowered the cord yet again, the female actually caught hold of the loop in her mouth and gave a mighty, irritable yank. Matt was snatched violently forward and his chest came up hard against the low balustrade. A section of the old woodwork broke away before him and crashed down onto the hippo. Only the fact that I grabbed him by the back of his shirt and jammed my feet against the surviving bit of rail saved him from going down as well. The mother had not budged an inch under the surprise aerial bombardment. Splintered wood littered her back but she was intently nuzzling the cold, dark form lying between her fore legs.

'Sure, there's only one thing for it,' puffed Matt, getting over the shock of his narrow escape from death either by breaking his neck or by being chomped by the hippo. 'Lower me down on the rope, Doctor—ye'll need two or more fellers to help ye. Then oi'll grab the little 'un whoile she's distracted somehow.'

It sounded perilous to me, not least because for over twenty-four hours now this animal had shown itself immune to every sort of distraction we had come up with. Matt would need at least five or six seconds to throw the rope round the baby and secure himself for the ascent. What could we do that would guarantee at least that much time? At the very best the mother would still be only a few feet from the head keeper, and hippos can turn their heads and the rest of their bodies like lightning.

'Oi've an oidea,' Matt continued. 'Jim!' he called to one of his keepers who was standing down below. 'Go to the souvenir shop and ask 'em to let you have three or four of those mechanical toys they're sellin'—the animals that move. The biggest they've got!'

Jim returned shortly with three brightly coloured plastic animals, a tiger, a pig and a dinosaur. Each had a clockwork motor that Matt wound up with a key. He put them on the floor, gave them a nudge and the three toys started to move round in loudly whirring circles. Matt seemed satisfied. We went down to the ground floor again and he cautiously opened the door of the pen containing our distressed mother. He wound up the mechanical pig, placed it on the floor just inside the door and set it off. Fizz-fizz-whirr went the toy, beginning to move in a wide circle. We watched the hippo. Her ears pricked, then she turned her head slowly towards the strange sound, fixed the mechanical intruder with a baleful gaze and advanced upon it, mouth agape. Stomp, stomp, crunch! The pig would never move or whirr again. Its clockwork spring remained impaled on one of her tusks.

'Foine! Foine!' crowed the head keeper. 'Oi reckon she was ten seconds away from the baby. We've two more of the same. We'll get into position and then when oi give the word, Jim can set both of 'em off in the same place.'

Reluctantly I went along with Matt's stratagem. I had nothing better to offer. With four keepers I accompanied him back to the gallery and we fixed a new length of one-inch rope to his waist, leaving a long piece free for him to attach to the corpse.

When all was ready and Jim had fully wound up the two toy animals, Matt gave a shout and the operation began. We took the strain and slowly lowered Matt from the gallery while Jim's animals did their bit like Trojans. The head keeper touched down gently as soon as the hippo was seen to be turning away and moving in to deal with this second wave of invaders. Crouching tensely, eyes fixed on the rear end of the hippo only a few feet from his face, Matt quietly fished in the straw for some extremity of the baby to pull on. Scrunch! One down—the mechanical tiger had bitten the dust. Matt had got hold of a leg and was hurriedly throwing a loop of rope round it. It was all up to the dinosaur now. Cra-ack, whirr—the hippo had lunged and split open its casing but the little hero was still going. The hippo was having difficulty biting satisfactorily at so small an object. Matt gave us the thumbs up and yelled 'Pull!' just as the dinosaur met a sticky end at last, stomped flat. The hippo whirled, we pulled like demons. Matt's broad head appeared over the edge of the gallery and the body of the little hippo bumped against the balustrade as the mother made her final charge. She missed Matt's boots by inches. It was done.

The autopsy showed the cause of the baby's death and of the dark-brown urine. It had been born without an anus, a congenital fault, and the large bowel ended instead in the bladder of all places. The deformity was too gross to have been curable, so there was some minute comfort in knowing that I could not have done anything for the little mite, but I was depressed by the evident psychological upset of the now lonely mother. Her milk would dry up without any need of drugs, but to ease her mind I put her on a course of euphoria-giving chemicals for a couple of weeks. She needed and deserved a bit of a 'high' for a while.

I congratulated Matt on his efforts. We had used toys in animal work before—for example cuddly ones for orphan monkeys and apes to cling to—but I had never thought of using clockwork animals as unmanned decoy missiles!

Any remaining worries I had about enough work coming my way vanished when Pentland Hick made me an offer. Frank, the curator of Flamingo Park, was leaving. Would I go to live at Flamingo Park and take the position of Curator and

Group Veterinary Officer? Hick said I could retain an essential degree of independence, visit Belle Vue regularly, go out to other exotic animal clients if they called, and use all the facilities of the operating room he was building for my use at Flamingo Park. More, he would pay for me to travel around the world, studying wild animals and visiting other zoos and animal dealers. I could keep the old farmhouse in Rochdale and would live a bachelor life in a caravan on the site set in a peaceful corner of the park. It would mean, too, that I could see even more of Cuddles, for whom I had developed something of an infatuation. The offer was a unique one and without hesitation I accepted: few zoo veterinarians have any experience of the other side of the fence, of general keeping, curating and management, yet they can never be fully efficient without it. It was to prove a watershed in my life.

Ten

Flamingo Park Zoo was built round an early Victorian manor house and occupied the house itself, the grounds and two or three outlying farms. The house and lake stood at the top of a rise, from which the ground sloped away to a stream and the caravan site. Across the Vale of Pickering, the hazy line of the North Yorkshire moors stretched across the horizon like a lilac-coloured rock garden. My first days as curator were highly discouraging. There was far more than I had ever imagined to running a zoo with a couple of dozen keepers and hundreds of assorted animals, not to mention the thousands of human varieties that arrived by car and coach each week. The veterinarian finds it salutary to see for himself that 99.9% of the important affairs in the life of the lions, camels, parrots and crocodiles, which he thinks he knows well, go on day after day in a subtly changing kaleidoscope while he is not normally there. Headline-grabbing, glamour bits of surgery on cute zoo inmates, the occasional dramatic intervention and the midnight emergency were not as central to my life from now on as keeping the drains unblocked and dealing with grumbles from visitors about catering, lost boys, too few lavatories, spectacles snatched by monkeys and coats ruined by wet paint.

I soon found caravan life too spartan for my more sybaritic tastes. Days that had started with one of Shelagh's fine breakfasts and time for a stab at the *Daily Telegraph* cross-word in front of the log fire were replaced by the miseries of tea stewed over a calor-gas heater, cold baked beans and no morning paper.

An unusually depressing spring, with icy winds and snow right through till May, turned the land round the caravan into a gumboot-removing quagmire. The caravan-site manager was a cussed individual who took a malevolent delight in switching off the lights in the cold, brick lavatory block just after watching me wade there across the mud in pyjamas and oilskins late in the evening. I resorted to carrying a box of matches with me when attending to calls of nature. As soon as the lights went off I quickly unravelled several feet of toilet paper and set fire to it. The blazing roll gave enough light for me to complete the ceremonies with a measure of decorum.

Apart from the visitors, the zoo stock and lesser beasts like the caravan-site manager, I also had my hands full with staff problems. I had to maintain discipline, try in vain to get them to clean their rooms and show them the rudiments of good stockmanship. One guy always stole the pennies thrown by visitors into the pools of the park. His intelligence did not match his greed, however, since he had no more wit than to spend the piles of verdigris-coated pennies in the zoo cafeteria or bar. Despite being warned by me, he continued to retrieve the coins which brought good luck to the throwers and Christmas comforts to the local charity to whom the pools' monetary contents were donated once a year. I had to fire the fellow for his own good, when I discovered him paddling about early one morning in the bear-pit pool. Two sweet-faced but lethal adult polar bears were standing on the water's edge, watching his treasure hunt.

Another keeper was asked to carry the bags of a newly arrived girl trainee to the caravan she had been allocated half a mile from the zoo. Neither of them returned for three whole days. Such instant passion had to be rewarded by instant dismissal when the two dreamily put in an appearance on the fourth morning. Even among my patients, I had never come across such importunate mating behaviour.

But by and large, the staff I had at Flamingo Park at that

147

time were a talented if colourful bunch. One is now the director of a famous safari park, another looks after the menagerie of the ruler of Abu Dhabi, another is a distinguished fine arts dealer, and there is one boy, who helped me to deliver the first baby dolphin conceived and born in England, who is now serving a life sentence for fitting an acquaintance with a pair of concrete boots and dropping him alive into the sea. If only he had stuck to the less flamboyant aspects of marine mammal studies!

Despite the weather, the drains, the staff and the visitors, I soldiered on. I had the animals, and for the first time in my life they were all under my care and not just with respect to veterinary matters. Want to hire an elephant for a store opening in Leeds? I was the chap who said yea or nay and organised everything. The rewards for putting up with the mud and the baked beans and the toilet roll torches were the opportunities to touch, see, smell and just be with a whole variety of animals all day long.

Everyone taught me something. I was initiated into the highly complex business of water treatment and filtration by the dophinarium staff. Violet, the head of the animal food kitchen, showed me how to present acceptable and appetising meals to some of the rare animals like lesser pandas, pangolins and Gambian pouched rats.

Most of all, the animals were always instructing me. Mangrove snakes went into convulsions when I experimented with what I had found to be a safe anti-tick aerosol on other sorts of serpent at Belle Vue. The great elephant seal demonstrated the uselessness of a dart-gun on him even at point-blank range; the near-liquid blubber in this species absorbs the shock of the syringe impact, and the charge that actually pushes the injection in does not detonate. Tigers, camels, elephants, cockatoos and kangaroos taught me respect—respect not of the kind I had always had for living things but for the way in which they insisted on certain standards of behaviour by human beings in the daily

148

routines of cleaning, feeding, watering and general maintenance. Break the routine, disturb their ordered lives, be brusque, cocky or absent-minded and they meted out punishment by employing one of the vast range of physical weapons they are fitted with, by embarrassing you in front of the public through non-co-operation or, worse, by escaping or by falling ill and dying.

I was learning the hard way, but I was learning fast.

With the arrival of early summer, caravan life at Flamingo Park became less stark. Shelagh and the girls drove over at the weekends and we would all swim with the whale. He was as good-natured with them as he was with me, which gave Stephanie and Lindsey something of an unusual advantage when talk among their school friends turned to dogs, cats and other more mundane pets. The light evenings meant the end of the site manager's jape with the lavatory switches, and it was my turn to discomfit him. I was rearing a lion cub in the caravan. On warm days it would roam round in the grass and play cubbish games of hiding behind clumps of weeds and springing out gleefully to give the legs of passers by a left, right with its paws. The site manager did not like cats, small or large, and suffered continual harassment of this sort. Worse, he watched with impotent chagrin as the cub lay in my caravan doorway, gnawing at the surrounding woodwork; the slow demolition of one of his beautiful painted mobile homes sorely grieved him.

There was lots of animal training going on at the park. Sharp-eyed macaws played pontoon with members of the public and always won. Their opponents never realised that the crusty-natured birds had been trained to spot marked cards which bore minute black dots on their reverse side. I learned how easy it is to train dolphins and how much easier it is for dolphins literally to train and condition their trainers. I also spent long hours watching the American girl, Jerry Watmore, turning Cuddles into a star performer. When she

149

had given him a full repertoire of jumps, rolls, handshakes and tricks of all kinds, and every one produced by kindness and rewards of mackerel, she handed Cuddles' presentation over to a young English boy who had the makings of a marine mammal trainer. He did well. Cuddles liked him and appointed him one of the select coterie, which included myself, who were allowed to ride round the pool sitting on his back either in front of the dorsal fin or, should one prefer a more exciting, bumpy journey, perched directly behind it. The training programme continued smoothly until one day there was a misunderstanding. Perhaps there was a foul-up in the system of signalling, the language of precise movement by which the man communicates his commands to the whale; perhaps the trainer was momentarily sloppy in his gestures; perhaps Cuddles was doing a spot of daydreaming about fat salmon or shoals of mackerel.

Cuddles was being trained to play the trumpet. He was to hold the toy instrument between his teeth with his head out of the water. The fanfare would in fact come not by his blowing into the trumpet (whales cannot exhale air through their mouths) but from loud hootings from his pursed blow-hole. There were a series of distinct signals governing the various stages of this performance: one hand movement caused Cuddles to raise his head and take the trumpet gently between his lips, another started him hooting, and a third stopped the hooting and persuaded him to release his hold on the trumpet. When things began to go wrong on that fateful morning, the trainer had got Cuddles to hold the trumpet perfectly and produce hoots that would delight the audiences in future but make Louis Armstrong turn in his grave. With the trumpet between his teeth Cuddles suddenly opened his mouth, no doubt impatient to receive his reward of succulent mackerel. Whatever the reason, the great jaws gaped, and the shiny plastic instrument fell onto the back of his tongue.

The trainer immediately took sensible action by giving a

hand signal which Cuddles had already learnt, and which meant that he was to shake his head vigorously from side to side as if rinsing out his mouth. Somewhere between man and animal there was a break in transmission. Cuddles closed his mouth, gulped and the trumpet was gone. Killer whales have wide, dilatable gullets; adults can swallow big tuna and seals whole. Within seconds the trumpet must have splashed down into the cavern of the first of the whale's four stomachs. As if he had not noticed a thing, Cuddles at once opened his jaws again in anticipation of fish for a job well done. The horrified trainer gave him a handful of mackerel and then dashed to the phone.

I was at the pool-side within minutes and went into urgent conference with Martin Padley, the head of the dolphinarium. First we had to make sure that the trumpet really had been swallowed. We grilled the poor trainer and sent a couple of scuba divers down to scour the pool bottom. We had had false alarms in dolphinaria before where trainers swore blind that they had seen an object swallowed by a marine mammal. Dolphins and sealions had been stomach pumped, X-rayed and dosed with emetics and purgatives. Then the object had turned up, thrown out of the pool by the animal and lying hidden behind seating, in someone's pocket or on the shelf in a locker. The cardinal rule was to check the pool and its surrounds meticulously, no matter who said they had witnessed the actual swallowing, before pursuing the foreign body into the animal itself.

Usually we had been concerned with nuts and bolts, coins, torch batteries and the like, things that can be overlooked on a pool bottom or elsewhere. You can hardly miss trumpets that are sixteen inches long and canary yellow with bright red valves. There was no doubt, we concluded eventually—the trumpet was inside the whale. I was pretty certain that it must be in the first stomach, since foreign bodies in cetaceans very rarely get through the tight little valve that guards the entrance to stomach number two. Being plastic,

151

the thing would not dissolve although it might conceivably break. In one piece it could do damage as the lining of the stomach contracted down onto it. Broken, it might cause severe internal bleeding.

I considered the medical implications. I would not be able to use my ex-army mine detector in the way that I did on ostriches that gulped down bits of old iron; the machine could not pinpoint the position of non-metallic objects. X-ray was out, too; there was not a set in the country, even at the University large animal clinics, that could have shot a picture through Cuddles' girth. Fibre-optic gastroscopy, the technique that Andrew was later to pioneer in dolphins, could not be used; even the longest fibre-optic instrument, the colonoscope for peering up humans' lower bowels, was far too short to reach down the whale's throat and gullet. Laxatives would be useless; the damned thing was safer in the stomach than trying to slide through the hundreds of feet of narrow bowel. Emetics? I baulked at the dose of sodium carbonate or hydrogen peroxide that I would have to use to try to induce vomiting. As for apomorphine, an injectable drug that causes retching in some species, it had never been used on whales and I feared it might rupture his guts. Abdominal operation on a killer whale was, at that time, totally beyond our capabilities.

So what was I left with? Only two approaches. One was the oldest medical therapy in the world (and arguably the safest)—do nothing but wait. The other was to use the good old stomach pump and try to flood the trumpet out. After much thought I decided to begin by doing nothing since I was sure that the trumpet would soon be regurgitated. It was a tough decision and even tougher explaining to Martin and Pentland Hick why I chose masterly inactivity. I went back to my trailer, poured a Glenlivet and tried to unwind by losing myself in Gerard Manley Hopkins' poetry, a sure remedy for tensions of the day.

Next day Cuddles was still in fine fettle but there was no

sign of the trumpet. The scuba divers searched again and we opened the pre-filters to look for pieces of plastic. Nothing was found. Cuddles ate a hearty eighty pounds of fish and played gleefully. Tests showed no blood or other abnormalities in his excrement. To keep everyone on their toes in case of a regurgitation, I promised a bottle of champagne for whoever brought me the troublesome Jonah of an instrument. I decided to wait another day. When that passed uneventfully I waited yet another.

By the fourth day I had lost enough sleep agonising over the possible ulcerating effects of the trumpet's mouthpiece, bell or valves on the soft stomach lining. 'I'm going to pump out his stomach,' I announced.

Like a genie conjured up by my words, Andrew Greenwood drove up to the dolphinarium at that moment. He walked blandly in as we rolled out the whale sling. His timing, as usual, was perfect. The grapevine extended down to his college in Cambridge and was functioning well.

'It'll be a wet business,' I told him, 'and I'm afraid there aren't enough wet-suits for everybody. If you want to get in close, strip down to your underpants.'

'Don't worry about me,' he replied, slapping a grip he was carrying. 'I've got trunks and towel in here.'

Once the dry-dock was in position it did not take a minute for the whale to cruise happily into it. We wound him up and I gave one keeper the job of wetting down Cuddles' entire body surface with a hosepipe.

'Don't let one inch of him dry out for an instant,' I warned. 'When we start pumping, his temperature will go up with stress and excitement and he'll steam like a Christmas pudding. Keep spraying the water, don't worry about soaking the people round him.' Stomach-pumping whales is never fun.

I had the plastic stomach tube and pump ready. Stainless steel buckets of warm water were lined up by my side. All I had to do now was pass the tube down the mouth and into

153

the stomach. In horses, stomach tubing can go wrong if you forget to check that the tube you have shoved gaily down the animal really is lying in the gullet. You begin pumping in the liquid, and may find you have a drowned nag on your hands; the tube has slipped down the windpipe. But any fool can stomach-tube a cetacean safely because there is no opening between the larynx and the back of the throat, so the tube cannot go wandering off towards the lungs. Whales and dolphins are vet-proof by design.

All the same, trumpet-chasing inside Cuddles was not going to be all that much of a piece of cake. Before I could pass the tube I naturally had to get Cuddles' mouth open, and whereas he would open it at the drop of a hat when floating in water, as soon as he was suspended in his hammock he resolutely clenched his teeth and refused to open them even a millimetre, not even for a mackerel dangled in front of his shiny eye. I tried prising them open with my fingers; I fancied he sniggered as he felt my puny hands working against jaw muscles that can wrench the entire giant tongue out of a blue whale at one bite. I had a tapered, four-inch-square piece of wood to use as a dental gag during the operation. I attempted to lever his mouth open gently by inserting the tapered end of the wedge between his lips. No go; Cuddles blew foamy bubbles through the fine spaces between his teeth. An onlooker suggested I might chisel out a tooth to provide a window for the tube. He quailed under the storm of ridicule and indignation. Multilate our Cuddles? The man must have been out of his mind!

The man with the hose was dutifully concentrating on his responsibilities and chilling us humans in the process. No-one complained. I noticed that when he sprayed his jet of water at Cuddles' lip, the whale would wriggle slightly and give some piggish squeaks. Taking the hosepipe, I rammed it hard up against the arcade of shining white teeth and told some-one to turn the water pressure on full. Tickly jets of tap water squirted through the gaps in the whale's teeth and struck the tongue and roof of the mouth. It must have produced some sort of fizzy sensation. Whatever it did, Cuddles suddenly opened his jaws a fraction and then clamped them shut again, cleanly amputating three inches of hosepipe.

'That's it!' I exclaimed. 'Two of you get ready to push in the gag when I do it again. Remember, once the gag is in place he'll throw his head around. Ride with him!'

I repeated the squirting business. Again Cuddles momentarily opened his mouth and the men rammed in the gag. Surprised and insulted, the whale threw his head to left and right, trying to dislodge the offending piece of timber. The two men holding the gag were flung about but clung on desperately as Cuddles beat them against the hammock framework. Suddenly one lost his grip. The gag slewed across the whale's mouth. The other gag-holder was pitched headlong into the pool and, with a final mighty shake of his jaws, Cuddles hurled the block of wood from him. It hit the shins of the water-spraying keeper with terrible force. As the poor fellow was carried off in agony with what turned out to be a fractured tibia, Cuddles contentedly shut his empty mouth tight.

Beefier gag-holders were recruited and the whole rigmarole was repeated. This time the men managed to survive the whale's onslaught. The gag was well and truly jammed into the space between the back teeth. As it was made of soft, white wood, Cuddles' teeth sank into it slightly, which was just what I wanted; it could not skid away like one made of resistant hard wood.

Cuddles protested with hoots and querulous squeals. I greased the stomach tube with liquid paraffin and passed it quickly over the back of his tongue. It slid easily. I felt the slight resistance as it curved round the larynx, then a fast transit of the gullet and finally more resistance as the tip pressed through the weak valve at the entrance to the stomach. I was in.

155

'Right, Andrew,' I said, 'start pumping as fast as you like. Go!'

Andrew bent to the machine lying in the first bucket of warm water and started working the handle rapidly up and down. Within a minute the bucket was empty. Nothing had changed at Cuddles' end of the tube.

'Start on the next,' I ordered.

That bucket also was quickly empty. Cuddles blinked but that was all.

'Next! Fast as you can!'

Andrew puffed away with the effort. The third bucket was half empty when suddenly Cuddles' stomach responded at last to the involuntary expansion. There was a rumble and a retch and Cuddles opened his mouth. I was drenched in a tidal wave of warm, fishy-smelling water. Wiping partially digested fish bones from my eyes, I looked around. No trumpet.

We did it all again. Four buckets went in this time before the wall of water inundated me. Still no trumpet, but at least there were fewer fish remnants.

Andrew inspected the whale, feeling the flippers and tail-flukes to test the temperature reaction. 'He's heating up noticeably,' he reported.

I could not risk much more stress. 'Just one more try,' I said.

It was another failure. The water returned promptly and in full measure; of musical instruments there was not the slightest sign, not even a grand piano. Despondently, I ordered the whale to be lowered back into his pool. Now all I could do was return to the so-called Turkish treatment or, as we say in Lancashire, 'doing nowt'.

I 'did nowt' for the next two weeks. Cuddles remained outwardly hale and hearty and the daily searches for the trumpet continued. I began to wonder if the whale would carry the object for life. I had been slightly consoled by talking by phone to Dr Sam Ridgway of the US Navy marine mammal research unit. He had told me of some of the large radio-telemetry packs which they were placing in the first stomachs of dolphins and which stayed in place for long periods without producing any signs of discomfort or disease. As the days went by we came to accept the fact that maybe Cuddles would have to live permanently with the trumpet.

I was surfacing from sleep one morning when there came a furious knocking on the caravan door. Half asleep, I tried to make sense of the noisy fool so rudely disturbing the delicate hour. Dammit, was this some keeper still drunk after an all-night binge? I pulled back the blankets and listened.

'Champagne, Dr Taylor, open the bottle of champagne!'

Suddenly, with crystal clarity, I knew what he was hollering about. Although it was raining hard outside, it was a wonderful, glorious, halcyon day.

I kicked open the caravan door. A dripping wet dolphin trainer stood on the steps with a grin like a slice of watermelon and a yellow and red trumpet held high above his head.

Cuddles had regurgitated the instrument without any fuss during the night and it had been found floating on the surface when the dolphinarium was opened up. I was overjoyed and immediately sent to the bar for half a dozen celebratory bottles. Forestalling the grapevine, I also telephoned Andrew to tell him the good news.

'Marvellous!' he replied. 'Like Benjamin Franklin wrote, "God heals and the Doctor takes the fee."'

I agreed, laughing, but reminded him in return of the Emperor Tiberius who claimed that every man at thirty is either a fool or a physician.

I could not have cared less into which category I fitted at that moment. All that mattered was that Cuddles was safe. There would be no more musical items in his repertoire.

Whitsuntide and its important bank holiday was approaching. There are three holy days in the year of a British zoo or safari park. These solemn festivals when the coffers are open and waiting to be filled to overflowing are the bank holidays at Easter, Whitsun and in the late summer. If the Gods smile and arrange for particularly favourable weather, these three days alone can put the zoo's accounts at the end of the year securely in the black. If it rains, or worse still snows or blows hard, these fateful few hours may well mean uncomfortable visits by the company accountants in October and bullets in the brain for a handful of lions.

Now you may well assume that the unwitting inmates of the zoo should be down on their paws, claws, fins and flippers praying to Pan for burning sun and bright blue skies on these three crucial days. Not so. Brilliant weather lures too many trippers to the beaches and swimming pools. Hot sun beating down on a car full of brats, with windows closed as per regulations while driving through lion and bear reserves, is a penance these weak souls cannot endure.

To be perfect, to lure human pilgrims to come and cough up their alms, to linger long at the hot dog stalls and treat the kids to elephant rides, these Holy Days must be warm enough to produce optimism and deter ladies in frocks from demanding an early return home, but cool enough to promote the sale of pies, jellied eels and hamburgers. The sun must be in evidence but without too much burning enthusiasm; as long as it nips unexpectedly in and out of small clouds, families considering a drive to the coast are uncertain, thrown off balance. As for rain, there is no harm at all in just a soupçon of the stuff around breakfast time. Not only does it put paid to the aspirations of would-be bathers and promenaders, it will without doubt prompt some member of the family to point out that zoos have shelters: you can always go to the monkey house if it pours down. Ah, you may say, but surely rain ruins the chances of an outing altogether? Might not the family opt en masse for television or the cinema? Not at all. At these great festivals, the British family Goes Out For The Day as Holy Writ commands. Obedience to these ancient traditions, together with faith that it might well clear up later, are all that it needs to get the family on the road. Once away, miles of traffic jams cannot stop these sturdy creatures from enjoying themselves—at the zoo, comes the chorus from the zoo directors.

Now you can understand why zoo directors can be seen actually going to church on the eve of the bank holidays, why some can be seen staring at the heavens, talking to old yokels wise in country weather-lore or scratching in the soil to see how deep the snails are burrowing, and why others take to drink, sorcery or self-flagellation.

These busy days are rough ones for zoo staff and animals alike. The latter engorge a surfeit of potato crisps, mouldy sandwiches, ice cream and foreign bodies that keep veterinarians in work for weeks afterwards. The staff sweat it out and wait for the blessed sight of the last human backside passing through the gates in the evening. As curator-cum-veterinary officer at Flamingo Park, I dashed at these times from drunkards throwing bottles at the bears to small boys locked in the lavatory to escaped monkeys causing havoc in the self-service cafeteria.

Pentland Hick always liked to have some special attraction for a bank holiday, something to get publicity in the press. That Whitsuntide it was a giant red Pacific octopus. We had had these monsters before and I had found them spectacular creatures but a bundle of trouble. The biggest problem was the shipping of them from the north Pacific. Although they were wonderfully packed in sea water and oxygen-filled plastic bags surrounded by ice and insulation and flown on non-stop jets, I was having great difficulty combating their tendency to poison themselves. On the journey they naturally emptied their bowels, and the nitrates which thus accumulated in the water made them mortally sick.

This latest octopus I met personally at London Airport. I gave him a fresh supply of sea water and ice, pumped pure

159

oxygen into his bag and drove north like a madman with the fifty pounds of angry red mollusc slurping about on the back seat of my Citroën. A refrigerated tank was waiting for him at Flamingo Park. I had three days to get him fit before the bank holiday. After showing promise on the first day, he collapsed and finally expired on the morning of the second, thirty-six hours before the big crowds paid to see the only giant red Pacific octopus in Europe, whose pictures had been in all the papers. Now he lay in a motionless heap on the floor of his tank, although I was intrigued to see that the animal's skin retained its ability to change its colour shade and patterning according to the background on which it was placed.

Pentland Hick took the news of the octopus' demise very badly. He had spent a considerable sum bringing the red monster the best part of seven thousand miles. 'It can't be dead,' he said in that ultra-quiet voice which indicated that he was very angry.

It was time to switch my veterinarian's hat for my curatorial one. 'It can't be dead,' I said to Martin Padley some time later. 'At least, not till the end of the bank holiday.'

For an instant he looked puzzled. Then he grinned as he understood what we were going to do.

The great day dawned perfectly and the coaches and cars began to roll up for what promised to be a bumper bank holiday. Down in the aquarium below the whale and dolphin pools, the first visitors ambled around. The big refrigerated tank in one corner was the main attraction. There, nestling in some rocks and illuminated dramatically by a pale spotlight beam, was the famous new arrival. From the other side of the armour-plated glass, the holiday-makers watched the tentacles tremble as if itching to unleash their fury and saw distinctly the flapping of the mighty creature's crimson mantle. It was surely breathing. It was alive. It was fantastic!

Martin and I were rather pleased with the octopus' resurrection. It had been a simple matter of running one of

160

the aeration pipes under the mollusc's body and adjusting the air flow so that the body vibrated just enough and the actual gas bubbles made their way to the surface through the rocks. The spotlight was a moment's work. In fact, terrible though it sounds, the dead monster presented a far grander spectacle than the live monster would have done. One thing live octopuses utterly detest is spotlighting, and it would have cleared out of the limelight in a cloud of black ink. Of course our deception was indefensible—except by the attention the beast received and by the shudders of delight from the onlookers, many of whom had come that day to see just such a sight and who went on their way none the wiser.

By noon things seemed to be going perfectly. The crowds were emerging from the aquarium and discussing enthusiastically their first face-to-face encounter with a real live Kraken. Then came the inevitable small boy, complete with small boy's earnest father. I was standing admiring our shameless bit of theatre when the pair came up to me.

'You the chap in charge?' began the father.

I nodded proudly. Now what have they lost, I thought, or have they dropped the lad's spending money into the dolphin pool?

'Clifford here, my boy, says that octopus is dead!' The words were uttered in a strident, Black Country voice. Nearby heads turned at the sound. The boy, around twelve years old, red-faced and weasel-eyed, looked up at me with a sly smirk as I registered what I hoped was incredulous horror at such sacrilege.

The father continued, 'See, Clifford knows about such things. Mad on animals, he is. Not much he doesn't know about 'em. And he says it's dead.'

I looked down at the horrid child and wondered whether I was looking at myself twenty-odd years before. I shivered at the thought.

'Why on earth should you think that?' I murmured with forced avuncularity.

More folk nearby were now paying attention to us. Were our sins about to find us out?

The boy spoke for the first time. 'Been down 'ere watching him for an hour. Been down as well before that. 'E don't move 'is tentacles one hinch.' He was speaking in confident triumph. 'No doubt about it, mister, that specimen of *Paroctopus apollyon* is gorn!'

Heresy! This couple of unbelievers were causing the faithful gathered in front of the great glass tank to begin muttering. Doubts were growing. Schism loomed!

To nip things in the bud I must tackle the precocious Doubting Thomas at once. Picking my words with Jesuitical care, I said loudly, 'Aha, sonny, but if you knew the giant red Pacific octopus like we know him, you would have learned that he is not given to dashing about his tank with the scatterbrained abandon of a guppy. He looks fine, to be sure.'

The boy was plainly unimpressed and wrinkled his nose. Mercifully the loudspeakers announced the beginning of the whale show and the crowd moved upstairs, including the boy and his father. When they had all gone out of sight I called Martin and dashed into the service area behind the octopus tank.

'Quick, get a pole,' I shouted. 'We must re-arrange our exhibit before that brat comes back.'

The ruddy corpse was not so co-operative this time. First it flopped over onto its back and lay looking very dead. I pushed and prodded frantically. When one tentacle did what I asked, the other seven lolled and drooped and snagged on stones. When I did manage to pose the creature in a suitable spot at the other side of the tank, the air tube secreted under its mantle released big bubbles that blooped noisily out of it and up to the surface.

'Looks like it's burping. It must be alive,' Martin grinned, keeping a wary eye open for intruders.

I groped about in the icy water with my sleeves rolled up. I was filled with uncharitable thoughts about the budding biologist, now no doubt casting a beady eye over Cuddles to make sure he was not a blown-up plastic dummy, and tried to get out of my head Sir Walter Scott's couplet about what a tangled web we weave, when first we practise to deceive.

At the exact moment that my fingers became blue and stopped functioning the octopus finally regained its composure, just as the crowd came pouring down the stairs again. The boy and the father appeared. I withdrew and watched. The boy looked puzzled, but he was a tenacious child. The afternoon drew on and during each whale show we moved the octopus about. The cunning child, with parent always in tow, popped back to the tank at unpredictable intervals. Martin and I sweated it out. It had become a battle between us and the boy, unspoken, undeclared but grim and determined. Then the boy switched the attack and appeared in the aquarium during a whale show. Martin countered neatly by innocently hosing down the concourse with a high-pressure spray. 'Sorry about this. It's the only chance I get of keeping things clean,' he explained to the couple as his powerful jet of water bouncing off the floor and walls kept them at bay long enough for me, behind the scenes, to work feverishly at moving the corpse yet again.

By the evening it was obvious we had won. The boy and his father made a final visit to the aquarium and then departed. The little fellow was looking somewhat chastened as they made their way to the coach park, and his parent was heard peevishly to remark, 'Clifford, you're not always right. Now damned well let the matter drop!'

The aquarium concourse had never looked so clean.

Martin and I paid for our duplicity when at the end of the bank holiday we removed the octopus and laid it decently to rest. Nothing, but nothing, smells more awful than a three-day dead giant octopus when it is out of its tank of water. Clifford would no doubt have been ecstatic if he had known that the experience put us off our food for the rest of the day.

Eleven

That summer was rich in fragrant, shimmering days. I saw my first adder basking on a rock on the moors above the Vale of Pickering. Evening skies were shimmering cyclamen. As the park's Chilean flamingoes seemed desperately in need of someone to give them fatherly chats about birds and bees and gooseberry bushes, I built some mud pies for them by the lake. They caught on, doubled the height of the mounds by adding more mud themselves, laid eggs on the uncomfortable tops of these spartan nests and hatched out a trio of fluffy grey chicks. I broke a rib trying to catch harbour porpoises off the Yorkshire coast, and discovered a marshy hollow where sundew plants grew wild and snapped up flies. An olive-green toad came to live in the long grass under my caravan; to save him the effort during the baking days and humid nights I brought him mealworms that I had taken from bush-babies' dinner plates. Purloining two mealworms from each of eight bush-babies did not harm them a bit but kept my toad plump and genial.

In early July, Rolf Rohwer telephoned from Rio Leon: it was time to collect the giraffe and two elephants from the defunct safari park near Madrid. Lloyd's of London were insuring the animals and insisted that a veterinarian was present while the animals were being transported, not least to tranquillise them if necessary. Yet again I found myself getting the jitters at the thought of doping a giraffe.

I flew over and met Rolf in Madrid, then we drove out to the safari park. When we arrived, a mobile crane and a brand new articulated lorry, which had been specially hired for the job, were waiting ready for the loading. The lorry was the entire fleet of a one-man firm whose sole proprietor, driver and driver's mate was standing proudly by the vehicle, pointing out to a knot of former would-be fox-lynchers the glories of the gleaming, yellow-painted, spotlessly clean monster. It was immensely long, but we saw at once that it was far too high: normally a low-loader is used for moving giraffes by road. But it had come all the four hundred miles from a village near Rio León and like it or not, we were going to have to use it.

I went to look at the giraffe, which had already been lured into a box whose sides reached up as high as her elbows. She was plainly very apprehensive and was beginning to strike with her hooves at the box walls. When anyone went close to her she started to stargaze, with her head and neck held in a straight line pointing up to the heavens or even tilting grotesquely back towards her tail. It was all frighteningly like poor Pedro. The crate was useless—she could vault out of it with ease—and to make a new one would take several days. Rolf made numerous phone calls and eventually arranged to borrow an old giraffe crate from the zoo in Madrid. It would arrive next day.

The first day had been wasted, but we found an isolated farmhouse where an old lady filled us with fresh bread, olive oil and tomatoes from her garden and cold, cloudy yellow wine from her cellar. Before dawn we were back in the safari park. The crate from Madrid had arrived. It was indeed old. The wood had been patched innumerable times, the leather padding of the interior had rotted into shreds, there was damp everywhere and rusty nails protruded dangerously in a hundred places. While the men set to work lining the box with hay-filled sacks and flattening the nails with hammers, we began loading the elephants onto the front of the open lorry.

The vehicle was brought alongside an earth bank and planks were placed to make a bridge. The elephants were let out of their house and we tried to tempt them on board with apples and bananas. Despite our proffered fruits, the nearby olive trees proved more attractive, and the two animals spent three hours squealing with delight as they rampaged through the groves, vandalising trees and scoffing foliage to their hearts' content. When we finally got them under control they settled down, walked up to the plank bridge and the first elephant put a tentative foot on it. The bridge gave slightly. That was enough. No great mammal with its wits about it is foolish enough to walk on unsteady ground. The elephants backed off and dug their heels in.

Another day was lost, and more of the old lady's victuals and yellow wine were called for. We had not gone a yard on our long journey towards Barcelona.

The third day started more promisingly. The elephants still distrusted profoundly the bridge onto the lorry, but with chains on their legs and an improvised winch we slowly hauled them on. Once they were in place side by side, looking out over the driver's cab, they seemed to relax and tucked in to a meal of fresh alfalfa and carrots. Now for the giraffe. The crate was ready and the crane stood poised to pick it up with steel cables. It was up to me: the insurance did not come into effect and the animal was not Rolf's until I gave the word to begin loading.

I walked round the old box. It had been repaired as much as possible, it seemed. The floor was the only doubtful part, but it looked strong enough.

I watched the giraffe nervously pacing her loose-box and wondered about tranquillising her. Pedro's sudden collapse had unnerved me—suppose this one fainted under the sedative or, like the Flamingo Park giraffe, had some physical condition which might combine with my drug to kill her. I made my decision. 'Get her into the crate with food,' I shouted. I was not going to give her a shot unless absolutely necessary.

I was surprised how quickly the gangling animal was

boxed, but once trapped in the wooden container she began to kick and her breathing rate increased tremendously. If anyone got within twenty feet of the box, she rattled round in a panic. It did not look good.

I gritted my teeth and gave the order to start loading. The giraffe was Rolf's from that moment. Back in pin-striped London EC3, underwriters with bowler hats and high blood-cholesterol levels would about now be leaving the Underground at Bank, unaware that I had just put them on risk to the tune of £3000.

When the crane's jib with its four cables swung out over her little prison, the giraffe became even more alarmed. She began stargazing again. I reached for the dart-gun and syringes—anything more and I would have no choice but to sedate her. Four of the Spaniards darted in and attached the cables. The crane took the strain. With much creaking and groaning, the crate started to rise. Soon the boxful of unwilling giraffe swung in the morning air ten feet above my head. The animal's long neck curved round the steel ropes as it waved its head from one side to the other. Bits of wood and puffs of dust fell from the crate. The jib reached maximum height and began to traverse steadily towards the lorry.

Suddenly there was a loud crack. The crate lurched and shuddered. A stout plank of wood whistled past my head and crashed to the ground. From the bottom of the box I could see the two hind feet of the giraffe protruding as far as the fetlocks. The floor of the old crate was breaking up. Any second, the whole one and a half tons of animal could come plummeting sickeningly down to the sunbaked ground.

'Move it, move it!' I yelled, dashing towards the crane driver's cabin. 'Lo mas rapido que posible! Fast as you bloody well can!'

The man understood at once. The crane accelerated, the jib swung over towards the lorry at full speed and the cables were begun on their descent simultaneously. Unceremoniously, the giraffe crate made a bumpy landing on the metal flooring behind the elephants. Chunks of rotten wood fell away. The animal reeled but remained upright as her feet were pushed back through the holes in the floor. She was aboard safely.

Rolf and I were both visibly shaken. Each of us could visualise the scene if the beast had gone through the crate bottom at that height. It would have been a surprise but nothing more for a tiger, maybe even a bear, but a giraffe's legs fracture if you no more than look at them: a stumble over a fist-sized rock can snap them. We had had a narrow escape, and neither of us dared think about how we were going to unload the beast.

'Let's have a word with the driver and then get going,' said Rolf, rolling his eyes. 'Mad onagers, fox-hangers, lousy crates—this place is bad medicine.'

The lorry driver was standing in front of the shining silver radiator grille, looking proudly down the length of his enormous vehicle. The elephants were calmly munching away at the front and the giraffe seemed less nervy now that the cables had been taken away. She blinked down at the assembled men gathered round the back of the lorry. The distance from the ground to the tips of her 'hat-pegs' was a daunting eight yards; it looked like an attempt at the altitude record in animal transporting. 'My right arm for a low-loader,' I muttered as I reflected on what our journey was going to be like. I did not know the roads we would be using, but I knew for certain that there would be a bunch of bridges, pipes, cables and other impedimenta strung across the road at just the right height to decapitate our lofty purchase.

'Now, Señor, about our trip,' Rolf was asking the driver. 'How long do you think it will take us to reach Rio Leon?'

The driver was a tubby man in his mid-thirties who sweated continually and who took a swig every few minutes from a litre bottle of red wine which he carried in his boiler-suit hip pocket. He looked at the sky, screwed up his face and scratched thoughtfully at his buttocks. After a few moments he replied, 'Mas o menos, around about a week, I guess.'

'A what?' I gasped. 'A week to do 350, maybe 400 miles? What's he talking about?'

The driver looked resentful and reached for his red wine again.

'The doctor's right,' said Rolf. 'How do you work that out?'

'Pero señores, the distance. The roads I must take. I have to obey the permisos. The authorities, the policia, the Madrid municipal office, the guardia civil, they have laid down the rules in the permisos.' He fumbled inside his shirt and pulled out a sticky sheaf of papers covered with the grandiose stamps and innumerable signatures of Spanish bureaucracy.

'What rules?' growled Rolf.

'Señor, there are so many. We cannot cross Madrid by day, there are some roads we must not use and under no circumstances must we travel on the bits of motorway between here and Rio Leon. Also I need to eat, siesta and sleep. So you see, we arrive no problem in one week, I think.'

'Balls to that!' I exclaimed angrily. 'I'm not having those animals up there for a week, unable to get them off for exercise. Let's get cracking and keep motoring. We'll run through the night, permisos or no permisos. One of us can take turns with him at the driving. If we're stopped we can blarney our way out of it. I've always found policemen intrigued by the novelty of big zoo animals on the move. I've never had any trouble bending the law in such matters.'

Rolf nodded. 'I agree. Bulldust baffles brains. We'll have to try it.' He turned to the driver again. 'Now then, Señor, we must get there quicker than one week. We must travel by day and by night if possible. I will arrange the permisos.'

The driver became agitated. 'But I can lose my licence just like that, pouf! I must obey the permisos.'

'Give me the permisos, my friend,' said Rolf. 'I'll carry

them and have them altered and stamped officially as we go along. Dr Taylor and I are going to be in the car driving directly behind your lorry. When we need to have a permiso changed, we'll overtake you, drive to the guardia or wherever and explain the problem.'

'But, Señor, the night driving! My siesta!'

'Don't worry. We'll relieve you. And there'll be a fat bonus for you in cash on top of our agreed price for the transport.'

Looking less than happy, the fat man agreed. We began loading bales of alfalfa onto the lorry and instructing the four fox-lynchers who were to travel on the back of the vehicle how to keep an eye on the animals. They cut tree branches with small forks at one end and put them on board; with these I hoped they would be able to lift and manoeuvre cables and wires in our path without themselves or, more importantly, the animals getting electrocuted. We did not forget buckets and two galvanized tubs, since in this heat the massive creatures would require frequent watering. At last we were ready. The lorry engine roared into life, the men clung to the vehicle sides as it began to judder forwards, and Rolf and I in the car took up our position three yards behind the sparkling yellow tailboard. We were off.

Rocking and reeling over the hard-baked uneven ground, we slowly approached the road outside the safari park. The elephants leaned for support on the yellow slats that ran along the sides of the lorry. The giraffe bumped and banged in its crate.

'She'll have swollen joints and deep abrasions before we've gone a mile at this rate,' I told Rolf gloomily. 'If things don't improve when we hit the road, I must call off the whole affair.'

As we went through the gateway onto the road, the heavy section of slatted metal on the left side gave way under the elephants' weight and crashed onto the tarmac. A moment later the right-hand section followed suit. They lay bent and chipped in the gutter. Everyone stopped. Rolf jumped up and down on the metal to try and straighten it. I hammered at the distortions with the car jack. Yellow paint-flakes flew. The driver held his head. With wire and rope we fixed the bits of the lorry back into place, but a certain newness had already departed from the front half of the vehicle.

Under way again, the animals settled down remarkably. The giraffe seemed surprisingly soothed by the movement. She turned to face the front and became as quiet as a mouse. Perhaps it was the flow of air over her face that she enjoyed, or maybe it was the constantly changing scenery. As we entered clumps of overhanging foliage, I was delighted to see her take mouthfuls of buds and leaves, quickly coiling her tongue round twigs and letting her momentum rip the morsels away. On corners she balanced herself expertly, and she was no longer coming into contact with the sides of the crate.

The elephants, too, were interested in the abundance of herbage passing above, around and even below them. They used their trunks to grab bigger helpings than the giraffe behind them, and sizeable branches came toppling down into the lorry. The two elephants considered themselves to be off on a tour gastronomique. The first few miles were on a twisting road through forests of pine trees whose cones were fat with succulent kernels. Having tried some of these, the elephants found them to their tooth and began feasting happily. Little squeals of joy would greet another branch brought down with a hollow clang onto the roof of the driver's cab. More yellow flakes of paint were left behind us in the dust.

The animal keepers on the back of the lorry had, in the usual Spanish style, stocked up copious supplies of red wine for the journey. I had always been alarmed by the way in which Spanish keepers began a day working in the reserves with deadly and powerful wild animals by having a couple of large brandies for breakfast and then taking bottles of wine with them on the job. These would be consumed while guarding the gates of the tiger section or standing in a kiosk in the bear enclosure armed with something about as big and lethal as a walking stick. Our chaps on the lorry were true to form and more ominously we saw that the driver had apparently swallowed his private supply and was being passed more by one of his compatriots who squeezed past the elephants and handed a couple of bottles in through the cab window as the lorry bowled along.

By late afternoon we drove into the outskirts of Madrid and faced the first test of our permisos. The lorry driver pulled up and declared that he would not go a foot further unless Rolf did what he had said he could do: get the permits altered by the hundred and one civil servants who had signed, stamped, initialled and endorsed them. It was four o'clock and the offices were closed. Only the policia head-quarters was still open, so leaving the lorry by the roadside surrounded by whooping children and ancient ladies in black who stared incredulously, Rolf and I went to see the Chief of Police.

We sat for what seemed like hours in the corridor outside El Jefe's office, while the permits were inspected, shuttled back and forth by a bevy of minions and finally stacked on the big man's desk. When we were called to his presence, he went through the necessary rigmarole of 'being busy on other important matters', made some phone calls, sniffed, coughed and pulled faces as he thumbed listlessly through some papers and finally sat in ominous silence, staring out of the window at the view of a bleached brick wall. At last, when my kneecaps were beginning to protest their boredom painfully, the Chief spoke.

'No es posible,' he said. 'It can't be done. You must travel only by night. You cannot come through Madrid. I am sorry but the Mayor's office alone can alter that. You must see them tomorrow.'

Rolf started to argue, at first reasonably and then loudly, with an occasional daring thump on the Chief's table. Here

172

comes my first peek inside a Spanish dungeon, I thought.

'Dammit, it looks like we're going to have to push on and risk them grabbing us,' Rolf eventually murmured to me, exasperated. That is the snag of asking permission: if we were caught now, we could hardly plead ignorance or innocent mistake.

'I assume, Rolf,' I said loudly and clearly in simple Spanish, 'that you have explained to El Jefe the nature of the giraffe and two elephants?' Before he could begin to look puzzled I continued, staring him hard in the eyes, 'That these creatures for your safari park are travelling in exchange for a flight of Imperial eagles that you have obtained for Madrid, to be presented to El Caudillo, General Franco himself?'

Rolf shook his head solemnly.

'No, Doctor, I haven't,' he said, also in Spanish, 'but no matter what happens I shall feel obliged to keep my side of the bargain. The eagles will still be sent to the Generalissimo.'

As one we stood up, trying to look resigned and dignified in defeat. 'Muchas gracias y adiós, Jefe,' said Rolf.

The police chief began to cough loudly as we turned away. 'Er . . . uno momento, Señores,' he said sharply as we reached the door. 'I cannot promise what will happen beyond Madrid on the rest of your journey, but perhaps I can, just on this one occasion . . .'

Ten minutes later we were back at the lorry and showing the driver our amended permiso. 'Get going at once,' Rolf instructed, 'straight through the middle of the city. Rush hour, daylight, it don't matter a damn! Pedestrian precincts, Triumphal Arch if you have to—straight as an arrow! Let's clear the city and make some good mileage before we begin night driving.'

'B-but how?' stuttered the driver.

There was no need to answer. Six blue and white uniformed motor-cycle cops roared up to us on BMWs.

Their leader explained that they were the personal escort of the Chief, and were to see us safely through the capital and on the road to Guadalajara. With three of the cops in front and three behind, the lorry and our car charged through that delightful and bustling city at 5.30 pm. Sirens screaming and red lights flashing, we swept up the grand avenues, through traffic lights that were against us, across squares closed to traffic and down the normally choked back streets of the old city. Taxis and buses screeched to a halt, folk flattened themselves against walls around the Plaza Puerta del Sol, windows were flung open as we careered along. The giraffe carried herself with the poise of a Queen of Spain making a Royal Progress. With her two bulky grey equerries in place at her feet, her aristocratic features looked down upon the common herd that thronged the pavements.

On the far side of the city we stopped to thank our police escort, water the animals and do a general check. The sky was cloudless and the deep pink of a Cuban flamingo as our driver and the keepers disappeared into a bar to replenish their wine bottles. Climbing up onto her crate I found that the giraffe was now much more approachable and could actually be touched by hand without lashing out. Obviously travel was broadening her mind. Her legs were in good condition, with no rubs or abrasions, and she took alfalfa and water greedily. The elephants were still content, though the lorry was now carrying a fair load of elephant droppings, which steamed away on the once spotless yellow floor.

'What do you think about night driving?' Rolf asked. 'Not much trouble with wires so far, but it could get worse.'

Although the city run itself had been fast and furious, elsewhere we had already been brought to a slow crawl by all sorts of wires and cables that crossed the road. Unless you do move giraffes by road, I suspect you never really appreciate the vast numbers of cords, ropes, cables, wires and conduits that infest the landscape. They are like Father Brown's postman, invisible through being utterly commonplace.

Spain certainly must be well in the running for first place in the most wired-up country competition. Carrying electricity, telephone conversations and often, we came to suspect, nothing at all, the wires festoon poles and masts and lamp standards at all levels. We had to avoid them all if I did not want to handle my first case of electrocuted giraffe or have her garrotted in true Spanish style. On the other hand we were anxious to avoid bringing the whole of Spain between Madrid and Barcelona grinding to a halt by severing power and communications links along our way. Wine or no wine, the men with their forked poles had quickly become adept at judging which wires were likely to be too low, neatly intercepting them and lifting them up so that the giraffe's head passed underneath.

'Yes, the wire lifting is going well,' I agreed. 'It should be possible to do it at night as well as long as our headlights pick out the overhead cables.'

When we got rolling again I calculated our average speed. The escort in Madrid had been a great help, but still we were not doing much better than ten miles an hour. Barely had we picked up speed after lifting one wire before we had to slow down for another. What was more, we found that the wires were often laid across our path in fiendish groupings of six or seven at different heights, tensions and thicknesses; it was a sort of minefield in the air. Our men soon had little time for their wine. We were getting out into the dull, flat country of red earth that stretches north-east of Madrid. Little groups of houses dotted the roadside every few kilometres and they positively bristled with wire traps. Even an isolated half-ruined hut by the edge of a cornfield was likely to be wired up for some purpose.

The sun set and we continued to press on. The men were working fluidly, passing the overhead obstructions from one forked stick to another with considerable skill. If they were quick enough, it meant that our driver did not have to reduce the speed quite so agonisingly low. Twilight set in, and the pink sky rapidly filled with smokey violet hues which deepened as the moon rose. We could still all see the wires sharply outlined against the cloudless sky. What we were slow to realise was that our sense of perspective was about to be lost. Slumped in the seats of our Seat Saloon, Rolf and I dawdled along at a snail's pace with our eyes fixed on the giraffe. Suddenly we saw her head snap back. A wire had caught her momentarily. I cursed, Rolf honked and we both shouted. Then it happened again, and again—nothing serious, just quick pluckings of the animal's head by a wire. There was no sign of spark or shock, just an occasional metallic twang. We had to face it: the twilight had destroyed our ability to estimate the distance and height of the wires as the lorry approached. At our slow speed I was not so much afraid of a serious neck wound as of the strand of metal damaging the large, delicate eyes of the animal.

A hundred yards ahead we could see a restaurant. 'Let's stop there,' I said. 'We must wait until it's completely dark and then see if our headlights and the moonlight change matters.'

We pulled in, parked the lorry under some trees where the animals could use self-service and, after watering them again, went in for beer and tortillas. After the meal we took the car on a short wire-hunt. It was useless. There was no reflection on overhead wires from our headlights or from the moon. Night travel was out. We prepared to camp.

Next morning when the grey-blue sky was just light enough for us to be able to see the wires and judge their height, we set off. It was tedious sitting behind the lorry, constantly moving up and down between second and third gear. The countryside was unspectacular as we approached Guadalajara and we were under a permanent, horn-blowing barrage from motorists behind who could not understand why we did not overtake the slow lorry.

The originally straight sides of the lorry were now grotesquely distorted. Our view from directly behind was one of a once sleek vehicle that had developed alarming bulges round its waistline. The elephants seemed to prefer leaning outwards into the slipstream. The metal sides did not fall off any more, they were simply buckled outwards.

Not long into the second day we encountered our first really low bridge. With some trepidation we crept up to it. Forked sticks would be no use now. The best we could do was to drive down the centre of the road and try somehow to persuade the giraffe to lower her head. We tried to get her mouth down to some tasty food, but alfalfa proved no attraction, so we offered apples, bananas and finally, under protest, the sugary buns which the men had bought for their mid-morning snacks but which Rolf ordered them to place before her. She licked them briefly but did not keep her head down for more than a second or two.

'Try tapping her very gently on her hat-pegs with one of your sticks,' I called up. One of the men tried it, but she calmly swung her head away from him.

Rolf sighed deeply. 'We'll just have to take a chance,' he muttered. 'There'll be lots more beside this one, I reckon. Roll on slow!'

The driver heard his shout and inched forwards. Closer and closer came the keystone of the archway. The giraffe was around two feet too high for the bridge. I held my breath. Then, as naturally as could be, when the stone was almost touching her, she ducked just enough and found herself under the bridge.

'God don't let her suddenly crack her head up onto the roof,' I said aloud. I had seen too many giraffes scalped by blows against their short, firmly fixed horns.

The lorry edged on. The giraffe stayed sensibly down, clear of the roof by three or four inches. Two minutes later we pulled out at the far side. The humans involved cheered with relief while the giraffe looked down benevolently, wondering what the dwarfs were making such a fuss about.

When we had gone through Guadalajara, where Rolf quickly avoided wrangles over permisos by passing out a bottle of vintage Osborne brandy to a policeman in a white helmet controlling traffic at a roundabout, the day became a succession of wires, cables and bridges. Past houses of red adobe, blood-red soil, fields of stubble stretching into the heat haze and hills of ugly, fractured, yellow rock, our strange caravan made its painstaking way. Old men in berets crossed themselves as we went by, frowning in door-ways at glimpses of beasts they had never believed existed. Boys clambered up the sides of the lorry to touch elephant skin, and knots of blushing girls clutched one another when the giants gushed waterfalls of urine. Shopkeepers came out and offered bunches of radishes and artichokes for the animals to eat; to us they gave slices of Serrano ham and glasses of wine as we waited for some particularly intricate web of wire to be unravelled.

Approaching Zaragoza we found ourselves weaving down from the high plain along narrow rocky gorges dotted with scrub and sheets of scree. When we reached the first of a series of tunnels cut through the hillside, the giraffe showed once again how eminently sensible she was. Tunnels were just long bridges to her—head well down, turn your long-lashed eyes towards the glow of light at the far end and caramba! There's nothing to it. Not once did she touch rock or raise her head suddenly to scrape painfully against the ceiling.

Out of the final tunnel we found ourselves being waved down by a pair of green-uniformed Guardia Civil. This para-military organisation is built up of men who are tougher, brighter and often meaner than the average Spanish policeman. Our lorry driver was out of his cab and nervously hopping about the two Guardias when we walked up. We were on the right road at the right time and our permisos for this section up to Zaragoza should be in order. Rolf handed them over and the two unsmiling Guardias pored over them. They asked for everyone's driving licences, inspected registration plates and went through their usual routine, oblivious to the elephants which were clumping about above them and giving an impatient trumpet or two. Rolf gave them the patter about the amazing trip we were on, giraffe, elephants going all those miles, animal doctor from England in attendance, Rio Leon Safari Park—great place to go, would they like a couple of free tickets—and so on, but they continued humming and hawing, peering and cross-checking, without so much as a glance at the animals. Perhaps they thought we were Basque terrorists indulging in some fiendishly elaborate exploit using elephants as a distraction.

As the Guardias stood sternly by the side of the lorry, grunting and passing sheets of paper to one another, the elephants decided they had had enough of this waiting. If I had been a bit quicker I could have averted what happened next, but I was too busy wondering what, if anything, might be wrong with our papers. The rushing sound from above warned me too late, and a pungent, warm cascade of yellow liquid poured through the gap at the bottom of the lorry's side. To the elephants' relief and our horror, the two Guardias were drenched instantly in strong-smelling urine.

Swearing, they both staggered away from the lorry and began spitting furiously. Their faces were wet. Some had gone down inside their shirt-collars. Their holsters were dripping; I hoped their guns were waterproof. It was nobody's fault, although we apologised profusely. What else could we do? There was nothing we could wipe off them. They were just soaked through—and smelled awful.

'A million apologies, Señores,' said Rolf, with a face that was incredibly straight and sincere. 'If our papers are in order, then, may I offer you some advice? Even after washing with water and soap, the smell of elephant urine clings to the skin.' The two Guardias listened with misery written all over their brown faces. 'So to remove it, rub the damp used grains of coffee all over your body. I have found that this will remove the unpleasant odour. But be quick now, before it gets embedded deep.'

Thrusting a soggy collection of documents towards us, the two men swore some more and hurried away to their motor-bikes. With a kick and a roar they set off at speed in the direction of Zaragoza.

When we had stopped laughing so much that I gave myself cramp, I said, 'Can you imagine what their Captain will say when they report they've been peed on by elephants?'

'And when they start grabbing all the police-station coffee for an after-shower talc.'

'That bit about coffee grains. That wasn't just a leg-pull, was it? Does it work?'

Rolf grinned. 'It sure does. I've used it a hundred times in Zambia.'

He was right: the next time I had to rid myself of elephant essence after taking a urine sample at a circus, coffee grains proved a remarkable deodorant.

The lorry driver was obviously weary by now, but refused to let one of us take over. At each stop he would walk slowly round his vehicle, lugubriously taking note of its steady deterioration. The comfortably leaning elephants had now pushed a deep bulge into the slatted sections of metal on each side. The cab roof was dented and chipped as if raked by shrapnel, and it was becoming plain that a man with entrepreneurial flair might make a million by bottling elephant urine and selling it as the ultimate in paint removers; the yellow had vanished from the front of the lorry and the wondrous solvent was now making short work of the rust-coloured undercoat. The driver was having to travel and drink his wine in silence, for his radio aerial had been thrown away by one of the elephants doing a bit of tidying up during a boring stop while a cluster of particularly devilish sets of cables was outwitted.

180

The Windsor Safari Park that the Smart's Circus family set up on an estate once occupied by President Kennedy's father. (*Both Tony Evans*)

Baby wallabies – 'joeys' – look secure in their mothers' pouches. After the use of tranquillisers I found I had threatened their security alarmingly. (*Welsh Mountain Zoo*)

A very happy ending. Wunn, now totally integrated into the Windsor baboon colony and even possessed of two adoring wives, faces the camera (centre front) in summer 1979. (*Tony Evans*)

Andrew Greenwood was always popping up when I was about to treat wild animals, and he eventually became my partner. Here he is taking an electrocardiogram of an Indian elephant with suspected heart trouble at Belle Vue Circus, Manchester in 1978. (*Syndication International*)

The general anaesthesia of the giraffe presented serious problems which were at last overcome. Andrew checks the colour of the tongue, keepers and curators prepare to support the head and I inject a powerful reviving drug into the jugular. (*Doug McKenzie*)

Our growing expertise at wire-raising, coupled with the giraffe's impressive commonsense approach to each and every obstacle, had increased our average speed considerably. By the evening of the second day we were on the outskirts of Zaragoza city. Rolf and I went ahead and persuaded a small and impressionable traffic policeman in a blue uniform and white topee who was standing in the centre of a dusty plaza whistling and waving furiously and being totally ignored by a mêlée of motorists, to come with us and conduct us through the centre. He took one look at the lorry with its usual crowd of curious spectators and puffed up visibly. His dark eyes gleamed with excitement as he snapped his coat cuffs and pulled his white gloves tight. Then, pointing to the space between the two elephants just behind the cab, he proclaimed firmly, 'I will stand there.'

Inside with the driver would have been the sensible spot, but our policeman was having none of it. He obviously felt that a leader must be seen to lead, and had no qualms about standing so close to a pair of four-ton giants. I admired his style, but warned him about the dung on the floor, the possibility that he might have his official topee forcibly removed and eaten or that his uniform could be drooled on.

He was deaf to such cautions. 'I will stand there,' he repeated, 'and give directions to the driver. It is no problem, Señores.' He explained that by shouting and banging on the left or right side of the cab roof he would guide the man sitting below without any difficulty.

We watched as the policeman climbed up onto the lorry, squeezed into position and then stood with his elbows on the cab roof, looking proudly down at the crowd. It was a fine sight. Flanked by the two impassive beasts, his diminutive uniformed figure reminded me of the Viceroy of India in the days of the Raj turning out for a Durbar. To the cheers of the folk on the pavement the lorry set off, its big engine roaring. We heard the policeman starting to shout, we saw his gloved hands beat on the cab as the lorry pulled out into the swarming traffic, then all was hidden behind a haze of exhaust fumes. We jumped into our car to catch them up.

Three hours later, we found them. It had taken innumerable calls to the police department and much driving to and fro and round and round the city by us, who were worried at losing a giraffe and two elephants, and by the police department, who eventually realised that they had lost an officer who was supposed to be on point duty.

They were run to earth finally on the road to Pamplona, ten miles north of the city and going steadfastly in the wrong direction. It was almost dark. At any moment the overhead wires would become invisible. The policeman was still in his cockpit, his topee was straight and unblemished, his gloves were intact and there was no ropy saliva on his blue coat. He climbed down to face the music. Two car-loads of his colleagues, Rolf and I, tired and worried, and a brace of Guardia Civil listened po-faced as he gave forth a torrent of words and gesticulated like Quixote's windmills. Apparently his communication system with the driver had been faulty from the start. His shouts had been drowned by the engine noise, and his banging had been confused by his elephantine companions hammering with their trunks. He had tried to get back to our men who were lifting wire busily from positions beside the giraffe crate, but he had been squashed and impeded repeatedly by the elephants. He ended his explanation with a shrug and a salute.

One of his superiors spoke for the first time. 'Mire! Look at your boots, Garcia,' he snarled, pointing downwards.

We all peered through the gloom at the unfortunate policeman's feet. Unlike the rest of him, they had not avoided trouble, and he was walking on two massive cakes of elephant manure that totally enveloped his regulation boots. Rolf's elephants seemed to be delighting in discomfiting the Spanish constabulary.

The matter was closed over several bottles of cognac which all of us, in and out of uniform, consumed in a nearby inn. We also bivouacked there for the night, drawing the lorry up beside a tree-covered bank. The animals began browsing enthusiastically over the side.

Before turning in, I managed to get a phone call through to home. Shelagh was coping with worried owners of parrots and gerbils fretfully awaiting my return. She had passed a falcon with what sounded like severe respiratory trouble down to an eager Andrew at Cambridge University, put a stitch in a hedgehog and been over to Oldham to console a distraught old lady whose even more ancient Patas monkey had collapsed suddenly and died. There had been trouble with a bison at Belle Vue; she had asked my old partner in general practice, Norman Whittle, to go and see it. Flamingo Park was running smoothly.

'One of these days you're going to have to get a partner in the zoo business,' she said. 'What happens if there's a really serious emergency while you're off on one of your trips?'

It was good to know that she was looking after things, but she was right. Not only was the practice keeping me fully stretched, but at this rate there would soon be enough work for another partner, who could also cover for me when I was away and so take some of the pressure which at the moment I was unfairly loading onto Shelagh.

Next morning I was wakened before daybreak by a cacophony of extraordinary sounds. The elephants were making a fearsome din, trumpeting, bellowing and squealing. There was a clanging of metal and splintering of wood, men's shouts and the dull thudding of feet running across hard ground. Bleary-eyed, I went to the open window and looked out. Our men were scuttling excitedly round the lorry, but the dark bulks of the elephants were indistinguishable.

I ran downstairs, pulling on trousers and sweater against the early morning chill. It did not take long to find the cause of the bedlam: the two elephants were reeling drunk. They were smashed, sozzled, pie-eyed. Wobbly-legged and droopy-faced, they staggered and stumbled against the lorry sides, making a thunderous noise. There were sections of twisted metal panel on the ground all around. Only the restraining chains on their hind legs, bolted into the steel flooring, kept them from blasting their riotous way to freedom. Like human drunkards they were maudlin one moment, genial the next and then again argumentative and ill-tempered. Their eyes rolled as mischievous jollity alternated with red-rimmed malevolence. Stroke one and it would rub dreamily against you for some time and then suddenly flail you irritably with its trunk.

I had seen the same thing before, not in zoos or circuses but in Africa, where at certain seasons of the year elephant herds will travel miles to have a week-long binge on the over-ripe, fermenting fruit of the so-called miracle tree. It is best to steer clear of such gargantuan bacchanalia, for there are always a few over-indulgers around with hangovers and long tusks. Here there were no miracle berries. I went over to the trees on which our elephants had been browsing. They were medlars. Fruit lay in the grass. As I picked some up and pulped it between my fingers, I caught the winey aroma. The elephants were high on medlars that had rotted so far that they were fermenting and producing alcohol. They would have the headaches today; I would have them tomorrow, when the inevitable diarrhoea ensued. For the first time on the trip I would have to give the animals an injection. I filled 60-cc syringes with vitamin B complex to speed the breaking down of the alcohol in the blood and smaller, 10-cc ones with a light sedative. Jabbing the haunches of the swaying sots, I started the drying-out process.

An hour later our troupe set off once more. All was silence on board the patched-up lorry. Two elephants lay drowsing and exhaling steamy, fruity fumes, while from on high the giraffe, who had apparently either eaten none of the alcoholic vegetation or possessed the liver of an Irish navvy, looked down with a faintly disapproving gaze.

Although forbidden to use the motorway on the last lap, we could not resist the thought of the time that it should save us. It took only a few furtive minutes to alter the wording on one of our permisos and to fudge up some imposing signatures. We joined the motorway but soon found that although it was free of overhead wires, there were far more bridges than on the older roads. Our average speed did not rise much, so forgery had yielded meagre rewards.

At last, at the end of the third day, we reached Rio Leon and prepared to unload at once in the light of car headlamps. First to be tackled was the giraffe. We had a crane ready for the crucial lift. Sheets of wood were dropped into the crate and pushed under the animal's legs to block the holes through which she might slip again. Rolf gave the order and the crate slowly moved upwards. The giraffe stayed put. The wooden walls had broken away from the floor. It looked slightly improper; as if the lady's wooden skirt was being ripped off. 'Down!' yelled Rolf, and the walls bumped back into place.

Whereas the elephants could be walked off onto a bank and then rounded up, the nervous, fragile giraffe could not be let loose that way. Eventually we hit on the idea of bringing another box onto the lorry, moving the giraffe into it and then, once she was secure, lifting the new, sound box off. It took all night for a suitable box to be found, modified and strengthened. As dawn broke on the fourth day, we at last freed the giraffe at the entrance to her new quarters. She walked sedately in to meet her new mate.

The two chastened boozers were no trouble to unload. Meekly they trooped off the lorry. Their sedatives had worn off and I had buckets of boiled rice and hay tea prepared to ward off any stomach upset following their celebrations. They swallowed their bland medicine politely. Both looked fit enough, although perhaps a little distant in the eye. I could imagine them wishing for a football-sized Alka-Seltzer. I sympathised and looked towards the lake at the valley bottom. 'I suggest, Rolf,' I said, 'that they do what you or I would do on the morning after the night before—have a refreshing shower.'

Minutes later the two animals were happily squirting cool water over themselves and dunking their foreheads with relief. I could relax; all the animals were safely delivered, and I had managed to avoid another confrontation with the need to dope a giraffe.

Twelve

In my office at Flamingo Park I was going through Andrew's dung list. While I was in Spain he had collected samples of droppings from every animal in the collection. With a microscope he had painstakingly searched for parasite eggs, identified them and calculated the actual number contained in every gramme of dung. Now complete and neatly tabulated, Andrew's figures gave a valuable run-down on the present status of everything from elephants to egrets. The complicated cycles of parasites passing through a variety of hosts, the ingenious methods they use to protect themselves and to find and enter their prey, their amazing reproduction rate and the subtle damage they can inflict deep inside the body are of crucial importance to zoo veterinarians. Andrew was providing valuable intelligence.

The telephone rang. It was the main gate. 'Someone to see you. Big car. Posh,' said the cashier. 'Urgent, they say.'

'Send them over, please.'

As I walked outside, a pre-war Daimler limousine, gleaming black with headlamps like frogs' eyes, drew up. A uniformed chauffeur leapt out, opened the rear door and stood smartly to attention. After some seconds a lady emerged. The chauffeur saluted crisply and closed the door behind her. My visitor was a tall, skinny woman of at least seventy years. She did not stoop, nor was her back hunched, but she somehow tilted the whole of her body forwards as if supported by invisible wires. I wondered why she did not fall flat on her face. The way she slanted, together with her scrawny long neck and aquiline features, reminded me strongly of an Egyptian vulture. She was wearing a big black straw hat and a long green velvet dress that smelled of camphor, eau de Cologne and mentholated vapour rub. Deep-set behind curtains and palisades of waxy flesh, two lizard eyes fixed me.

'Dr Taylor? How do you do. I'm Philomena Rind, from Harrogate.' Harrogate is the spa town near Leeds where the woollen merchants and others who, as they say in the North, 'think they're no cat muck' dwell in stone mansions behind thick privet and rhododendrons.

As I showed the old lady into my room, I wondered what animal she had got wrapped in a blanket on the floor of the Daimler. Animals resemble owners in my experience, and I weighed up the possibilities. Hardly a vulture or condor, despite the strong resemblance. Macaw? A strong possibility. Monkey? No, Miss Rind was not one of the distinctive monkey-owning types. Hawk or falcon? No: once upon a time maybe, but not now with her powdered throat and fingernails as long as a mandarin's. Her vibrations were of something quite different. Reptilian? Yes, that was it. She was going to send for the chauffeur in a moment and he would bear in a dyspeptic alligator or some such.

'An urgent matter, I believe, Miss Rind,' I said.

She sat clutching a large velvet handbag and scrutinising me intently with the lizard eyes. 'Yes, indeed, Doctor. It's Hugo.' She unclasped the handbag and put a hand inside. 'Hugo, my dear old friend.' Her hand emerged from the bag and carefully set something on my desk top.

It was a terrapin, as big as a saucer and with handsome striped head and red flashes behind the eyes. It began to row its way clumsily over the surface of my blotter.

Hugo's owner leaned even further towards me and spoke again in confidential tones. 'Do you see his eyes, Doctor, how they're becoming sore? And he's not eating a thing. That's why I've come to see you.' Her voice became a whisper. 'Mr Lawrence sent me.'

I picked the terrapin up and looked at it closely. The under-shell was softer than normal, yielding easily to finger pressure. The eyes were indeed inflamed and oozing cloudy tears. It was typical terrapin trouble—a deficiency of vitamin A and probably vitamin D and minerals too, most likely brought on by a diet of too much raw meat and no nourishing pond snails with their livers rich in the essential vitamins. Under that dark green shell there would be a pair of kidneys starting to pack up. An injection of vitamin A in oil might be just in time. It is an irreversible and lethal disease once it is well established.

'Mr Lawrence?' I remarked. The name was not familiar to me. 'Is he your vet in Harrogate?'

Miss Rind sat back and looked miffed. 'Dear me, no. Certainly not.' She seemed to soften slightly and leaned forwards once more. 'Doctor, do you know D. H. Lawrence?'

'D. H. Lawrence? The writer? *Sons and Lovers*, you mean? I thought he died years ago.'

'Yes, passed on. Have you never read his poetry? He wrote beautiful poems about tortoises.'

Oh Lord, I thought, a time-wasting crank. Poetry— what next? Anyway I never realised that Lawrence wrote poetry, let alone anything about tortoises. This must be a batty old bird with more money than she knows what to do with.

'I'm afraid I haven't,' I said coldly. 'I thought sexy gamekeepers were more in his line. Now, about this terrapin, the problem undoubtedly is . . .'

Miss Rind stood up abruptly and loomed over me. 'I haven't come for a diagnosis on Hugo, Doctor,' she interrupted with a boom. 'All I want is what Mr Lawrence instructs—Balm of Micomicon.'

I was totally at a loss. I had better start from the beginning, slowly. 'Please do sit down, Miss Rind. Just tell me the whole story.'

She lowered herself into the chair and started whispering

again. 'Are you a believer, Doctor? In the after-life, the world beyond?'

'Well, er, yes. I suppose so.'

'Good. You wouldn't be one of us, I suppose—a spiritualist?'

'Afraid not.'

Hugo was snuffling about the plastic sachets containing Andrew's dung samples. He did not appear to be paying any attention to the conversation. Was he supposed to be a spiritualist, I wondered.

'Well, I am a believer, Doctor,' Miss Rind went on. 'I'm not fortunate enough to have been gifted with clairvoyant powers myself, but I have been greatly helped and uplifted by Mr Pickersgill.'

'Mr Pickersgill?'

'Our wonderful leader at Otley Road Spiritualist Church. A most talented medium.'

'And Hugo?' I interposed quickly.

Hugo had just recklessly launched himself over the edge of my desk when Miss Rind shot out an arm that looked like a flamingo's leg and took the catch in mid-air.

'Hugo here became ill, like he is now, about two weeks ago,' continued the old lady placidly, as though nothing happened. 'Mr Pickersgill held a wonderful séance shortly after Hugo stopped eating, and that's when Mr Lawrence came through.'

'Came through?'

'He's on the other side now but still interested in animals—tortoises and things. He wrote so beautifully about tortoises when he was among us. "You draw your head forward, slowly, from your little wimple . . ." That's from his poem, "Baby Tortoise". Odd you've never read it, someone like you.'

I was losing the thread again. 'I'm sorry, Miss Rind, but I still don't understand.'

For the first time, the old lady smiled. 'No, of course,

Doctor. Anyway, Mr Pickersgill suddenly found that Mr Lawrence was coming through, trying to communicate a message. And it was for me. I'd spoken on previous occasions to my father and to a Red Indian chief called Fire Mountain, but here was a famous writer concerning himself with me!'

It was interesting, but I must get back to being a zoo vet. Again I said, 'And Hugo?'

'That's who the message was about. Mr Lawrence said he knew Hugo was ill, that his eyes were diseased and that there would be no difficulty in curing him if I anointed them with—and he was quite clear about the name—Balm of Micomicon.'

'I'm afraid I've never heard of the stuff,' I said.

Miss Rind sighed heavily and flapped her arms. 'Just what the vets and doctors and chemists in Harrogate and Leeds all say. They've never heard of it and have no suggestions to make. That's why I came to you, knowing you have so many reptiles under your care.'

'But perhaps the name's wrong, garbled. If it's not in the drug lists, maybe it doesn't exist, unless it's some obscure old herbal remedy.'

'Dr Taylor!' She stood up again. 'I hope you're not suggesting that one who's passed into the Greater Awareness would lie. Mr Lawrence was quite specific. What's more, we used the ouija board afterwards and it spelled out Balm of Micomicon for all to see!'

I fetched a dictionary. There was no mention of Micomicon or anything like it.

'I'm sorry,' I said finally. 'I can't help with this balm, but I do know what's wrong with the terrapin. An injection is needed. Eye drops and ointments aren't the way to treat what is in fact a general deficiency.'

There was a long silence. Miss Rind sat motionless with her eyes glued on the reptile in her lap. Bubbles of liquid came out of Hugo's nostrils. He looked as if he had a rotten head cold, but he was far sicker than that.

'I don't know what Mr Lawrence will say, nor how Mr Pickersgill will take it,' she murmured eventually. 'They were so adamant, and said nothing about injecting the little mite.'

'It would be wise, I can assure you. If you like, I'll make you up a balm to apply to his eyes. It's the best I can do. Not this Micomicon, of course, but something soothing.' Then, like a sycophantic prig, I heard myself add, 'Mr Lawrence might understand the substitution in the light of our failure to locate the precise thing he prescribed.' Lord, I'll be spouting ectoplasm before long, I thought.

That did it. The old lady nodded. I prepared an injection and mixed a little chloramphenicol cream with a teaspoonful of colloidal silver. I jabbed Hugo in his groin and showed his owner how to apply the quasi-Balm of Micomicon.

Then, with the terrapin back in her handbag, Miss Rind thanked me, said she would let me know how Mr Pickersgill and others took things, stuffed a ten-pound note in my top pocket and swept out to the limousine.

Ten days later there came a phone call from Harrogate. Hugo was fighting fit, eating again and no longer having trouble with his eyes. 'Mr Lawrence says he's very pleased with you, Doctor,' Miss Rind purred. 'He came through again last Sunday. He thought your concoction was an admirable second-best.'

I put the receiver down and had an interesting thought: maybe if I ever got to Heaven I could swap my harp for a microscope and syringe and find plenty of work as a zoo vet?

Cuddles, the corsair of the oceans with a computer for a brain and the lethal power of a wolf-pack submarine, was like a lamb, as gushily soft as a Liberace with water wings. Martin Padley and I and the others working in the dolphinarium knew that; the public did not. The very name, killer whale, the vague recollection of stories by polar explorers of how these creatures had lunged up onto ice floes in

192

pursuit of human prey, the way whaling fleets detested marauders who blatantly freebooted among the coveted blue and fin whale herds, memories of old seafarers who had seen the sea turn red as packs of the distinctively marked assassins slaughtered whole dolphin schools just for the hell of it; all this patchwork of myth and reminiscence and folk memory made a reputation for his kind of which Cuddles, as he basked in his pool with love in his heart and his belly full of prime herring, was quite unaware. He liked people and seemed to try to reach out mentally towards them. People got delicious goose-pimples as they looked down at him. They thrilled and admired and shrank back. There was a chasm of incomprehension between the whale in the water and the primates with smaller brains that gibbered on the pool-side.

Martin and I did not include ourselves among these landlubbers. With much delight and more than a touch of exhibitionism we continued to swim daily with the whale. The crowds thought us ever so daring. In fact, I had never felt safer. Not noted for intrepid acts of derring-do, a fair to middling swimmer only, and with a concern to preserve my own skin from the attentions of nature red in tooth and claw, I nevertheless felt at home with the whale from the very beginning. I had been frightened by horses that lashed out with both hind feet at the slightest touch—not to mention a mad onager—cornered by hysterical Alsatians that made me sweat, and forced to back down by bloody-minded alligators. But Cuddles I knew instinctively to be benevolent. It was in his eyes, the carefully measured pressure of his jaws on my hand or leg, the squeeze of his flippers round my trunk, his very presence, We had our lingua franca of squeaks and whistles. Like making love to a girl from Venus, it was the way things were said and done rather than the actual meaning of the words exchanged that mattered. Looking through the literature, I could find no authenticated cases where killer whales had been proved to attack humans. The polar explorers' story of the animals breaking a pathway through ice to reach them did not end in actual assault and was, I believe, more probably just sheer curiosity on the whales' part. Americans had already swum among schools of wild killers and come to no harm. Eskimo lore contained no hard evidence, only tales of hunters paddling their kayaks into a fog-bank, never to be seen again and presumed taken by one of the 'Lords of the Sea'.

Scientifically, we were convinced that unlike the dim-witted and primitive shark which will snap at anything, even its own entrails after being disembowelled, the highly sophisticated whale does not do anything without thinking first with fine precision. It is equipped with sonar that can not only judge ranges but identify the nature of objects with a precision far beyond the capabilities of man-made devices: in pitch-black water it can distinguish between one kind of fish and another and even read the emotions of another of its species by 'looking' into the skull sinuses to detect internal blushing. It has an intricate communications system that uses unjammable codes so far uncracked, and eyes that see well above and below the surface. It seizes only what it wants to seize, never attacks blindly. And whereas it counts dolphins, seals, walruses, fish, diving birds, jellyfish, squid and, no doubt, ships as familiar inhabitants of its environment to be eaten, hunted, ignored or avoided in the natural order of things, free-swimming, awkward humans are outsiders, objects merely of curiosity and of less significance than a clump of floating seaweed. Killer whales do not waste time on seaweed, so we romped with Cuddles in the water during his first year without qualms. My own children did it. Nude model girls did it. The whale treated each and every playmate considerately and benignly.

I had overlooked one very important fact. Bright as they are, killer whales are not omniscient. Wise in the ways of the deep waters, of hurricanes that madden the breakers above and of the fire-jewelled shrimps that troll the abyss below, they know nothing of fellow mammals who stayed on land when they, aeons ago, went back to the seas. They assume that creatures plying their trade in the ocean can survive in a liquid world. Watching, touching, tasting me, Cuddles must have assumed too much. I imagine he was amused by my inelegant paddling around and impressed by the way in which so clumsy a beast could evidently hunt. This flailing pink ape had a knack of somehow coming up with an inexhaustible supply of fast-running fish like herring and mackerel. In my bathing trunks I showed no sign of possessing much in the way of weapons and my feet seemed very inferior to flippers and flukes. Still, the proof of the pudding was in the eating, and I appeared good at catching fish.

The crunch came when Cuddles assumed that I was good at something else. Killers can hold their breath underwater for more than a quarter of an hour. While it is true that a man has stayed under without special gear for $13\frac{3}{4}$ minutes, most homo sapiens, including pearl divers, have a far lower limit of endurance. Cuddles could not be expected to know such statistics when we began a new game one rainy morning in late summer after I had dived into his pool for our regular daily mixture of fun and veterinary checks while Martin and his trainers prepared the whale's food downstairs in the fish kitchen.

It all developed out of something we had enjoyed many times before. Cuddles would push me round his pool with the point of his snout stuck in my navel. I was expected to tickle his throat with my toes as he propelled me backwards through the water. Sometimes he would angle me down a bit and we would take a quick swoop towards the pool bottom, then up he would soar, balancing me perfectly as I crashed through the surface in a welter of foam. This morning Cuddles decided on a further variation. He would push me as usual, then he would stop abruptly. I quickly caught on that I was supposed to flounder away, escape him even, and when I was a few yards off he would come after me and gently pick me up once more on the tip of his snout. It was a sort of tag. Cuddles enjoyed the competitive aspect of the new game immensely. He would roll slightly to one side and, with one syrupy eye held well above the water, watch me make off. There was the glint of an excited puppy in the eye.

I did quite well and on the odd occasion almost managed to sideslip when he took up the pursuit, which is not to be sniffed at when you realise that killers can turn on a sixpence and use their great tail-flukes to brake to a dead halt from sixty miles per hour in a second. I tried rolling under him; that worked quite often. The pink ape was learning. Cuddles thought it was all a marvellous wheeze but unlike a dog or cat, that will repeatedly make the same error at ball-games where humans are involved such as 'pig-in-the-middle', Cuddles used his vast expanse of grey matter to neutralise my evasion tactics. He began to come in twisting like a snake so that I could not see him for foam, or climbing up like a fighter plane to intercept me at my blind spot, below and behind. Always his final attack was gentle; I felt the round, warm smoothness of his muzzle press into me and I knew I had been caught again.

Next I tried deflecting his muzzle at the last moment rugby-style by pushing him off with a hand so that he cruised by me. Full marks to me. That, and a kick back with one foot pressed against his side, and I was away. Cuddles squealed contentedly and turned to follow me. I raised a hand to deflect him again. Before my fingers could touch him, he stopped dead, sank vertically a few inches and zoomed in for my stomach. With consummate ease he made contact, and to secure his hold dived slowly at a shallow angle. Holding my breath I went down, expecting any second to be taken up to the surface as usual for the next round.

But no. With a soft thwack, my back was flattened against the wall of the pool. Not painfully—Cuddles was far too careful with folk to act roughly, even in the heat of a good game. He simply pressed me against the concrete. I could almost hear him clicking through the water, 'Now, old friend, gotcha! Get out of this one if you can!' All of which was fine, good, clean, healthy fun—except that we were four feet under water. He could hold his breath for fifteen minutes and I knew it. I might manage no more than two at a pinch, and he did *not* know it.

I pushed. Cuddles increased the pressure just enough by the minutest vibration of his tail fluke. I wriggled, tried to squeeze sideways, thumped on his fat-filled forehead. Cuddles did just enough to make sure I was fixed. My wriggles and thumps no doubt showed how much I was enjoying myself. Cuddles liked being thumped.

Fear swept through me. My lungs were ready to explode. I must breathe, even if it was only one last inhalation of sparkling blue water. I remember the resentment I felt at dying accidentally, the ridiculousness of it all. It seemed absurd to be drowning in fun instead of dying in a rational, professional manner under the fury of a badly tranquillised polar bear, lanced unexpectedly by an oryx or even from some virus picked up at an autopsy. As my fear turned to terror and my resentment to despair, Cuddles remained motionless but transfixing me as surely as a pin holds a butterfly in its glass case.

The haze of green and blue, the dancing white bubbles, the black fuzz of the whale's head were beginning to spin when I heard through the rising roar in my ears a far-off whistle. Instantly the pressure on my stomach disappeared and I felt my hair grabbed and pulled painfully. The next moment my head was above water and I was pulling in chest-fulls of precious air. Martin was kneeling on the pool-side, holding me up by my hair while the rest of me dangled like a string of frog-spawn. Cuddles was floating a few feet away with his mouth open and his eyes fixed on the gleaming bucket by Martin's side. By good fortune the head trainer had come up with the first fish of the day at exactly the right moment. He had taken in the situation immediately and blown his whistle to give the 'come and get it' signal to the whale, who had at once left our deadly game and gone to breakfast.

Martin helped me out. When I had got my nerves under control I issued an instruction that no-one was to swim alone with Cuddles ever again. Killers may not attack human beings but I knew now how easily they could kill accidentally.

Things were never the same again. Children and model girls were no longer invited to have a dip with the genial giant. When we went in, there was always someone on the side with a whistle and a bucket of fish, just in case. About that time we found out that some of the American marinelands always had a baseball bat on hand when their killers were being ridden. They did not like talking about it, but it was plain that other folk had had their doubts about the safety of these whales.

Before long it was Martin's turn to revise his ideas about our cuddly Cuddles. 'I can't put my finger on it,' he said to me one day after a session swimming with the whale, 'but I don't feel as secure with him any more.'

We discussed it, but could not arrive at any precise reason for his apprehension. Perhaps it was Martin's knowledge of my experience. Certainly Cuddles was playing games with greater gusto than ever, but he was still good-natured and cheerful all day long.

Then Cuddles developed a fetish for rubber flippers. First he started refusing to release the grip of his teeth on the black, webbed footwear of a diver in his pool. Quickly this worsened to the point where he was obsessed with the things and, with a jerk of his head, would wrench the flipper off the wearer's foot. A pink and white unclad human foot, complete with toes, was of no interest; Cuddles was just kinky about frogman's gear. His pursuit of a man wearing the flippers became doubly keen to the point where he would surge up and snatch them off as the swimmer scrambled over the pool edge. The first Achilles tendon sprains appeared. Martin's fears deepened, but we decided to continue swimming with the whale whenever necessary for veterinary inspections and for cleaning and maintaining the pool.

The next stage was more serious. Like an underwater commando, Cuddles would neatly break the air-pipe of a diver's scuba gear, forcing him to surface rapidly. The latter was not so easy if the attack then turned, as usual, to the flippers. We stopped the use of scuba gear unless absolutely essential and made do with masks and snorkels. Cuddles soon found he could rip the masks off, breaking the rubber retaining bands with ease.

Finally, Martin walked dripping into my office with his wet-suit in tatters. There were blue weals on his skin below long tears that had shredded the rubber in half a dozen places. He looked pale and grim.

'I went in to seal a leaking window,' he said, shivering. 'Cuddles came up like an express train and tried to rip my suit off. His teeth bruised me for the first time. I can tell you, I was bloody scared.'

So our salad days were over and swimming with Cuddles came to an end. On special occasions when we had to go into the water, we wore bathing trunks and hung protective nylon netting between us and him. I believe that the wet-suits were the key to the problem. In them men became sealions. Sleek and shiny, with a changed outline and a different, more facile movement through the water, maybe these mermen awakened memories in Cuddles' subconscious of those fin-footed creatures like seals which, while of the ocean, have not totally forsaken their ancient home on land and which, while able to dart like arrows through the dark water, are not able to out-think or out-manoeuvre the killers who find them such tasty morsels.

Thirteen

Once the busy spring and summer holiday periods at Flamingo Park were over, I decided to go on one of what I called my 'walkabouts'—a wander around places abroad where things of zoological interest were to be found. Increasingly, I was combining pleasure, work and study in such a tour: my list of clients overseas was growing, and most of them were in places like the Côte d'Azur, the Spanish coasts, Switzerland or the German Rhineland. In such places blood samples, vaccinations and hysterectomies could be neatly blended with sunshine, sea, old cities or mountain villages. After the wrestling with gorillas or gnus came the opportunity for wines of Rüdesheim or Cariñena, for fruits de mer, chorizo or rum topf. A good example was, and still is, my association with the river Rhine. I could not get away from the charms of the greatest of all Europe's rivers, and on its banks from its sources in the Swiss mountains, down through southern and then northern Germany to where it reaches the sea in Holland, I found myself dealing with all sorts of exotic creatures and getting the chance to taste the variety of cultural styles through which the dark water runs.

At its head, near the Bodensee, there was a tiny hamlet, just a church, a post office, an inn and a farmhouse. In a quiet meadow behind the farmhouse was an old wooden barn, the inside of which had been converted by a travelling flipper show into a miniature dolphinarium, the winter quarters for a bunch of porpoises under my care. Visits there meant staying in the most cosy yet sumptuous hotel rooms I have ever seen, at the Drachenburg in Gottlieben, with wild boar and morels for dinner, with excellent Swiss wine, and afterwards riotous dancing with the Yodelling Club, a form of music that elsewhere I utterly detest.

Further on, where the quiet Alpine stream has become broad and busy with barges, the Rhine passes by the vineyards and orchards of the German Pfalz region. Beyond the woods and farmland that surround the ancient four-towered cathedral at Speyer is a holiday park with more very un-German animals—sealions, flamingoes and chimpanzees. After sunset, with my patients settled down for the night, my samples labelled and my instruments cleaned, here I could sit in the scented air beneath lime trees, drinking cold golden beer and watching the inn-keeper roasting his kasseler, smoked loin of pork.

More dolphins were to be found near the Rhine at Bonn, and at Duisburg is the zoo with another sort of marine animal that was on my list of patients, a beluga whale. There was always time after emergencies had passed to walk round Cologne Cathedral, sample hot wurst from kerbside stalls and rubberneck around the Eros Centres.

On its last miles, slipping strong, flat and oily by Dutch water meadows, the Rhine passes close to the gates of Rhenen Zoo, where I actually watched for the first time a baby hippopotamus being born, and where an eland antelope bull I was treating fatally impaled its keeper on its horns in one terrifying, unexpected sweep of its head. In winter, when all the animals had been checked at one of my routine visits, Henni Ouwehands, the director's wife, would warm us with steaming plates of boerenkool-met-wurst. In summer I tried to make my visits to Rhenen coincide with the town's street market, where green herrings and onions were sold. The succulent slivers of raw fish were washed down by cold Genever gin and Amstel beer and the evenings spent at the shooting club in Wageningen.

I was not finished with the river until it actually swirled

under the keels of ocean-going vessels in Rotterdam. Even there, dolphins from Florida swam in a floating dolphinarium made from four converted Dutch barges and moored to the quayside. Rotterdam meant Indonesian rijstafel and gossip in harbour bars, with salt in my hair and lanolin under my fingernails after unloading and checking a couple of new arrivals.

One way and another the Rhine is a very zoological sort of waterway for me, but on this particular 'walkabout' I decided to go far away from the Rhine, up to the edge of the quite Teutoburger forests of Westphalia. I would have a look at the animals in a safari park on the edge of Bielefeld, which oddly enough is Rochdale's twin town. There the Wurms family had cleared a vast area of pine trees on the sandy soil of a village named Stukenbrock and turned it into a place where lions, tigers, elephants, antelopes and ostriches roamed. There were the usual gastronomic and other attractions: the district teems with trout farms and little gasthofs that serve the fish fresh in a dozen different ways, and it is an easy drive to places like the famous Hamelin, with the church whose carillon and moving figures I find eerily compelling, or Karlshafen, where the carp in the river chomp with audible, lip-smacking noises at bread thrown to them by folk like me. Nothing in the world is more satisfying than watching a hungry animal obviously enjoying its food.

It was a typical early autumn evening as I drove up to Stukenbrock. Flags of grey mist were hanging from the trees, and the road through the forest glistened with sticky condensation. The visitors had all gone. In the lowering gloom I could just make out the upper halves of yaks and Watusi cattle standing silently, black, featureless torsoes floating on a sea of eddying vapour. Fritz Wurms, the director, whom I had never met before, invited me to his office for a glass of schnapps. By the time we came out it was fully dark. The mist had turned into a dense fog that was biting cold.

'The new tigers should be all bedded down by now,' said

202

Wurms. 'Come and look at them. We have the finest tiger sleeping-quarters in Germany.'

With the director leading the way we set off on foot into the foggy night. I was walking in a cloud of eye-stinging mist. The torch held by my companion cut a narrow beam in front of him for a yard or so and then was swallowed by the fog. I could see my knees if I looked down, but my feet were invisible. Fortunately Herr Wurms knew his way. We went through a wooden gate and began to trudge across a flat expanse of what felt like grassland. From time to time I would wrench my ankle in a rabbit hole bored into the sandy soil.

'We're in the main reserve,' my companion told me. 'We'll have to watch out for the lake-side. Careful with the tree trunks.'

He told me that after hundreds of trees had been cleared for the safari park, their stumps had been left projecting a few inches above ground level. It was like stumbling through a minefield. Unable to see the low obstructions, we advanced cautiously.

'What animals are out at night in this reserve?' I asked, stubbing my toe and staggering awkwardly as my feet found my first stump.

'Oh, yak, Watusi, ostrich, zebra. Nothing troublesome.'

We plodded on. I heard the dull thud of hooved feet nearby. The dark mist billowed and something snorted its way past me. I could smell animal. Was it a yak, or a sweating zebra? I could not tell. Wurms' feeble torch beam lit for an instant on a dark flank of hair. It quickly dissolved into dripping wreaths of black cloud. 'Watusi bull,' said the director. He was right. I felt my foot sink into a warm pile of sour-smelling droppings.

'A bit to the left here and we should be at the gate to the tiger reserve.' Wurms stopped and fumbled in his pocket. In the light of his torch I saw he held a small walkie-talkie. He spoke into the transmitter. 'Hallo, hallo. Ulli, bitte melden—please report. Are all big cats in compound?'

The walkie-talkie crackled and a voice confirmed that the lions and tigers had been called in for their dinner of cooked tripes. Reluctant diners are rounded up by rangers in Land Rovers. I wondered how they would have fared, chasing lions and tigers in this pea-souper of an evening.

'Good. Ulli says we can go into the reserve.' Wurms put the walkie-talkie back into his pocket and pulled out another device. It was a box the size of a cigarette packet bearing two buttons, one red and one green. He pressed the red button and I heard a humming noise. Flicking up the beam of light, the director picked out the steel gate of the tiger reserve. It was opening after receiving a signal from his remote control device. As soon as we had moved through, Wurms pressed the green button on his box and the gate began to close behind us. After a couple of steps we were once more cocooned in dank and chilly steam. I could smell cat now. The acrid stink of tiger excrement and urine hung in the clinging vapour all around us.

'Only a hundred metres to go,' came the voice from in front. Any moment now and the torchlight should give way to the glow from the big cats' warm and well-lit night-houses.

Wurms walked carefully on, swinging the light beam from side to side to avoid stepping into a drinking pond. I stuck close behind him. All at once he stiffened and stopped dead in his tracks. I blundered into him and very nearly brought us both down.

'Scheisse, look at that,' he hissed.

I looked down the short beam of milky light. It ended in two shimmering orange discs. That was all—two glowing coins, newly minted from red gold, were suspended on invisible strings. They hung steadily in the coiling mist. Beyond them was impenetrable darkness. There was no doubt what they were. They were the clever, light-reflecting, starlight-gathering devices that nature invented millions of years before human snipers were equipped with night-sights and image-intensifiers. They were the layers of scintillating cells behind the retinas of the eyes of certain animals. Such as tigers.

'It's a tiger,' I whispered lamely. I was astounded to find myself smiling. This was ridiculous. Even in horror films they did not come up with scenarios as bizarre as this: two unarmed fellows on foot in the fog, finding themselves face to face with a tiger. It was like a horrible mismating between a Victorian gaslight melodrama and *The Jungle Book*. Except it was really happening.

'Hold the torch just as it is, straight in the eyes,' Wurms said without turning his head. 'I'll call that verdammte Ulli again.'

Carefully I took over the torch. I looked at the unblinking eyes. I tried to distinguish other features, nose, ears, whiskers, but they were invisible. Somewhere I had read that attacks from big cats are not particularly agonising, the damage is so severe and shock numbs sensation so quickly. But could anyone be sure? What were those reports of humans who had survived attacks? Was Cecil Rhodes one? Or was it Teddy Roosevelt? At that moment these seemed the most important things in the world to remember. My mind shuffled thoughts frenziedly.

Then Wurms' voice was rasping into the transmitter. 'Ulli, du Idiot! How many tigers did you count in, man?'

There was silence for a while and then I heard Ulli's voice, worried, explaining, excusing. Ulli was feeling as bad if not worse than we did at that moment. There were numbers I recognised: 'Zehn . . . neun . . . nebel (the word for mist) . . . schwer' (difficult).

'Come on,' I said aloud. 'The fellow's going to talk us into our graves if he goes on any longer.'

'It's Rajah, a male, one of the most dangerous,' Wurms whispered presently. 'Let's start moving towards the house but keeping the light in his eyes. Go carefully sideways'.

We began to edge away. The gold coins remained hung on

the end of the torch beam. When we had travelled seven or eight paces they had not dimmed or changed their size.

'He's coming with us,' said my companion.

'And he's not had a meal since yesterday.'

'Worse than that, I'm afraid. Yesterday was the weekly fasting day. He's not had a bite for almost forty-eight hours.'

My stomach went into intricate contortions.

I had always enjoyed talking to tigers. It does not matter if you have not been formally introduced or never met before; just make a lip-flapping imitation of a tiger purr and nine times out of ten the animals will answer back with friendly civility. I tried it: 'Prr-prr-pch, prr-prr-pch.' It sounded louder than usual and echoed faintly in the oppressive fog. No answering purr or chirrup. I tried again. The gleaming eyes were still there but not a sound came in reply. To my dismay I saw that the light beam was now no longer white but a feebler yellow and did not reach into the gloom as far as before.

We continued in a nervous, slow-motion pirouette. Somewhere in the gloom there was the sound of an engine starting up. Ulli was coming to get us. A minute more, his headlights would cut through to us and we would be OK.

Wurms stopped suddenly again. 'Dr Taylor, with all this turning in the fog I've lost my bearings. I'm afraid I can't be sure we're still going towards the night-house. We'd better go in a straight line and try to make for one of the fences.'

I was cold and frightened. The thick water vapour was searing my lungs. I cursed my decision to go walkabout. Next time, blockhead, I said to myself, an end-of-season laze-around at Reid's Hotel, Madeira—if you get out of this.

The torch battery was definitely on its last legs. The light began to flicker. Suddenly the tiger eyes vanished.

'He's gone,' I whispered. My tongue was dry and made speaking difficult.

The German must have been holding his breath, for he

exhaled explosively between clenched teeth. 'Stand back to back,' he muttered. 'Let's wait for Ulli.'

There was the sound of a revving motor and the harsh grind of gears off to our right. It was difficult to judge the distance. Wurms waved the torch and spat some words into the walkie-talkie. The engine noise became distinctly louder. I strained to see the first glow of the lights. 'Come on, Ulli,' I prayed. Wurms began to shout at the top of his voice, 'Over here, here, here, here!'

Somewhere in the spongy darkness a tiger, lord of the jungle, crouched listening. The sweat of man-fear permeated the dripping darkness. The tiger's sensitive nose was at that moment telling him loud and clear that the two humans were terrified, and with a puny, two-legged, ill-defended scrap of a beast like the human being, terror meant that the battle was half won. But did the great cat want to do battle? The one thing on our side was that tigers are as unaccustomed to hunting in dense fog as we are. Still, I could not forget what Wurms had said about yesterday having been fasting day.

Suddenly there was a thunderous crash. It was followed by some yelling and the frantic revving of an engine to screaming pitch. There was the roar of spinning tyres and then silence. The walkie-talkie crackled with voices. Ulli had gone over the edge of one of the drinking pools. He was stuck, with the Land Rover's exhaust pipe submerged.

Contrary to what is written in books and films in the English language, annoyed and exasperated Germans at moments of crisis do not say 'Gott in Himmel!', 'Schweinhund!' or even 'Donner und Blitzen!' What Herr Wurms uttered as he fired the unfortunate Ulli by walkie-talkie was unprinted and unprintable.

All we could do was to go on again in a straight line, hoping to find a wire fence sooner or later.

Every sense alert, we linked arms and began the twisting, turning, laboriously slow dance. The torch penetrated only a foot or two by now but it was our best hope of locating the tiger eyes should they re-appear. Our complicated footwork made keeping a straight course extremely difficult. After what seemed like half an hour but could have been only minutes, we were relieved to find ourselves with our noses up against the wire fence. Then we realised its mesh was too small to provide footholds.

'Shall we walk round the fence until we come to a gate?' I asked.

'I'm not sure where we are, and the length of fencing in this reserve is as much as three hundred metres between gates. We're perhaps more likely to meet the tiger near the fence, too.'

As in most big cat compounds, the tigers liked to pace the boundaries of their territory. There was a well-beaten track just inside the fencing. No doubt every few yards there would be invisible 'markers', where the animals had sprayed urine to lay claim to their patch.

'What shall we do, then?' I was shivering more than ever.

'Try to get over the top, Doctor,' said Wurms. 'Stand on my shoulders. With your height, maybe you can reach the top and scramble over. Find one of my men and tell him to fetch Poludniak, the curator, and to make sure Poludniak brings the guns.'

He clasped his hands into a stirrup and I climbed onto his broad shoulders. Taking a hold on the wire mesh and unceremoniously putting all my weight on one foot planted on his head, I strained to reach the top of the fence. I was feeling around blindly. Jagged twists of wire cut my hands. Then my heart sank; the top twelve inches of fencing was angled inwards. A baboon might have got over it with ease but I had no chance. I thudded back down onto the ground beside Wurms.

At that moment there was a shout from nearby and a dark shape loomed up out of the fog on the other side of the wire. 'Herr Wurms, Herr Doktor!' called the shadowy figure.

'It's Poludniak. He's found us.' Wurms gave a relieved

208

laugh. 'Over here, Poludniak,' he called. 'Got the guns? Good man.'

The curator levered open a gap in the wire with the steel barrels of one of the two shotguns he was carrying and pushed both weapons through. Things were improving. We were armed, although with the fog as dense as ever we might not get a chance to pull the trigger in self-defence.

'Hold on a moment,' I said. 'It still isn't safe to walk towards the gate. How far is the nearest one, Herr Poludniak?'

'150 metres, I reckon.'

'That tiger could be anywhere and on us without warning. Get back to the drug cabinet as quick as you can and fetch a bottle of ammonia and two 20-cc syringes.'

The curator disappeared at once.

'Let's stand back to back and keep moving the torch around,' I said.

Twelve-bores at the ready with their safety catches off, we must have looked, if only we had not been shrouded in fog, like Custer's Last Stand. The first barrel contained a blank charge. The second held a lethal cluster of elephant-shot. One flash of a golden eye and I was ready to let fly. Apart from destroying dogs when I was a student with the bloody, ear-shattering but humane captive-bolt pistol, I have never shot any sort of animal in my life. Clutching the shotgun and seeing phantoms swirling in the mist, my dislike of firearms was as strong as ever.

Poludniak lumbered up out of the cloud. He passed a bottle and two syringes through the wire.

'Now we are safe, Herr Wurms,' I said, as I filled the syringes with the pungent ammonia. 'We take one syringe each and spray a little of the liquid around us as we move towards the gate. No tiger will come through ammonia vapour.'

We began to spray and walk along the fence line. The chemical hung in the thick air and caught our breaths. We coughed but kept moving. If it was irritating our nostrils six feet up, it would be even more obnoxious and repellent to anything stalking us closer to the ground. Matt Kelly at Belle Vue had introduced me to the defensive uses of ammonia when in a tight spot—only orang-utans would keep coming through showers of the stuff.

The torch battery gave up the ghost just as we reached the gate. One final burst of ammonia, a press of the button on the director's remote control box and we were out. As the gate clanked to behind us, I leaned up against the fence and laughed with relief until my ribs ached. The tension drained away and my legs felt like soft rubber.

All at once a piercing pain shot through my backside. I yelled, fell away from the fence and crashed to the ground. The curator shone his torch on my offended rear parts. There was a V-shaped tear in the seat of my pants and blood was welling out. 'Was ist?' gasped Wurms, and swung the light onto the fence.

There, wreathed in smoky haze, was the tiger, one paw pressed hard against the wire and each scimitar-shaped claw extended and glistening white. He had got me after all—just.

Next morning the telephone rang early in my hotel. I had not finished with the Stukenbrock tigers, it seemed. One of them was apparently choking on a lump of meat; would I go round at once. I jumped into my hired car. This walkabout was becoming anything but a relaxed toddle round Europe's beauty spots. And my bum was sore.

Back at the safari park I found everyone in the tiger house gathered round a year-old tiger that was obviously in serious trouble. It was fighting for air, heaving desperately with its mouth agape. Its gums and tongue were a delicate and sinister violet shade. Despite its frantic efforts to breathe, only a faint squeak came from its throat.

'It must be a chunk of the tripe from last night. You can feel it in the throat, Doctor.' The tiger was too agonised to object as Wurms poked a finger at a lump in its neck.

I dropped to my knees and examined the animal's throat. As so often happens, the 'lump' was the perfectly normal Adam's apple or larynx. The tiger did not care as I thrust my fingers down its throat and probed rapidly round his tonsils and epiglottis. I ran a hand down its neck. Nothing. I could find no evidence of an obstructing foreign body. The larynx was not swollen. Maybe something was lodged well down in the windpipe. I decided to do a tracheotomy straight away. There was no time for skin-shaving, asepsis or carefully balanced anaesthesia.

'Get the oxygen from your welding equipment in the workshop,' I ordered. 'I'm going to open the windpipe.'

I reached in my bag for a scalpel. No time to sterilise it. Fixing the gristly cartilage rings of the trachea with two fingers, I stabbed a hole low down in the centre of the underneath surface of the neck. The tiger was groaning and completely oblivious to me. I twisted the scalpel blade in the incision to open up the hole in the windpipe. Bubbles of froth emerged but the tiger's breathing did not ease noticeably. I needed a tube to keep the hole open. Grabbing a 2-cc plastic hypodermic, I sliced off the front half with my blade. That would fit nicely and the plastic finger grips should stop it slipping completely into the trachea. As I started to insert the tube into the hole in the neck, the tiger gave a strangled cry that sent shudders through me. It stopped breathing. I pumped its chest furiously, massaged its heart, got three men to hold it vertically by the hind legs and swing it, jabbed a shot of theophylline into its tongue vein. When the oxygen cylinder arrived I stuck the welding head down the end of the improvised tracheotomy tube and turned the tap on gently. Nothing worked. I felt the pulse in the animal's groin fade, flicker and finally become imperceptible. The tiger was dead.

'I'll do an autopsy at once,' I said. 'Let's have him in the hospital.'

There is something troubling about doing a post-mortem on a newly dead animal. The body is warm, fresh and vital. Muscles still flicker. Cells still truly live. What is the dividing line between life and death? I sometimes feel like an intruder irreverently rooting round the remains where dignity still lingers. Yet in cases like this, and indeed in post-mortem work in general, the fresher the material the more the knowledge that can be obtained.

No piece of tripe was jammed in the windpipe. The body was that of a plump adolescent tiger in first-class condition, except that the cause of death was as plain as a pikestaff. The animal had literally drowned. Every nook and cranny of both lungs was filled with water.

'Drowned? But how? In his sleeping place with a small automatic water bowl on the wall?' Herr Wurms looked incredulous.

Drowned the tiger certainly had, but not in water from outside. Somehow it had produced the water itself. It had seeped rapidly and in vast quantities out of the lungs' blood vessels and had filled up the essential air spaces.

There was no sign of inflammation, no pneumonia, and indeed the whole course of the tiger's suffering had been witnessed and seemed too rapid for infection of any sort that was known to occur in cats. The keeper cleaning the house early in the morning had actually seen the animal begin to behave strangely, to breathe heavily and finally to collapse, fighting for air. The entire course of the attack before I arrived was no more than thirty minutes. I was mystified. I went with Wurms and Poludniak back to the tiger house to check on the others. Surely, I thought to myself, this must be a one-off, sudden dropsy of the lung caused by allergy, as can happen when sensitive folk are stung by bees. Allergic reactions are often extremely speedy; I was to find this out when a year later I unaccountably became sensitive to zebra and horse blood and nearly got jammed inside a zebra's womb when foaling it. My arm swelled up as if inflated by air.

If, as seemed likely, the tiger was an odd case of allergy, the others would not be at risk. No doubt it was something in the cooked tripes that had triggered off the trouble. It was odd, though, that it should happen this morning when the last feed had been the night before.

The three of us walked slowly up and down the passage-way in front of the tiger cages. It is a fine building with perfect heating, ventilation and lighting. Each tiger has a comfortable bedroom, fitted with all 'mod cons' including a soft straw mattress. I had slept myself in worse places in Spain and the Far East.

'Everything looks OK with these others,' I said as the big cats yawned and stretched at the beginning of another day. 'Prr-prr-pch,' I went.

'Prr-prr-pch,' responded each tiger, including a sleepy-looking Rajah, who after frightening the life out of us the previous evening had eventually been lured by hunger into the night-house.

'Allergy', I declared confidently. 'Something in the food or possibly the straw. We'll do microscopic tests of course, but I don't think there's any likelihood of a recurrence.'

We walked towards the door. Just then I heard a soft noise. It was a faint, hoarse wheeze and it was repeated regularly. I looked round. A magnificent young female stood looking at me from behind the bars. Each time she breathed out she made the noise.

'Prr-prr-pch,' I purred. The tigress blinked at me calmly but did not answer.

'She's eating fine. No problem,' Wurms told me. 'Maybe she's always been a little thick in the wind and we've not noticed it.'

It was certainly nothing very dramatic. Perhaps I was wrong. But . . .

'I tell you what,' I said. 'Get a pole or something and chase her about in the cage. I don't like to do it. Just enough to make her move.'

Poludniak got a brush handle and poked it through the bars. He rattled it against the metal and waved it up and down. Annoyed, the tigress snarled and ran up and down at the back of her cage, well out of reach.

'Good. Now stop,' I said after a minute. 'Let her settle again.' I wanted to see what effect the slight exertion, running perhaps a hundred yards, had had on the cat's breathing.

Poludniak withdrew his brush handle and we watched. The tigress slumped onto the straw as if exhausted. Ribs heaving, mouth dribbling foam and tongue protruding, she puffed and panted like a chronic asthmatic. We were stunned. The faint hoarseness was now a bubbling, rasping torrent of sound.

Within five minutes the tigress was dead. Once again the lungs were bursting with water.

The whole complexion of things had changed. I considered the possibility that we were faced with some new form of virus, perhaps a vicious mutant of the bug that causes influenza in domestic cats. I prepared for the worst.

'A twenty-four hour watch on the animals. The welding oxygen to be kept in the house. Change the food and the bedding. Shoot all stray cats that are found scavenging for food round the park,' were my orders.

For hours on end, Wurms and I walked along the line of cages, listening intently for the first signs of hoarseness. We were not long in finding number three; again it was a healthy-looking one-year-old. As its breathing worsened, number four appeared: Rajah. I injected all the cats with anti-allergic drugs, but unfortunately it had to be done by dart-pistol, which excited the beasts and did not help their respiration. Numbers five and six were revealed by the darting process. Within twenty-four hours I had seven gasping, groaning tigers on my hands. Only an undersized runt of a cub, the weakest of the bunch which had been retarded in its growth by bowel trouble months before, and all the lions were unaffected. Antibiotics did not appear to make any inroads into the disease, but if it was a virus that was to be expected.

By dashing up and down with the oxygen we managed to keep the air-hungry creatures alive, but there was no sign of improvement and the strain on the animals' hearts was becoming severe. I wracked my brains. Why not the lions? Although in a separate house, they had been given the same food of tripes. There was nothing else with which the cats had come into contact, except the bedding and the reserve outside. Could it really be a virus that selected only tigers? I wandered over the grass and round the tree-stumps, now warmed by autumn sunshine. There were rabbit droppings, pine cones, mosses—all manner of objects that conceivably could cause allergy, but nothing that I saw was a serious possibility. Anyway, the lion reserve was identical.

I turned my attention to the bedding. 'Where does the straw come from?' I asked the director as I filled a batch of syringes with cortisone to see whether this potent drug could reverse the deadly accumulation of water in the tigers' lungs.

'A local farm, Müllers. It's stored in our barn in bales.'

I tackled the keeper who bedded the tigers down. 'Show me exactly what you do when you put new straw down for the tigers each night,' I asked, 'right from the beginning.'

He showed me the neat stacks of bales in the barn. 'I take two of these each afternoon, load them on the cart and make up the tigers' beds with them before the animals come in in the evening.'

'And the lion keeper does the same?'

'Yes. We both use the same bales.'

'On the night before all this began you did nothing different?'

'No, I don't think so. I took my two bales from down there.'

I walked over to where he pointed. There was a pool of water on the barn floor where a broken roof panel had let rain in, and a few bales at the bottom of the stack had soaked up the moisture. Bending down, I saw that they were becoming mouldy.

'You might have picked up a bottom bale, then?' I asked the tiger keeper.

'Very possibly. As long as it was dry I didn't mind a bit of mould; tigers don't eat straw.'

Light was beginning to dawn. I went to the lion keeper and questioned him. Yes, he knew the damp spot in the barn. He had never drawn bales from there. The old straw from the beginning of the outbreak was now all steaming away on the manure heap and there was no point in rooting about in that. But no matter how I looked at things, the only significant difference between the tigers and the lions was the bedding quality. This must indeed be a rare outbreak of allergy to mould fungus spores, an acute form of a disease that in humans is called Farmer's Lung. The tigers were drowning because of musty bedding. Why the retarded tiger remained unaffected we shall never know.

The cortisone injections produced a perceptible improvement, but the tiger house remained a grim place full of loud wheezes, hoarse rattles and tortured breathing. Much more cortisone, and the animals' ability to fight off penumonia germs might be affected. Before long the bacteria would be joining in on the act. What I needed was a drug that acted similarly to cortisone in some ways but did not reduce the body's resistance. There was one available—phenylbutazone, a preparation normally used in treating rheumatism and arthritis in old humans and show-jumping horses. What its effect on drowning tigers would be I had no idea. I decided to try it anyway, darting small doses of the chemical into the seven tigers' rumps.

It was not turning out much of a fun trip to Stockenbrock: I had not worked so hard for years. But with the phenyl-butazone injected, there was nothing to do but sweat it out over beer and frankfurters.

Two hours after the injections, the tiger keeper came into the restaurant where I sat with the director to say that the animals were looking distinctly easier. We went over immediately. It was true. The tigers were more relaxed, breathing less laboriously and even sniffing at their food trays.

Next day there was no doubt. The tigers were all on the mend. Everyone was still breathing hard but there were no more groans. Dishes had been licked clean and I was given the odd 'Prr-prr-pch'.

Progress continued dramatically, and at the end of a week I was able to leave seven bouncing tigers behind and drive down to Dusseldorf for the plane back to England. The tigers, or at least old Rajah, had left me a souvenir, but I had been too preoccupied to worry about my clawed posterior. Now, inspecting the wound awkwardly in a Viscount washroom while flying to Manchester, I discovered that it had gone septic.

'Physician, heal thyself,' said Shelagh, laughing as she swabbed the claw-hole and I knelt, trouserless, in an undignified position on the bathroom floor.

Fourteen

The following summer was exceptionally busy. It was the height of the craze to open safari parks, following the lead of places like Woburn and Longleat. Every duke, earl or impoverished fellow who fancied he had a teaspoonful of blue blood in his veins, and who was certain of the jaundiced tinge to the Inland Revenue inspector's eye whenever the stately pile cropped up in conversation, was scattering lions and giraffes around the Nash terraces and along the rose-walks. Capability Brown was turning in his grave and being dug up to make room for dolphin pools.

The safari parks undoubtedly saved a number of aristocratic residences from having to be taken over by the National Trust and contributed a great deal to our knowledge of keeping wild animals in captivity. Jimmy Chipperfield showed at Longleat, Woburn and elsewhere that properly acclimatised tropical mammals, with their built-in heat-regulating systems, could prosper in the depths of an English winter without fancy heated housing. Town folk got a taste of the African bush without driving far from London or Liverpool. Species such as the cheetah, notoriously difficult to breed in traditional zoos, began to reproduce at an increasing rate.

There were problems, however. The wide open, grassy spaces of the parks, with an abundance of food lying around, encouraged rodents and other pests to move in, join the fun and import troublesome diseases. Parasites thrived comfortably in the semi-natural terrain. Animals were not as easily inspected and handled as in the closer confines of a zoo.

Not all of the problems were purely veterinary ones. The controlling of social groups of creatures like lions, zebras and baboons in extensive parkland presented many challenges for the pioneers. I found myself one of those pioneers when, through my connections with the Smart circus family, I became involved in helping them to set up a safari park at one of the finest sites in Britain, on a hillside looking towards the Royal castle at Windsor.

Baboon reserves are one of the commonest and certainly one of the most entertaining features of a safari park, and the baboons were some of the first animals to take up residence at Windsor. They, and their cousins in other parks, gave us a heap of headaches in the early days, mainly because of their obsession with escape. Compared to baboons, prisoners of war with their wooden horses and other feats of mental and physical ingenuity were mere beginners. If they could talk, some of the baboons I know and respect, with names that sound like hoods in a Cagney film—'Scarface', 'Tin-Ribs', 'Wart' and 'Squint'—could confidently drawl, just like Cagney, 'The jail hasn't been built that can hold me!' and mean it. At Windsor the baboons were originally corralled, or so we fondly thought, by a high wire fence with a sheet of smooth, slippery plastic on the top. The idea was that they could not get a grip on the plastic; that was what was going to keep them in. The baboons solved this minor problem by climbing up the wire until they reached the bottom of the plastic sheet and then, like a troupe of circus acrobats, forming a baboon pyramid to by-pass the puerile device. Sitting on the top edge of the fence, the first escapers would then reach down, if necessary with someone holding their ankles, and give a hand up to their mates who had been the sturdy-shouldered base of the pyramid.

To make the baboon pyramids unstable and unworkable, we stepped the plastic sheet inwards a foot or so from the fence. Back went the baboons to the secret drawing-board. The next schemes involved either unpicking the slippery green sheet with the persistent patience of a few dozen Counts of Monte Cristo or mounting diversionary attacks on the Alsatian dog that guarded the gate to the reserve whilst the main bunch of escapers slipped out on his blind side.

In the end the Windsor baboons opted for a peaceful life within their compound, mainly because their successful break-outs led either into the tiger reserve, where they got the fright of their lives and quickly 'escaped back in', or into less lethal parts of the park where meal tickets were hard to come by; meals in their reserve were plentiful and toothsome. Also there were lots of fun things to do inside, like dismantling cars. The baboons could take the trimmings off a moving car far quicker than any automobile worker on the production line could put them on. As I discovered to my cost when I first drove my own car into the Windsor baboon reserve to visit a patient, Citroën saloons were bristling with lamps, bits of chrome and other trimmings that French workmanship had neglected to make monkey-proof. Having dealt with my sick baboon, I returned to the car to find the exterior denuded of everything portable. Aerial, screen wipers, lamp glasses—all gone. It was not as if the animals wanted to do anything useful with the articles that they stole. Like their human counterparts with birds' eggs, butterflies or beer mats, they just collected them for collecting's sake.

I at least knew where I might find the looted bits of my car in a day or two. Along with the baboons in the reserve at Windsor lived a lugubrious coven of Egyptian vultures. These harpies never caused anybody any trouble and were remarkably diligent in building nests, not nests of twigs and sticks in the manner approved by the ornithological rulebooks but jazzy, glittering, pop-art bowers, comfortable lattice-work constructions made from screen wipers and radio aerials gathered from the ground after the baboons had knocked off for the day.

At a safari park which I visited in Spain, the wire fence of the baboon reserve was topped not by slippery plastic but by a strand of electrified wire of the sort used to corral cattle. Here the baboon POWs adopted a method of escape which might have been copied from the way soldiers are supposed to deal with barbed-wire barricades. One individual would fling himself onto the wire and lie there, twitching and jerking, whilst the others would quickly scurry over the bridge made by his gallant little body. When all had gone, he would drop back exhausted. It would be his turn to go out with the next batch, when someone else would act as the insulator.

Unlike the prisoners of Colditz, the baboons did not need to fudge the numbers at roll call to give fugitive comrades valuable time to get well clear of the camp. Keepers and curators do make regular checks of the stock list, but by their very nature the shifting, fidgety bands of baboons in a spacious reserve are as uncountable as a flock of sparrows. So some who 'make it' are not missed for a long time and their disappearance can remain permanently undiscovered or forgotten as numbers are built up by breeding or as the keeping staff change. I know one deep wood of birch and fir trees, fringed with palisades of brambles and wild roses that are heavy with juicy hips and blackberries in the late summer. Its inner fastnesses are carpeted from June with succulent red-cap boletus mushrooms, and edible blewits can be found even in the first frosts. White truffles sleep just below the beech mast. There are breaks in the trees where the grass grows tall and is speckled with vetches. Shallow, reedy pools tremble as water beetles, caddis-flies, water snails and frogs go about their business. In the depths of that wood live at least three baboons with long and glossy coats. They supplement the harvest of food, which each season naturally brings and which hunger, curiosity and intelligence revealed to them, with occasional forays for eggs, vegetables and discarded goodies from the gardens of cottages just outside the wood.

There was another baboon, a female, in the fugitive band

but she was caught in an illegal gin-trap and died miserably. I was brought her emaciated and multilated corpse. At autopsy I found the pieces of insect carapaces, seed husks, toadstool stems and bone fragments from small creatures that revealed how she and her comrades feasted in their woodland territory. And there is an abandoned badger sett, which I found at last after days of searching, where the gang holes up, dry and snug, during the dripping chill of winter.

I would not reveal the location of these English baboons for a king's ransom; unlikely to be able to trap them, but fearing claims for damages from folk who have been relieved of a few apples or radishes, their former owners would send in the shotguns. Like slaves in ancient Rome, these doughty creatures have earned their freedom; they have been on the run for more than a year and a day.

One of the first parks I visited in Europe was the superbly designed and beautiful zoo at Kolmården, on the Baltic coast of Sweden. I was there to study, among other things, their well-built baboon compound. High fences with their top sections angled inwards, deep foundations to thwart tunnellers, electrified mats at the exits and entrances—this was surely a maximum security unit. But they said that about Colditz.

Beyond the baboon compound was a lovely wooded reserve of pine trees in which a number of bears ambled about. The ground was covered with delicious pine kernels. The baboons could see and smell the tantalising morsels through the wire, but how were they to get at them? The 'goon squad' of keepers at the gates was very alert. The first attempts were not up to the expected standard: they tried stowing away on the roofs of coaches or sneaking along beside a car, keeping the vehicle between themselves and the guards and then, as the car reached the electrified mat, jumping up, holding onto a door handle and keeping their feet clear of the ground until they were safely through. Using a pair of guards, one at each side of the mat, soon put a stop to that. The Escape Committee had to put their heads together. It took time but in the end they came up with the answer. As a coach approached the exit gate, the baboons would nip smartly between its wheels and with both hands and both feet latch onto the chassis. Best of all, on some models they could pull themselves up into secluded recesses in the bodywork or behind the mudguards. Out went the coach with its stowaways, who dropped from the undercarriage like autumn leaves when they reached the pine trees. The answer to that one was to equip the guards with angled mirrors on the end of long poles. Before each coach left the reserve they inspected its underside carefully for contraband apes, just like the stony-faced East German border guards at Checkpoint Charlie.

Baboons are a hardy breed, and the group at Belle Vue needed my attentions only once in about eight years. Manchester air and the carefully planned diet agreed with them and they, a peaceful, well-balanced social group, agreed among themselves. At the safari parks, on the other hand, I was kept busy patching up the bruises, cuts and knocked-out teeth of the day-to-day squabbles which regularly arose from disputes over marital and territorial matters, from greed, jealousy and the eternal clash between youth and age. To watch them at it reinforced my opinion that the naked ape in New York, London, Ulster or Moscow is barely a step ahead of his simian cousins in the evolutionary race.

Although my baboon friends did not pose any exceptional veterinary problems for me, I did meet a certain baboon, named Wunn, who had had a whole bundle of surgical problems heaped on his little shoulders by mankind. Wunn was an experimental baboon in a University laboratory involved in advanced transplant research. After being captured as a youngster in Africa, he knew no home other than the small galvanised box with a metal grille at the front, one of many identical one-man cells that stood in rows in the antiseptic, green-tiled room. He grew well enough on a scientifically perfect but unutterably boring diet of monkey pellets with the occasional half-orange and, when his turn came around, was experimented upon. Bits were taken out and put back in, plastic tubes were inserted to replace portions of his natural ones, miniature electronic gadgets were buried in his flesh to record this and that and always, always he was being sampled—a biopsy today, blood tomorrow, urine catheter the day after. For years Wunn bore it all stoically and displayed a gentle and warm nature towards the laboratory staff. Eventually the series of experiments came to an end. The men and women in white coats were pleased, and moved on to tinker with other baboons that Wunn could not see but only smell and hear.

Wunn had made his contribution to medical science. Now, instead of an OBE, there was only one remaining thing: death. According to the strict vivisection laws which operate in Great Britain, a laboratory animal which has played its part in a series of experiments must be put to sleep. There are no exceptions, no question of finding it a good home like a retired greyhound or redundant pit pony. The Home Office is adamant.

The girl laboratory technicians who had worked all along with Wunn had become particularly attached to the sweet-natured baboon. With the tacit approval of the surgeons involved, and with even the august head of research turning a Nelson's eye, they contacted me. Could I find a zoo where, without any chance of Government snoopers finding out, Wunn might for the first time in his life rattle about with a troupe of other baboons just like baboons are supposed to do? I was all for it. The secret of the bionic baboon would never be leaked to the Government but there was one possible snag: baboons live in strictly organised social communities where everyone knows his place. Singleton strangers are rarely tolerated and at worst are beaten up and driven off or killed.

Windsor Safari Park agreed to acccept Wunn, and we decided to put him first in the baboon reserve in a cage normally used by nursing mothers. Wunn could see and be seen by the other animals but was protected from them by the wire. They became used to his presence and his smell. But what would happen when the newcomer was eventually let out into the main bunch? When should we try it? It was my decision, and I knew that if I saw Wunn at the receiving end of a lot of punishment from the other adult males, I would have to dart him and put him painlessly to sleep.

After Wunn had spent three weeks in his separate cage, during which time he had aroused a certain but not inordinate amount of curiosity from a few of the other baboons, I decided to release him. My heart was in my mouth as a keeper opened the cage door and Wunn shuffled out into the grassy reserve. Now for it, I thought. My dart-gun was ready and loaded in case of a mugging. Wunn went a few yards, sat down and blinked towards the sunlight. He picked idly at this funny but tasty green matting all around him. His eyes followed a great grey and white cloud moving gently across the blue sky and then flicked across to where the cloud was suddenly pierced by a 707 climbing out of Heathrow airport. Slowly, nonchalantly, the baboons began to gather round him. To my surprise, instead of marching up to him and demanding to see his credentials, or beating up the stranger first and asking questions afterwards, they drifted up in twos and threes diffidently and almost respectfully. As would happen were a white explorer to stumble into the camp of a band of nomadic tribesmen, the first individuals to come right up to Wunn were the children. Within minutes, one or two of the smallest baboons were climbing over his hairy mane as if he were their long-lost favourite uncle.

We were overjoyed. So far, so very good. After the kids, one of the dominant male baboons cautiously approached the stranger, sniffed at him from a couple of feet away and then walked off unconcernedly. Wunn gazed benignly after him. I had already noticed that Wunn's testicles were abnormally small, probably because of his lifetime of acting as a surgical swap-shop. Perhaps he did not give off enough of the masculine scent to provoke the males; if so, I thanked God he was so poorly endowed. A few of the females came closer, emboldened by the first male's display of disdain. They gave Wunn the once-over, but from their reaction it did not seem as if the baboon equivalent of Richard Burton had arrived. It was all going far better than I could ever have hoped. The main group moved off and carried on with their foraging, feuding and courting. Wunn was left peacefully alone to begin doing amazing, novel things like sticking a finger into the soil or finding his first discarded screen wiper.

Not once in the days that followed did we see Wunn get into trouble. The kids liked him and a gang of them were constantly in attendance on him. The women continued not to be turned on by his charm, but then there was obviously more of the philosopher than the philanderer in his sage countenance. And the bellicose, butch leaders of the pack ignored him; the newcomer, they had concluded, was not going to make any waves. Gradually, as the months passed, Wunn was absorbed smoothly into the troupe. He seemed, and still seems, one apart, a member of the society but with no precise place in the hierarchy. The important thing is that he enjoys the sunshine and the rain, chasing the vultures, climbing over the rocks, taking handfuls of warm meat and vegetable stew in the winter and riding round the reserve on car bonnets during the summer. Two recent events have given me the utmost pleasure: Wunn has acquired a timid and devoted lady companion who grooms him whenever he feels lordly; and I have watched him deftly steal the chromium-plated wheel-trim from a coach—a coach carrying a visiting party of eminent surgeons.

It was at Windsor that summer that I was approached by 'Mac' McNab, the head keeper there, a plump, genial individual and a dead ringer for film comedian Oliver Hardy. 'We're going wallaby catching,' he announced. 'Do you know much about them?'

The honest answer was 'No'; I had already found these mini-kangaroos from down under to be unco-operative in responding to the medical ministrations of a Pommy veterinarian. With the aid of a certain brand of mint which these animals adore, a tip that I had picked up from my professor of surgery whilst at university and the only piece of exotic animal know-how I had been given as an undergraduate, I had been able to come into close contact with the timid marsupials from time to time but had found the early diagnosis and effective treatment of their ailments difficult. They are particularly prone to infection by a germ called actinomyces, which is carried into the jawbone and later to deeper parts by the tiny, barbed awns of grass on which they graze. The awns get jammed between their teeth and gradually work their way down into the gums. It was not an easy condition to tackle: the wallabies' struggles while they were injected often overstrained their hearts fatally and the surgical attempts I had made to cut out diseased areas of bone had been dogged for many years by the animals' unpredictable reactions to the only anaesthetics available.

'Not really, Mac,' I told him, 'but I'd dearly love to come on the catching.'

'Right,' he replied. 'We're going down to Hampshire. Leonard's Leap, a private estate, has a surplus of the little beauties. We've got to grab them ourselves, though. It'd be best if you came along in case they need doping.'

Although McNab's words made it sound as if I were a key member of the hunting team, I had a feeling that I was being invited for the sake of appearances, more as a professional scapegoat than as an insurance against mishap. My old partner, Norman Whittle, had warned me early in our days together of how often the zoo vet finds himself playing this role.

With an assortment of wooden crates and three vehicles we set out from Windsor and drove down to Hampshire. Leonard's Leap is buried deep in the countryside and is to be found by strangers only with much difficulty after wending through a maze of leafy, un-signposted lanes that fork a hundred times. Not only that, but wallabies at the time were hard to come by, yet the owner of Leonard's Leap, a gentleman apparently quite unaware of the going rate in the zoological business, was asking a ridiculously low price for his animals. No wonder McNab, a wily Scotsman, went to great pains to keep the source of the bouncing bargains a close secret. The keepers who drove the vans carrying us and the crates were given maps in case the convoy became split up. The maps had been carefully drawn by the head keeper and bore only the barest details necessary for arriving at our destination. When all three vehicles finally reached the estate, a network of small valleys thickly scattered with large rhododendron bushes, McNab dashed round retrieving the maps from the drivers and put a match to them. It was all rather melodramatic but to this day, although I have got the name right, live within forty miles of the place and have occasionally driven around on a summer Sunday trying to find it, I have never been able to locate the hidden haunt of the wallabies. McNab is an ex-gamekeeper and knows a thing or two.

The rhododendron bushes at Leonard's Leap have dry and hollow centres where the wallabies could be found, snugly holed up and proof against the elements. All that McNab, I and the keepers on the expedition had to do was to chase the wallabies out of their rhododendron hideaways and into a funnel-shaped trap which the estate gardeners had made with wire-netting at the head of one valley. This was the athletic side of a zoo vet's life. All through that hot afternoon we panted and puffed, running up and down the grassy slopes, crashing headlong through bushes and hurling ourselves in futile rugby tackles at the lithe, grey-brown bundles of fur that sprang silently over the ground as we approached. By late afternoon we had at last bagged our quota. Although not as winded and worn out as we were, the wallabies had begun to pant and their heart rates were almost too rapid to count. I decided to give each animal a shot of tranquilliser before crating it so that it would be able to relax on the long journey home.

McNab held the wallabies by the base of the tail while I gave the injection and checked to see how many of the females were carrying babies or 'joeys'. Of the twelve wallabies we had caught, ten were females and eight of them had sausage-sized infants firmly attached to the milk teats in their warm pouches. Safely on board the vans, the animals settled down quickly and without fuss in their boxes. I felt confident that I had done a good job in helping to catch the wallabies, and that my little drop of tranquilliser had set a seal of professionalism on the proceedings. McNab had told me that previously wallabies had been captured and moved without drugs being used. Sometimes an animal or two had died, probably of heart failure. Get this load back alive and well and McNab would undoubtedly appreciate the superior virtues of modern veterinary science in the zoo field. We set off home, map-less, following our noses towards a main road.

Back at Windsor, as the light began to fade, the wallabies were released into their grassy paddock. Ten, eleven, twelve: I counted them out. They were all alive and looking fit, and immediately began jumping uncertainly around their new compound. They bounced nervously along the perimeter and glanced with darting dark eyes at all the strange surroundings, at the humans peering through the fence and at the giraffes strutting in the adjoining paddock. They cocked their heads to listen to the sound of roaring lions, the screeching of bus brakes on the road outside and the thunder of jetliners making their final approach into London. McNab and I watched them, but suddenly he cursed and leaned forward. As the wallabies hopped, wriggling pink lumps of what looked like denuded mice fell onto the ground from the pouches of some of them. Within a minute or two, eight helpless baby wallabies, still with the foetal appearance of marsupial young, who are normally ejected from the womb to spend the latter half of 'pregnancy' in the pouch, were blindly writhing on the grass.

'Jeez, will ye look at that!' exclaimed McNab. 'Every mother's lost her young 'un!'

Quickly but carefully, we began to collect the hairless infants. They felt red-hot in the palm of my hand.

'Why, why d'you think that could have happened?' mused the head keeper as we stood looking at the adults springing quietly around us.

Suddenly the answer came to me: my wretched tranquilliser. It had done the trick all right on the mothers during the journey, but a proportion of it must have passed from their blood into their milk. Taken in by the babies, it had made them slightly drowsy and, when their parents were released at the park and began to leap about, they had lost their hold on the teat in the pouch and had been thrown out. I had given them each an indirect Mickey Finn.

I explained my theory to McNab, who nodded grimly. 'Hrrumph. Never did like the idea of all these new-fangled chemicals. Too much of it. Far too much of it,' he growled.

His opinions had been confirmed, but there was no time for further recriminations. Something had to be done—fast. The awful thing was that all the babies looked alike in their shiny, frail nondescriptness and so did all the mums. There was just no way we could tell which infant fell from which pouch, but back into someone's pouch each would have to go. McNab called in some keepers and the job of re-catching the wallabies began. Carefully, and with fervent silent entreaties to the gods to forestall what might turn into a joey holocaust, I stuck a couple of fingers into the pouch of each female. If I found a damp teat from which a drop of milk could be drawn, I plugged on one of the rudely evicted innocents.

Back in the security of a pouch, each joey latched firmly onto its allotted teat and snuggled down, but the chances that I had paired the right mother and offspring in each of the eight cases was something like one in five thousand. What if wallabies were like many other mammals and identified their own babies by scent, rejecting all imposters? In that case there would be de-pouched youngsters on the ground again in a little while and the deadly game of snap, using flesh and blood creatures instead of cards, would have to be played over and over again. Please God, let them be like caribou cows who willingly accept infants not their own, I prayed.

'Let's put them all in the night-house now,' I suggested to McNab. 'That way, at least they won't be bouncing around and it will give more time for any tranquilliser still in their systems to wear off.'

He agreed, and we released the nursing mothers into their indoor quarters. Now there was nothing more to be done except to leave them in peace for a few hours and hope that St Francis was listening. There was no point in saying anything to Shelagh about the affair when I telephoned her that night. I felt wretched enough as it was, without re-hashing everything. Nothing even she might have said could have provided any mental loophole through which I could wriggle away from the brutal fact that I had put the joeys' lives at great risk.

After a sleepless night I went down to the safari park early. It was seven o'clock. McNab and the rest of the staff would not be in for another hour. My heart was bounding as I went to the wallaby night-house and opened the sliding door an inch. Peeping in with my stomach anxiously churning, I scanned the sawdusted floor. There was no sign of any still, pink sausages. I went over every square inch again, straining my eyes till their muscles ached: not a joey in sight.

Only then did I raise my head a little to look at the crouching wallabies. All twelve of them seemed in good order, but there was no way of knowing how things were going in their pouches. Maybe the flattened corpse of a joey was underneath one of them or hidden under a layer of bedding. I pulled the door right open and gently shooed the animals out onto the grass. Nothing fell out of them as they hopped off into the morning sunlight. On hands and knees I meticulously picked through the sawdust, the bedding and the droppings, sweeping clear every inch of the floor with my bare hands. Saints be praised! Not one single baby could I find.

I went outside and watched the wallabies moving about, busily cropping the short grass. All seemed perfect. I hurried off to see if McNab was in yet and to give him the good news. In the days that followed, frequent inspections by McNab and his keepers turned up no evidence that any of the willy-nilly adoptions had failed. To my delight, it gradually became obvious that all eight babies were none the worse for mum-swapping; after a few more weeks furry brown heads began to peep out of the pouches on sunny days.

'Well, Mac,' I said, when it was clear that the wallabies were out of danger, 'it seems that they must be very civilised and tolerant creatures. One kid's as good as the next to those little ladies.'

'Yes,' he murmured, 'but no thanks to your tranquillisers, David. How many millions of years have wallabies been happily bringing up their young without 'em?'

He had a point, and a good one, but it struck me then how generally accepted on the zoo scene the veterinarian had become. Of course some of the old prejudices still lingered on, and calamities like the wallaby affair did not help, but most zoo men appreciated well enough how veterinary science could make their jobs easier and raise the standard of zoo care by—and this was the fundamental and important thing—improving the health, diet, handling, breeding and day-to-day welfare of the animals. I thought back to my early days at Belle Vue, when I despaired of my medical knowledge ever matching the wisdom and experience of Matt Kelly, or of showing him that modern drugs and other developments could go hand in hand with his innate animal-craft. Now even old hands like Kelly and McNab would grudgingly admit that perhaps my potions, flying darts, autopsies and analysing did have something to offer. That battle was all but won at last, I felt, and it would be together that we would tackle the numberless problems that lay ahead.

Fifteen

Andrew Greenwood spent less time with me during that summer. He was on the run-up to his final examinations. Nevertheless, he took time off to come up to Flamingo Park when he heard that one of Cuddles' regular blood samplings was due. He had asked me over the phone if it would be OK for him to take a biopsy of the whale's skin. Professor Harrison at Cambridge was working on the curious problem of why dolphins and whales can swim so fast with such little expenditure of energy and without setting up turbulence. The secret, he suspected and was later to discover, lay in the skin itself. I had given the go-ahead until Andrew arrived at the park with a fearsome kit of biopsy instruments like miniature apple-corers. Science or no science, I was as proud as Punch of Cuddles' billiard-ball-smooth skin and I worried over every little nick and pimple it developed. I chickened out of having him sampled like a cheese at a gourmets' gathering and sent Andrew back empty-handed and, I fancy, rather niggled.

I was a trifle embarrassed by my change of mind, but I had come a fair way since my early days of reckless postgraduate enthusiasm, when I would dash into major, complex surgery at the drop of a hat, stick needles into and take innumerable samples from every long-suffering patient that came my way. With the benefit of time, that precious, unteachable, elusive thing, clinical judgement, had grown, as it does in all medical practitioners. Leave well alone was its cardinal maxim: if in doubt, do nowt, as the Lancashire farmers would say. Cuddles was a big responsibility, and I was not prepared to risk the slightest chance of anything going wrong with him because of interference that did not contribute directly to his well-being. The question of how these creatures slip through water so easily was fascinating, but not important to Cuddles and me. As essentially a clinician, though now working with unusual and glamorous animals, I have often had to dowse with iced water the enthusiasm of academics for the advancement of pure scientific knowledge. I had learned this as a student, when a bunch of keen young anaesthetists from the Manchester Medical School had been let loose to experiment on some lions at Belle Vue. They had dashed joyously back to their laboratories and seminar rooms—while Matt Kelly had had to arrange the disposal of several overdosed cadavers.

No, I stand for the animal. If not me, who else? I am happy to think of myself as nothing more than the family doctor, but to a dumb family of extraordinary folk.

In June, Andrew telephoned to say that he had qualified. He was now a fully fledged Member of the Royal College of Veterinary Surgeons. After congratulating him, I asked about the future.

'I'm going to stay on in Professor Harrison's department at Cambridge and do some research in diving animals.'

'You're still keen on exotic creatures, then?'

'Most certainly. I'll be able to help out, do locums when you're away, that sort of thing.'

I was at least glad about that, but once the mill that grinds out PhD's had swallowed him, I feared he would be lost to the real world of animals with aches and pains and pestilences.

'What diving animals will you be working on?' I asked. 'Seals, dolphins?'

'Nothing so grand,' came the reply. 'I've got a research grant from the Royal Navy and they do their diving experiments with far more prosaic species.'

'Such as what?'

'Would you believe, goats? Goats that get the "bends".'

Over dinner that evening I said to Shelagh, 'Pity about Andrew. What a waste of a good man. Research! Goats! And I thought he had the makings of a first-class zoo vet.' Thoughtfully, I stabbed at a potato.

My visits to cases outside Flamingo Park had meanwhile become steadily more frequent. Pentland Hick was very patient; sometimes I would be gone for two weeks at a time. I was driving 70,000 miles a year, flying four times as far and becoming accustomed to sleeping by the roadside in my car. Rochdale to Stirling to London and back to Rochdale all in one day by road was nothing abnormal: 850 miles virtually non-stop except for fuel between a sick dolphin in Scotland and a dying sealion in southern England. I existed on a diet of peanuts, Haydn and Bach from my cassette player and the banter of the girl operators who manned the car radio telephone transmitters round the clock. It was a cracking pace that was required, manning a practice that had grown to be almost a thousand miles square.

I saw Rochdale and my family less and less and I formed the opinion which I still hold: that being a peripatetic, single-handed zoo vet is ideally work for a bachelor. I sympathised with Shelagh when I rang her from a hotel bar in San Diego or Nassau. She was at home, running this one-horse practice, bringing up the girls and keeping the house together in the rainy north-west, while I was grumbling about being delayed for an extra day on Grand Bahama Island by airline foul-ups, or about the indolence of a laboratory in Venice which meant that I must pass yet another salmon-skied evening watching the world turn round the Piazza San Marco. I could not see any obvious solution. One thing I was certain of: nothing, but nothing, would tear me away from exotic animals in a million years. Cats, dogs, pigs and sheep were things I seemed barely able to remember.

After a year and a half at Flamingo Park, I decided the time had come to return to full independence: there was an abundance of cases and little likelihood that I might have to sit in the office at home, waiting for the telephone to ring. I was not sorry to leave. Pentland Hick had sold his zoo empire out of the blue and, as happened in so many similar cases around that time, the big public company moved in. Anxious to diversify into what they believed to be a lucrative sector, these experts in bingo, casinos, catering and discos looked at animal collections and assessed them like banks of one-armed bandits or seats in the dress circle. Animals became units. Targets, budgets, productivity were words bandied about when animal diets were adjusted to suit the changing seasons or repairs to houses had to be made. The dead hand of the Accountant lay on the beasts' backs and the Public Relations Officer held sway over all.

Cuddles the whale suffered a grave attack of intestinal ulceration with massive bleeding, but after intensive treatment he rallied and pulled round.* Against my advice, the animal was moved shortly afterwards to Dudley Zoo in Worcestershire, where he was put on show in a hurriedly adapted pool. He proved a great attraction, but the writing was indelibly on the wall. From now on, commercial considerations took pride of place, even where the health of a very valuable animal was at stake. I continued to act as Cuddles' doctor until 1973. Then, whilst I was on a visit to Communist China, he mysteriously broke a rib, developed an abscess at the site of the fracture which sent seeds to infect his brain, and died within three or four days of falling ill. Having been in at his beginning, I was heart-broken not to have been on hand when he was finally up against it. But I was pleased that Andrew did the autopsy and that I, half a world away, could not.

*See *Zoovet*

My life as a medical carpetbagger, a vagrant veterinarian-in-a-suitcase, here today and gone tomorrow when a gorilla hiccupped in Paris or Port of Spain, suited me, except for three things. First, I was seeing Shelagh and the girls but rarely; second, I was abusing my digestion in motorway cafés; and third, I still had this 'thing', this blue funk about doping giraffes. After the Belle Vue specimens with hypothermia, after Pedro, after the Flamingo Park giraffe which had died under my hands, giraffes gave me the jitters. I consoled myself with the thought that with a little bit of luck I might be able to keep dodging the issue. Deep down, I knew that there was no hope of things always going as smoothly as they had with the Rio Leon specimen. One day, probably soon, I was going to have to anaesthetise another giraffe.

So the familiar butterfly sensation started in my stomach when Matt Kelly telephoned from Belle Vue, where I was still veterinarian and which still provided a good proportion of my cases. The Irish head keeper sounded concerned but hardly panicky. 'Oi've got a giraffe with a tomato stuck in its gob,' he told me. 'Strange thing is, she's still eating foine. Not causin' her trouble. Mebbe it's caught on a tooth. The keeper thinks he got a glimpse of it two days ago.'

If it was a tomato, it should not take long before the squashy fruit disintegrated without causing any further trouble. Still, it sounded a rum story and I promised to go straight over, though I reckoned it unlikely that I would have to do much else but mutter a few reassuring words and let time do the rest.

Molly was a lovely specimen of Masai giraffe and had already produced three healthy calves. Standing looking up at her, I could see what Matt was talking about: a red sphere that protruded from the right-hand corner of her lips. It was smooth and shiny and about one and a half inches in diameter. It looked at first glance like a tomato but, encapsulated in a fold of gum tissue that had at last grown big enough to flop out of the animal's mouth, the spherical object was without doubt either a cyst or a tumour. The giraffe would not be able to feel any pain from the lump and it had not grown enough to interfere seriously with her feeding.

'What d'ye think, Doctor?' asked Matt after giving me a few minutes to ruminate while the butterflies in my stomach become bat-sized.

'A growth, Matt. It's probably been hidden in there for quite a while, but it's not causing problems yet. Let's wait and see first.'

There were two chances that I might be really lucky. If it was a saliva-duct cyst it might burst or subside spontaneously. If it was a papilloma, it might drop off like the related wart on a human hand or leg. 'I'll have a look at it in a couple of weeks,' I said as we went out of the house.

Two weeks later, the tomato had grown into an apple. Its presence was beginning to irritate the giraffe as she ate. There was not the slightest sign of bursting or separation, in fact the lump looked to be blooming with health and well supplied with blood vessels. I stood on stepladders to try and touch the thing, but Molly swung her head as I approached and sent me tumbling down onto the straw.

Picking myself up, I said the words that sounded in my head like a death warrant. 'There's nothing for it. I'll have to take it off—under general anaesthesia.'

I arranged the operation for the next day. Andrew was still messing about with goats. He was always ready and eager to do work for me when asked. I gave him a call and explained the position.

'We'll put her under,' I said, 'then I'll get the surgical side over as quick as possible while you keep an eye on her system reactions. Then we'll pull out all the stops to reverse her.'

We talked for a long time about what drugs to use and how we might approach the difficulties that we felt sure were associated with the giraffe's peculiar blood circulation to the head and neck.

'This fainting under tranquillising is the problem,' said

239

Andrew. 'If they do that, everybody rushes around trying to hold their massive heads up in a "normal" posture; it strikes me that's just the wrong thing to do. The beast should be laid flat and given deeper anaesthetic at such times.'

It made sense physiologically, I saw, although I had made the Belle Vue keepers hold Pedro's head up when he fainted. We would try it Andrew's way and, as well as using etorphine and xylazine, would experiment with Dopram, a new American drug that counteracts the respiratory depression caused by narcotics. Our armoury of drugs was increasing every day. We had not used Dopram on giraffes before and decided it would be best to base the dosage on human requirements. Molly weighed as much as eight adults, so we agreed on 500 milligrams. The animal would not be allowed up onto her feet until any chance of fainting had gone.

Next morning we all assembled at Belle Vue. Andrew had driven up from Cambridge overnight. Matt was organising his keepers and looking very apprehensive. The giraffe keeper was truculent and pale-faced. I tried not to let my own trepidation show, but I suspect I failed.

When everything was ready we began. First a small dose of xylazine was injected into Molly's shoulder then, when she went drowsy after a quarter of an hour, I jabbed the etorphine into her jugular vein. She went down onto the thick bed of straw and, while Andrew was still attaching the electrocardiograph leads and administering the Dopram, I splashed iodine over the operation site and grabbed the lump. A glance showed me that it was a benign tumour. My mind empty of thoughts, all my attention fixed on the cold, silver edge of my scalpel blade as it swept round the base of the tumour, I worked as if it were a small time-bomb. It fell free. Blood welled up. I staunched hard with a gauze swab punched into the wound and then clipped off the main blood vessel. One, two, three, four—I slapped in the sutures and knotted them furiously. Swab again. No blood ooze. Done. It had taken about two minutes.

'Right, Andrew,' I said, louder than I intended. 'Bring her round.'

Andrew moved to the animal's neck and shot the syringeful of blue antidote, cyprenorphine, into her vein. Almost at once, Molly gave a great sigh and blinked. She was coming round. If we were in for trouble, this was where we would run into it.

'Keep her head down at all costs until we give the word,' I instructed our helpers.

Andrew gave Molly more Dopram. He pressed the button on the electrocardiograph and more coils of paper bearing the characteristic tracings were spewed out. He disconnected the leads and bent over the giraffe's heaving chest with his stethoscope.

'How's it going?' I asked.

He gave me the thumbs-up.

I took two keepers to sit on her head and neck. When she struggled I added a third. Andrew stayed at her chest. I looked at my watch. After five minutes, Molly was obviously very conscious and wondering why she had the heavy bottoms of three men pressing down on her. I slipped a final two millilitres of cyprenorphine under her skin to guard against any anaesthetic that had still not been neutralised.

At last I took the bit between my teeth.

'Everybody off,' I shouted. 'Stand clear!'

The men jumped to their feet and we all moved smartly back. Molly lifted her neck, looked round at us and slowly fanned those long, glamorous eyelashes. Effortlessly, she gathered her legs under her and stood up.

I bit my lower lip till it bled. Molly walked slowly over to her feed-trough high on the wall. Was that a slight flicker of the muscles in her haunches? She caught one hoof in a twist of straw: was it a stumble, the first before she keeled over? Molly looked into her trough and cast a liquid eye over the pile of fresh fruit, corn and fresh celery that Matt had prepared. Then she curled out her grey tongue and began to eat avidly.

We all stood as the minutes went by. No-one spoke until a quarter of an hour had passed. Molly had cleared the trough and was looking round for dessert.

I cleared my throat and licked my now sore lip. 'Er, I think, gentlemen, she's going to be OK. Thank you very much. One stays with her. The rest come and have a beer.'

Andrew grinned. 'We've cracked it,' he said.

It certainly looked so. 'Look here,' I said to him as we walked over to the dispensary to wash up, 'why don't you pack up this research business and come into partnership with me? Do some real work.'

He answered immediately. 'Of course I will. I wondered when you were going to suggest it.'

Molly was to be the last case I treated as a solo zoo vet. We were on our way.